MANAGERIAL ACCOUNTING FOR THE SMALL BUSINESS

1ST EDITION

KENNETH CREECH

NorthAmerican
Business Press
Atlanta – Seattle – South Florida – Toronto

North American Business Press, Inc
Atlanta, Georgia
Seattle, Washington
South Florida
Toronto, Canada

Managerial Accounting for the Small Business
ISBN: 9780988919389

Library of Congress Control Number: 2013946290
Library of Congress Cataloging in Publication Division
101 Independence Ave., SE
Washington, DC 20540-4320
Printed in the United States of America
First Edition

MANAGERIAL ACCOUNTING FOR THE SMALL BUSINESS – BOOK INTRODUCTION

This textbook is written to provide the basics of managerial accounting to individuals studying to become small business owners or managers rather than for people planning to work as accountants or managers in large corporations. The book will cover the main points of managerial accounting from a unique position of being able to trace the development of the concepts with the same companies, rather than changing companies and information for every new concept. This tracing will be accomplished by the use of four trial balances presented in Appendix A. These trial balances will be used for exercises and problems in most chapters and they are unique in that the trial balances represent four different business types and the concepts are discussed for the four business types. These business types are: a manufacturing firm; a merchandising firm, a service company (in this case a hospital) and an agricultural production company (in this case a cattle ranch). Through the use of these trial balances the students will see how the concepts can be applied to different businesses. It is intended that the text provide information on how the concept can be applied to different business types so that students will have background on whatever type of business they end up being employed in or owning.

The focus of the text is designed for use in programs that are based on small business entrepreneurship or on communities that are primarily driven by small local businesses. In the book there are other unique coverage areas, besides the trial balances in Appendix A, including: a chapter on cash flow planning that focuses on what information should be gathered and how to use that information; and two chapters relating to small business taxes and possible ways to manage those taxes. The cash flow chapter is presented as cash flow is the most important issue faced by any small business.

Because they are not applicable to small business, due to cost and time required for set-up and maintenance, both activity based costing and the balanced scorecard have not been discussed in this textbook.

TABLE OF CONTENTS

CHAPTER 3 – BASIC COST TERMINOLOGY AND COST FLOWS

CHAPTER 4 – COST BEHAVIOR AND COST TYPES IN BUSINESS

CHAPTER 5 – PROCESS COSTING, JOB ORDER COSTING AND COST ALLOCATION

CHAPTER 6 – COST-VOLUME - PROFIT ANALYSIS

CHAPTER 7 – RELEVANT COSTS FOR DECISION MAKING

CHAPTER 8 – CAPITAL BUDGETING DECISIONS

CHAPTER 9 – BUDGETS AND THEIR USES IN PLANNING AND DECISION MAKING

CHAPTER 10 – VARIANCE ANALYSIS – A BASIS FOR PERFORMANCE EVALUATION

CHAPTER 11 – FINANCIAL STATEMENT ANALYSIS

CHAPTER 12 – CASH FLOW PLANNING

CHAPTER 13 – IMPACT OF TAXES ON SMALL BUSINESS

CHAPTER 14 – OVERVIEW OF FEDERAL INCOME TAXES

CHAPTER 1 – INTRODUCTION TO MANAGERIAL ACCOUNTING

LEARNING OBJECTIVES

1. Describe the current view of accounting information systems with an understanding of the differences between financial and nonfinancial accounting information
2. Compare and contrast the information and users of managerial accounting versus financial accounting
3. Understand the role of relevant factors in the use of budgets and performance reports for planning and control in an organization.
4. Understand why accounting is important in a variety of careers.
5. Understand the importance of ethical conduct in accounting.

INTRODUCTION

During the past several years business environments have gone through dramatic change. Companies of all sizes can now be involved in the global marketplace through the use of technology. The increased ability to transact commerce via electronic means (e-business) had led businesses to downsize. This downsizing, along with a more mobile workforce has caused businesses to place a premium on having a more talented, knowledgeable and technologically savvy workforce.

Businesses are driven by the needs of their stakeholders. Customers demand specialized products and services and the ability to get real time information concerning product availability, status of current orders and product lead times. Suppliers need information on their customers' sales and inventory levels in order to adjust their production and delivery schedules to ensure meeting their customers' needs. Owners (stockholders) are demanding greater returns on their investments. Employees are asking for the latest and best tools in order to work more efficiently. These changes require more effective use of knowledge within a given organization.

Frequently the terms knowledge, information and data are used interchangeably but they should not be confused with each other. ***Data*** relates to recording or tracking of individual transactions, such as inventory records or the number and types of products or services sold. When data is summarized and put in a form that can be used as the basis for decision making it becomes ***information***. When the information is shared and decisions are made that add value to the Company, it becomes ***knowledge***.

All types of organizations have a need for accounting information. It doesn't matter if the organization is for profit or not for profit, locally or globally focused, large or small. The nature of the organization also doesn't matter as it can be in manufacturing, retail, agriculture or providing a service.

ACCOUNTING INFORMATION

Accounting information is provided by the Organization's information system. These systems can be small systems used primarily to gather accounting data or the accounting information can just be a part of the information gathering of an extensive Enterprise Resource Planning (ERP) system. Any type of information system used for accounting information captures financial data resulting from the Company's accounting transactions. ERP systems integrate the accounting information system with other information systems to capture both quantitative and qualitative data within a single system. The ERP system is used to collect and organize the data into useful information that can be communicated and used throughout the organization thus creating knowledge. The exhibit below shows the traditional information that would come from an accounting information system on the left hand side and the additional information that would be captured in an ERP system on the right hand side.

Exhibit 1-1 - Financial and Nonfinancial Information

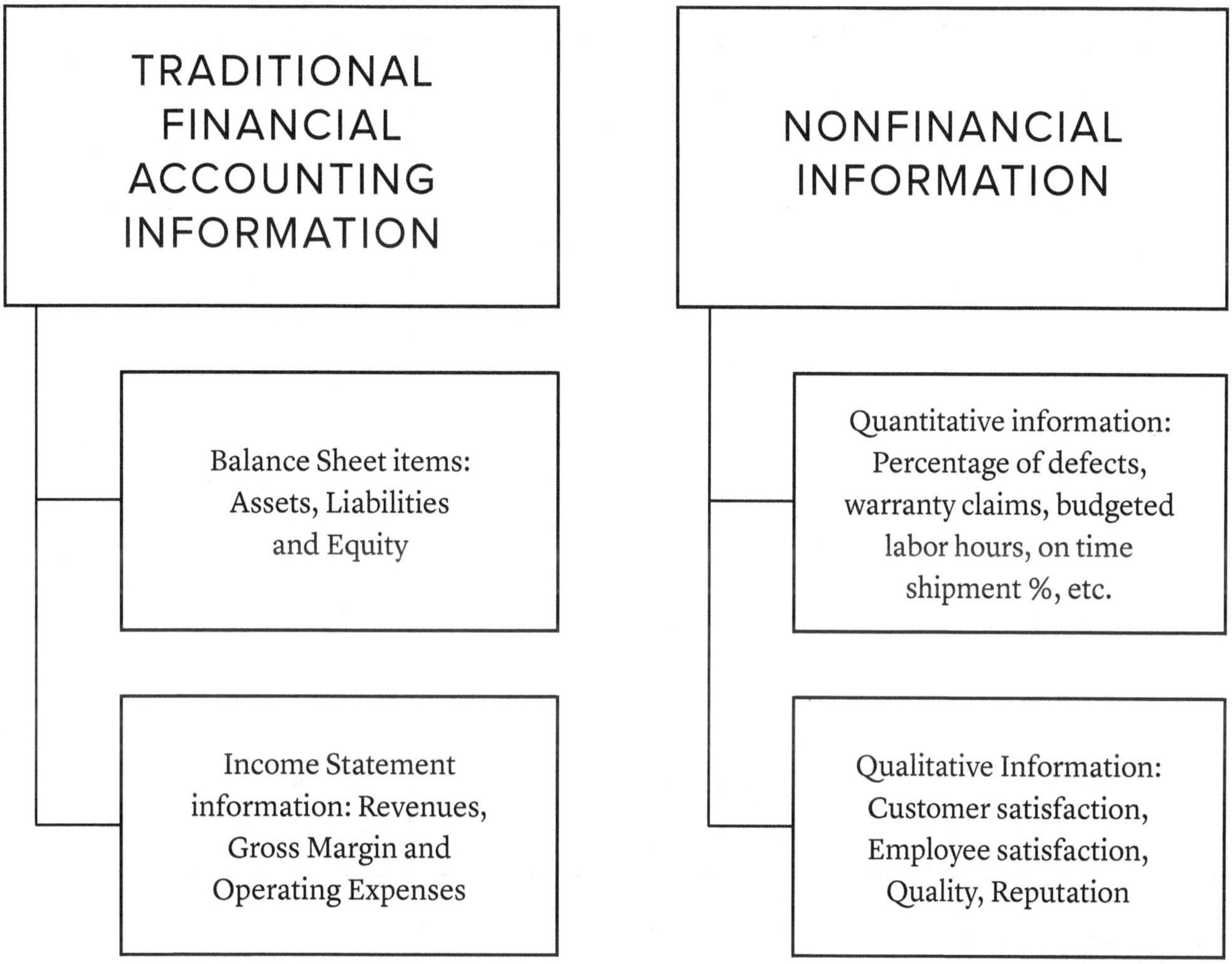

TYPES AND USERS OF ACCOUNTING INFORMATION

In general there are two types of accounting information: ***financial accounting information and managerial accounting information***. Financial accounting is primarily focused on the preparation and use of financial statements by external users. External users could include: banks; investors (stockholders); suppliers; customers; taxing agencies and others outside the Company. Managerial accounting is primarily focused on generating both financial and nonfinancial information that can be used for decision making purposes by internal users. Internal users could include: individuals, teams, departments, top management and others inside the Company.

Exhibit 1-2 - Differences between Management & Financial Accounting

	Management Accounting	Financial Accounting
Primary Users	Organization managers at all levels	Outside parties such as investors, but also internal mangers
Freedom of choice of accounting measures.	Only constraint is that the cost of providing the information cannot be more than the value derived.	constrained by Generally Accepted Accounting Principles (GAAP)
Behavioral implications	Consider how the information will affect managers' behavior.	Behavioral implications are secondary.
Time focus of reports	Future oriented.	Past oriented.
Types of reports	Detailed reports.	Summary reports.

EXTERNAL USERS

External users want the types of information that will allow them to analyze the current and potential future profitability of an organization. Companies that have issued stock to the public in the past have to report this information on a regular basis. The Securities and Exchange Commission require companies to report the information on a quarterly basis on form 10-Q and on an annual basis on Form 10-K. These reports are public information and are available through the SEC website. A company that plans to issue stock to the public presents this information in registration statements, prospectuses and other reports.

Smaller companies that are held by just a few family members or close friends (closely held) may need to provide this information to banks to obtain loans to run the business. Also, sometimes creditors wish to review financial statements to ensure that there is sufficient cash flow for the Company to pay its bills. Customers may request the financial statements so they can evaluate the likelihood that the Company will remain in business and be a source of supply.

In the case of nonprofit organizations, donors may wish to review the financial statements to make sure that the funds are being spent for the charitable purposes for which they were intended.

INTERNAL USERS

The internal users of information are those individuals or teams that are charged with making decisions on how the business is run. These decisions involve ***planning, operating and controlling activities***.

Planning involves the development of both the short-term (operational) and long-term (strategic) objectives and goals of the organization along with the resources and actions needed to make them happen.

Operational planning is focused on the short-term objectives (those typically to be achieved during the next operating cycle (usually one year)). Examples of this would include: planning for raw materials deliveries for manufacturing organizations; planning for the numbers of physicians and nurses needs for each shift, for the next month, at a hospital and planning for deliveries of merchandise to be put on the shelves of a retailer based on how often deliveries are received.

Strategic planning addresses long term questions of how an organization will differentiate itself from its competitors to achieve an advantage. These could involve the timing of introduction of new products, whether to enter new markets or the decision of where to locate a new production facility. Strategic planning also involves decisions that will affect the long-term performance and profitability of the organization. This will lead expectations regarding sales growth, market share and stock price. The primary focus of strategic planning has to be on the maximization of stockholder wealth over the long term.

Operating activities are those items that managers must do to run a business on a day to day basis. In a manufacturing company these decisions would include: how many parts or other raw materials to purchase, whether or not to accept a special order, whether to schedule overtime or additional shifts, etc. On the administrative side the decisions could involve what products to sell and at what prices, how much advertising to use and where to advertise, and which tasks to assign to individual employees.

Controlling activities involve the motivation and monitoring of employees and the evaluation of all resources used in the organization. Controlling activities are used to ensure that organizational goals are being attained. Normally, control involves the comparison of actual results to the operational plan (budget). The comparison focuses on sales, cost of products and all manageable expenses. The comparison leads to managers being asked questions about items that are either better or worse than the plan. Managers should only be asked questions about those areas that they exert control over and that vary from the plan (management by exception).

Exhibit 1-3 - Framework for Planning and Control

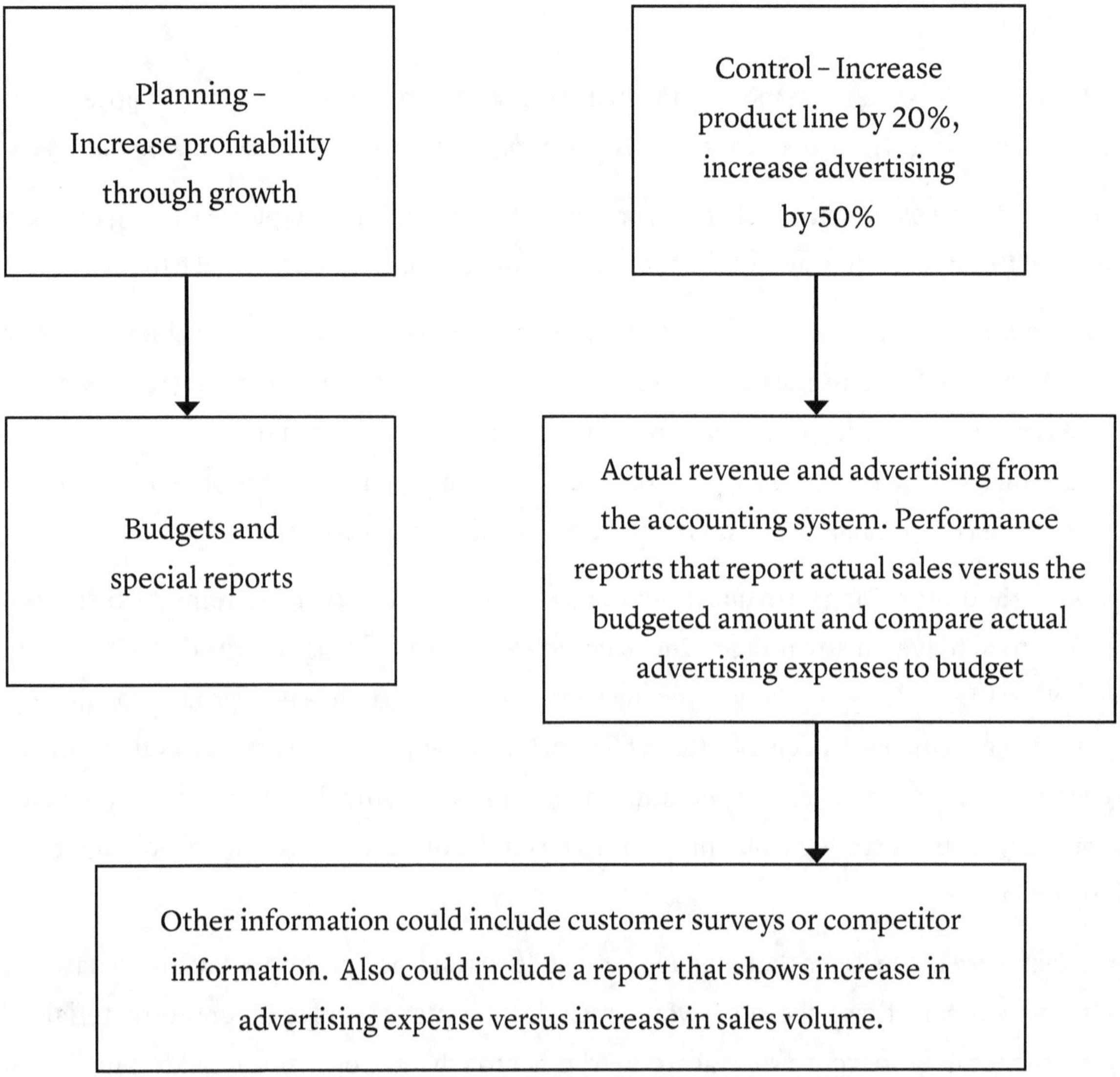

FUNCTIONAL AREAS OF MANAGEMENT

OPERATIONS AND PRODUCTION FUNCTION

The operations and production function has responsibility to produce the products and/or services that are sold to the organization's customers. Operations and production managers are focused on producing quality products, in a timely manner, that are competitive on a global scale. These managers need accounting information regarding the costs of production so they can work towards reducing those costs. In a manufacturing environment these costs will include: materials cost, labor cost, and other direct and indirect costs that support the production function as well as the cost of storing both the materials needed to produce the products and the finished products awaiting shipment to customers. In a service environment the primary production cost will be labor. An example would be a hospital scheduling the number of nurses on a given floor based on patient load on a given day or shift. In retail business managers have to decide both on the quantity and mixture of products to keep on the shelves and the number of people to have working on a given day to maintain the proper level of customer service.

MARKETING FUNCTION

The marketing function has the responsibility of developing, pricing, promoting and distributing goods and services to customers. Marketing managers need to know what products or services cost in order to set pricing for customers. They will need to design appropriate advertising campaigns to meet the advertising budget and at the same time increase sales to meet the sales budget. Based upon how the organization goes to market the nature of the advertising could vary as could items such as packaging. To make these decisions the marketing manager will need accounting information. In addition the marketing manager may need other information, such as customer surveys, to determine the types of products or services to be added or discontinued.

FINANCE FUNCTION

The finance function is responsible for managing the financial resources of the organization. They also are responsible for ensuring that the information systems provide the accounting information needed for proper decision making within the organization. Based upon the organization's plans the finance function will need to decide how to raise capital and how to invest it to ensure that the company can meet its goals.

Exhibit 1-4–Value Chain for Business

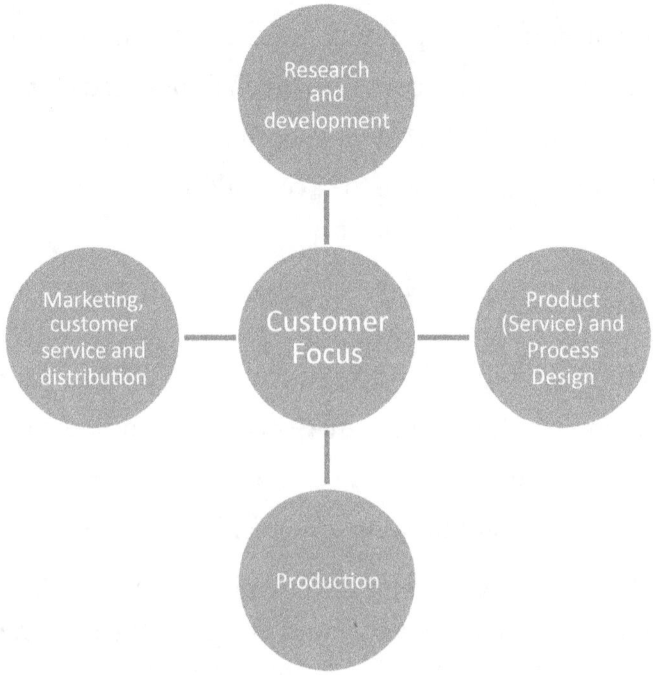

THE ROLE OF THE MANAGEMENT ACCOUNTANT

The role of the management accountant is to provide meaningful information to management to aid in decision making. The management accountant needs to have a focus beyond just the numbers as they relate to profitability. They need to be business partners that can provide diverse information and help coach managers on how to use the information in making decisions. Information that may be useful beyond basic profitability information could include: measurements of efficiency; measurements of productivity; tracking of shipments made on time; tracking of fill rates on orders; tracing of sales by product and any other information that can be used in decision making to support the organization's goals.

Management accounting has become a specialized area within the accounting profession. In The U.S., **The Institute of Management Accountants (IMA)** began the process of recognizing this separate area within accounting a few decades ago. They license individuals as a *Certified Management Accountant (CMA)* once they meet the established criteria for certification. The criteria involves, having a college degree, passing a 16 hour examination that has separate parts covering financial accounting, management accounting, accounting information systems, finance and economics. In addition the individual has to have a minimum of five years experience as a management accountant. Internationally, **The Chartered Institute of Management Accountants (CIMA)** recognizes individuals as a *Chartered Global Management Accountant (CGMA)* once they have criteria similar to those required by the IMA. **The American Institute of Certified Public Accountants (AICPA)** has partnered with CIMA to make the CGMA designation available to individuals in the U.S.

DECISION MAKING AND RELEVANT FACTORS

Decision making is the process of identifying different options for a given situation and the selecting the one most appropriate. Decisions require the use of judgment which is based on the background and experience of the individual manager making the decision. The quality of the decision will depend upon how good the given manager's judgment is. Judgment involves using a logical, rational approach to making decisions rather than making decisions on the spur of the moment. Typically, better decisions are made by managers with more experience making decisions in their given area of expertise.

In making a decision the manager needs to consider all relevant factors. Generally factors are only relevant if they differ between the options. Any factor that is the same between all options is not relevant to the decision making process. A key component in the decisions making process is the ability to recognize the relevant factors.

Many times the key relevant factors have to do with *relevant costs* (those costs that vary between the alternatives). One way to identify relevant costs is to identify those costs that can be eliminated by choosing one alternative over another.

Sunk costs are costs that already have been incurred. Examples of sunk costs would include: buildings and equipment in use at a manufacturing firm; cash registers, shelving and displays at a retail establishment; items of equipment at use in a service organization, such as computers at a CPA firm or beds at a hospital. Since these costs have previously been sunk into the business they cannot be avoided and therefore would not be relevant costs.

Opportunity costs are the costs avoided or the benefits foregone by choosing one alternative over another. As an example, a cattle rancher currently uses the land on the ranch to graze his herd. If the rancher were to feed his herd on hay and corn (or to rent land for grazing) and then use the land to grow wheat he would have several opportunity costs to evaluate. The first cost that would need to be evaluated would be the cost to grow wheat and the revenue to be realized by growing wheat (revenue would be $ 20,000 and cost would be $ 2,000). The next cost to evaluate would be the cost to rent land for grazing ($ 16,000). The final cost for evaluation would be the cost to feed the herd on hay and corn ($ 22,000). Because the costs and benefits differ between the alternatives these costs would be relevant.

Exhibit 1-5 - Relevant and Irrelevant Costs

Relevant Costs		Irrelevant Costs	
Future costs that differ between alternatives	As presented above these would be opportunity costs	Future costs that do not differ between alternatives	Sunk costs as presented above

Ethics and Business

Managers are faced with making decisions on a continual basis and these decisions will either lead to the attainment of the Company's goals or not. Managers could be faced with a dilemma where they could make an unethical decision that would lead to the attainment of the goals or an ethical decision that will lead to the goals not being attained. Business need to make sure they have policies and procedures in place that will lead to decision making being ethical rather than unethical.

Establishing an ethical business encourages employees to conduct business in a proper manner. Generally conducting business in a proper manner means making decisions that benefit the organization as a whole and do not unjustly or unfairly take advantage of anyone the Company is involved doing business with. It also would cause employees to take actions that do not violate any laws or regulations.

Ethics results from the interactions of personal morals and the objectives of business. The leaders of an organization need to make it clear that they act based on high personal moral principles and expect the same at all levels of the organization. This means that we will be applying our own views of what is right or wrong within a business setting.

Management accountants are in a unique position within an organization because they have access to all documentation and records that have to do with the day to day business. Having this access makes it necessary that the management accountant watch for anything that is not consistent with ethical behavior. The Institute of Management Accountants has a code of ethics for its members. This code is presented below:

Members of the IMA shall behave ethically. A commitment to ethical professional practice involves overarching principles that express our values and standards that guide our conduct.

PRINCIPLES

IMA's overarching ethical principles include: Honesty, Fairness, Objectivity, and Responsibility. Members shall act in accordance with these principles and shall encourage other within their organizations to adhere to them.

STANDARDS

A member's failure to comply with the following standards may result in disciplinary action.

COMPETENCE

Each member has a responsibility to

1. Maintain an appropriate level of professional expertise by continually developing knowledge and skills.
2. Perform professional duties in accordance with relevant laws, regulations, and technical standards
3. Provide decision support information and recommendations that are accurate, clear, concise and timely
4. Recognize and communicate professional limitations or other constraints that would preclude responsible judgment or successful performance of an activity

CONFIDENTIALITY

Each member has a responsibility to

1. Keep information confidential except when disclosure is authorized or legally required
2. Inform all relevant parties regarding appropriate use of confidential information. Monitor subordinates' activities to ensure compliance.
3. Refrain from using confidential information for unethical or illegal advantage

INTEGRITY

Each member has a responsibility to

1. Mitigate actual conflicts of interest. Regularly communicate with business associates to avoid apparent conflicts of interest. Advise all parties of any potential conflicts.
2. Refrain from engaging in any conduct that would prejudice carrying out duties ethically.
3. Abstain from engaging in or supporting any activity that might discredit the profession.

CREDIBILITY

Each member has a responsibility to

1. Communicate information fairly and objectively.

2. Disclose all relevant information that could reasonably be expected to influence an intended user's understanding of the reports, analyses, or recommendations.
3. Disclose delays or deficiencies in information, timeliness, processing, or internal controls in conformance with organizational policy and/or applicable law.

RESOLUTION OF ETHICAL CONFLICT

In applying the Standards of Ethical Professional Practice, you may encounter problems identifying unethical behavior or resolving ethical conflict. When faced with ethical issues, you should follow your organization's established policies on the resolution of such conflict. If these policies do not resolve the ethical conflict, you should consider the following courses of action:

1. Discuss the issue with your immediate supervisor except where it appears that the supervisor is involved. In that case, present the issue to the next level. If you cannot achieve a satisfactory resolution, submit the issue to the next management level. If your immediate superior is the chief executive officer or equivalent, the acceptable reviewing authority may be a group such as the audit committee, executive committee, board of directors, board of trustees, or owners. Contact with the levels above the immediate superior should be initiated only with your superior's knowledge, assuming he or she is not involved. Communication of such problems to authorities or individuals not employed or engaged by the organization is not considered appropriate, unless you believe there is a clear violation of the law.
2. Clarify relevant ethical issues by initiating a confidential discussion with an IMA Ethics Counselor or other impartial advisor to obtain a better understanding of possible courses of action.
3. Consult your own attorney as to legal obligations and rights concerning the ethical conflict.

Source: Institute of Management Accountants, Ethical Standards.

The Chartered Institute of Management Accountants has a similar code of ethical conduct for its members.

During the late 1990's there was a wave of corporate wrongdoing that led to several publicly traded companies going out of business. Also, it appeared that the auditors for some of the companies may have neglected their professional responsibilities, which led to one of the largest accounting firms in the world going out of business as well.

Because of this wave of problems Congress held hearings into some of the cases which ultimately led to the passing of the Sarbanes-Oxley Act of 2002.

The law includes a number of significant provisions. For example, the law requires management to assess whether internal controls over financial reporting are adequate. It also requires the company's external financial statement auditor to assess whether the controls are effective in preventing and detecting financial misstatements. To provide a significant deterrent for executives allowing or participating in financial misstatements the law allows for criminal penalties of up to a $5 million fine and 20 years in prison for being associated with financial statement fraud.

EXERCISES

1. Accounting information is used by various people both within and outside of an organization. Below as some potential users of accounting information:
   a. Banks
   b. Operations manager
   c. Production manager
   d. Customer
   e. Creditor
   f. Human resource manager
   g. Possible future stockholder
   - For the users identified above state whether they are internal or external users of financial information and whether they would be most interested in management accounting or financial accounting information.
2. Name three types of accounting information that would be provided by financial accounting and three types that would be provided by management accounting.
3. Contrast the rules governing the preparation of financial accounting information to those governing the preparation of management accounting information.
4. In decision making what causes information to be relevant. Identify one type of relevant information and one type of information that would not be relevant.
5. What are the four overarching principles in the standards of ethical conduct of the Institute of Management Accountants?

ETHICS IN BUSINESS

Case

Mary Jones works as the controller (she is a member of the Institute of Management Accountants) for Everyday Chemical Company, Inc. Everyday Chemical produces a variety of chemicals for both home and industrial use. Some of the chemicals that are hazardous and require special handling for the disposal of remnants of the manufacturing process, as Mary was gathering data for a footnote to the financial statements she came across a handwritten note addressed to the production manager, the note was unsigned. The contents of the note were as follows:

Fred, the disposal costs on the hazardous materials are really hurting our profitability. During the day to day business some of these chemicals inadvertently end up mixed in with the normal trash through minor spillage on the floor. I would like up to explore the possibility of mixing more of these chemicals with our day to day trash to see if we can reduce our disposal costs. The amounts should start out small and be gradually increased to see if our trash hauling vendor notices.

Mary was concerned about this as it would be both unethical and possibly illegal to intentionally mix the hazardous chemicals in with the normal trash.

Mary took the issue to her boss, the Chief Financial Officer, who told her not to worry about it as she was fully aware of what was going on and felt that it was good for the Company.

Mary does not want to drop the subject and feels that it needs to be stopped. She lives next door to a member of the Board of Directors, who does not work at the Company.

Mary has considered the next possible steps

1. Make an appointment with the CEO to discuss the issue.
2. Telling her neighbor on the Board of Directors about the issue.
3. Informing the appropriate legal and regulatory authorities about the practice.

Leaving the Company and remaining quiet about the issue.

Discuss each option she is considering with regard to the requirements of the standards of ethical conduct of the Institute of Management Accountants since Mary is a member.

Also, make a recommendation as to what step or steps you feel Mary should take both from a personal ethical perspective and based on compliance with the standards of ethical conduct.

CHAPTER 2 – REVIEW OF FINANCIAL ACCOUNTING

LEARNING OBJECTIVES

1. The student will understand the basics of the balance sheet as commonly prepared under U.S. Generally Accepted Accounting Principles (GAAP).
2. The student will understand the income statement as commonly presented under U.S. GAAP.
3. The student will obtain experience in creating a balance sheet and income statement from company trial balances.

Balance Sheet

The balance sheet is governed by a basic accounting equation as presented below:

assets = liabilities + equity

This equation gives us the basic classifications that the financial statement preparer will be identifying from the trial balance in order to create the balance sheet. It should be noted that the balance sheet is always prepared as of a given date and represents a snapshot of the balance sheet components at the close of business on that day,

Now we will look more in depth at the components and classifications of the balance sheet accounts. The major classifications of assets, liabilities and equity will each have sub-classifications on most companies' balance sheets. We will start out by looking at asset accounts and how they tie into the sub-classifications normally shown on the balance sheet.

Assets are classified based upon how quickly they will be used in the day to day operations of the business. Those items that will normally be used or turn to cash in the next operating cycle (for most businesses this would be one year) are sub-classified as *current assets*. The normal accounts that would be included in current assets would be cash, account receivable (net of any applicable allowance for bad debts), inventories (net of any inventory reserves) and prepaid expenses. Most small businesses would not have any other current asset accounts, some large businesses might have other accounts that would be sub-classified as current assets. These accounts might include cash equivalents and marketable securities. For purposes of the book we will only focus on the accounts common to small business.

Cash would represent any monies held in banks accounts, accounts at savings and loan associations, accounts at credit unions and any petty cash held on the business premises. Generally each account at a bank, savings and loan, or credit union would have a separate account on the trial balance as would the petty cash. These accounts would be combined into one line for cash when preparing the balance sheet.

Accounts receivable generally represents funds owed to the business by its customers. The customer make purchases on credit and based on the credit terms the customer has makes payment at a later date. Sometimes things cause customers not to make payment and so the company makes as estimate to amounts they probably won't collect. This estimate is based upon past history of the percentage of credit sales that go uncollected. The estimate normally doesn't identify a particular customer since if the business knew which customer was unlikely to pay they would not grant credit to that customer and would require cash payment for in advance for all sales. This estimate is called an allowance for bad debts (sometimes called allowance for doubtful accounts) and is deducted from the accounts receivable balance in calculating the amount that will show on the balance sheet as accounts receivable, net of allowances.

Inventories represent those items that will be used in production or sold to customers. Different types of businesses will have different types of inventories showing in their trial balance. Manufacturing companies normally have three types of inventories: raw materials, work in process, and finished goods. Raw materials are those items that the company purchases to use in the manufacturing process to make goods that will be sold to their customers, Work in process inventory represents the items that have been started in production but have not yet been finished and therefore are not ready for sale to customers. Finished goods inventory are those items that have been completed and are ready for sale to customers.

Normally, a service company such as a CPA firm or a law firm will not have any inventory. Some service companies that provide a product or a service that is not strictly an intellectual service may have some inventory. Examples of this would be fast food restaurants and hospitals.

Retail stores such as hardware stores or department stores will normally have inventory as their business is in selling products to the general public. They will only have finished goods inventory as they do not produce the items they sell.

Also, many companies will have some items that are obsolete or that sell slowly. In these cases the companies will make a reserve to recognize that not all of their products will sell within the next operating cycle. This reserve could be called reserve for slow moving inventory or a similar title.

In preparing the balance sheet all types of inventories would be combined and any reserves would be deducted from the total in calculating the net inventory line on the balance sheet.

Prepaid expenses represent those items that the company has paid for in advance and will receive the service over a period of time with the service to be completely consumed over the next year. An example for a business that is also applicable to individuals in their daily lives would be prepaid insurance. The company (or individual) pays for their insurance up front and the policy is for a given period of time (usually six months to a year). The unexpired portion of the insurance represents the prepaid asset.

After each of these items is shown on the balance sheet they would be totaled to show the amount of total current assets on the balance sheet.

Next on the balance sheet would the line for property, plant and equipment, net. This represents the long term tangible assets that the company has. These would include any land and buildings that are owned. It would also include any equipment or fixtures that are owned. These items could be large pieces of equipment used in a manufacturing facility, hospital beds and monitoring devices used in a hospital, cash registers or signs used by a fast food restaurant, or the shelving in use in a retail business. These are shown on the balance net of the accumulated depreciation for the items included.

Finally all other long term assets would be shown which would normally all intangible assets. These are assets that are used in or add value to the business but cannot be physically seen or touched. An example of an intangible asset would be a college degree. While the diploma can be seen or touched the degree cannot but it provides value for the individual. At the end of the asset section of the balance sheet all of the sub-classification totals and any lines not in a sub-classification would be totaled to obtain the line shown as total assets.

Next, we come to liabilities which have the same types of sub-classifications as assets. First are the *current liabilities*, those that will become due and payable during the next operating cycle of the business. This would normally consist of accounts payable (amounts owing to suppliers for purchase of inventory and other supplies) and accrued expenses (those items that will come due at a future point but within the next operating cycle) the most common type of accrued expense is for taxes, either payroll related or income tax. If the business has bank loans that require payments, those payments that will be due within the next year would also be considered a current liability and would normally be called current maturities of long term debt or something similar. These would be listed individually and then totaled for the line of current liabilities.

Next would be listed all of the long term liabilities (those that will become due and payable beyond one year from the balance sheet date). The most common items shown on a balance sheet would be bank loans or long term leases of buildings or equipment. These items would be combined with the sub-total for current liabilities to get the total liabilities line.

Following this would be the *shareholders' (stockholders') equity* section. This normally would have three lines: common stock (based on the number of shares outstanding times the par value per share), additional paid-in-capital (this represents the amounts that the original shareholders paid for their interest in the company that is in excess of the par value of the number of shares they acquired) and finally retained earnings (this represents the net earnings of the company since it began business less any dividends paid). The current year's income or loss would have to be combined with the retained earnings figure shown on the trial balance to obtain the amount to be shown on the balance sheet. These three lines would be totaled to obtain the line labeled total shareholders' equity.

The total liabilities line would be added to the total shareholders' equity line and this would be a line titled total liabilities and shareholders' equity. The total on this line must equal the amount on the total assets line to meet the requirements of the basic accounting equation.

Exhibit 2-1 - Sample Balance Sheet

ANY MANUFACTURING COMPANY

BALANCE SHEET

December 31, 20xx

ASSETS

Current Assets

Cash	$793,189
Accounts receivable, net	3,734,824
Inventories	5,375,132
Prepaid assets	722,818
Total current assets	10,625,963
Property, plant and equipment, net	5,882,036
Other assets	2,246,950
Total assets	$18,754,949

LIABILITIES AND SHAREHOLDERS' EQUITY

Current liabilities

Accounts payable	$1,964,317
Accrued expenses	$3,296,490
Current maturities of long term debt	100,000
Total current liabilities	5,360,807
Long-term loans payable	2,530,737
Long term lease obligations	1,836,666
Total liabilities	9,728,210

Shareholders' equity

Common stock, $ I par value	13,200
Additional paid-in capital	636,900
Retained earnings	8,376,639
Total shareholders' equity	9,026,739
Total liabilities and shareholders' equity	$18,754,949

INCOME STATEMENT

Now that we have reviewed the balance sheet we go on to a review of the income statement (sometimes called the statement of operations). The income statement will begin with a line for net sales (sometimes shown as net revenue). This line represents all sales made during the year less any sales deductions for items such as: items returned for credit, cash discounts taken by customers or possibly freight charges paid for shipment to the customer (if the customer was billed for the freight and the charges are included in the sales account).

If the business sells products then the next line will be the cost of goods sold (this could also be called cost of sales or cost of revenue). This represents what it cost the business to make or purchase the products that were sold to the customers. In a later chapter we will explore how to calculate this amount for companies that sell products.

The cost of goods sold will be subtracted from the net sales amount and will be shown on the income statement as gross margin (or gross profit). From this amount all general, selling and administrative expenses would be deducted to arrive at operating income (income from operations). In many cases this would be equal to an amount called earnings before interest and taxes (EBIT). However, in some statements the company will deduct interest expense before computing operating income. If interest is not deducted before computing operating income it will be deducted next and this will lead to a line called income before income taxes. Income tax expense will then be deducted and the result will be the net income (net profit).

The income statement is always prepared for a period ending with the balance sheet date.

Exhibit 2-2 - Sample Income Statement

ANY MANUFACTURING COMPANY

Income Statement

Year ending December 31, 20xx

Net sales	$36,477,460
Cost of goods sold	26,036,564
Gross margin	10,440,896
Selling, general and administrative expenses	6,590,110
Operating Income	3,850,786
Interest expense	629,602
Income before income tax	3,221,184
Income tax expense	647,587
Net income	$2,573,597

STATEMENT OF CASH FLOWS

The last financial statement we are going to discuss is the statement of cash flows. Like the income statement, the statement of cash flows is always prepared for a period of time ending with the date of the balance sheet. It is required to be prepared for the same period of time as the income statement. Therefore, if the income statement is for a year then the statement of cash flows must be for a year as well.

The statement of cash flows is broken down into three sections. These are cash flows from operating activities, cash flows from investing activities and cash flows from financing activities.

The cash flows from operating activities is the most significant section and involves the items that most investors, creditors and customers are most concerned with. The section starts with net income and then presents a reconciliation of non-cash items that will lead to identifying the final net cash flow from operating activities. The most common adjustments relate to depreciation, amortization and deferred income tax. If the company sold any fixed assets during the year and realized either a gain or loss the amount of gain or loss would also be recognized as an adjustment. If the company has made any adjustments to reserves, such as the allowance for bad debts then this would also represent an adjustment. Following any adjustments the company will then show the changes in the current assets and current liabilities as having an effect on cash flow from operations. If current assets, other than cash, increased they will be shown as a decrease to cash flow from operations while decreases in these accounts would show as an increase to cash flow from operations. If the current liabilities increased they would be shown as increases to cash flow from operations and decreases in the accounts will be shown as decreases to cash flow from operations.

Cash flows from investing activities relates to investments made for the good of the company. Typically these would involve fixed assets. They would include the proceeds from any sale of fixed assets and any additional investment in fixed assets (fixed asset purchases).

The final section of the statements of cash flows relates to the activities that provide financing for the business. These activities would include payments made on loans or long term leases, proceeds from loan advances, issuance of bonds, sales of additional common or preferred stock and payments of dividends.

The totals of these three sections account for the change in cash during the year and when the change is added to or subtracted from the cash balance at the beginning of the period it will provide the reconciliation to the cash balance at the end of the period.

Exhibit 2-3 - Sample Statement of Cash Flows

ANY MANUFACTURING COMPANY

Statement of Cash Flows

Year ending December 31, 20xx

Cash flows from operating activities	
Net Income	$2,573,597
Adjustments to reconcile net income to cash from operating activities	
Depreciation and amortization	1,546,816
Deferred taxes	(1,700)
Provision for doubtful accounts	(26,070)
Change in assets and liabilities	
Trade accounts receivable	(421,906)
Inventories	114,458
Prepaid expenses & other current assets	(107,648)
Trade accounts payable	(238,087)
Accrued expenses	(140,193)
Net cash from operating activities	3,299,267
Cash flows from investing activities	
Proceeds from sale of property and equipment	68,625
Additions to property and equipment	(1,460,133)
Net cash from investing activities	(1,391,508)
Cash flows from financing activities	
Payments on capital lease obligations	(59,466)
Proceeds from issuance of long-term debt	7,700,635
Payment on long-term debt	(7,624,793)
Cash dividends paid	(2,226,316)
Net cash from financing activities	(2,209,940)
Net Change in cash and cash equivalents	(302,181)
Cash and cash equivalents at beginning of year	1,095,370
Cash and cash equivalents at end of year	$793,189

In a complete set of financial statements issued in accordance with U.S. Generally Accepted Accounting Principles (GAAP) there would also be a statement of shareholders' equity included. It is not necessary to present that statement to accomplish the goals of this brief review of financial accounting and therefore the statement is not presented.

SUMMARY

In this chapter we have done a brief review of the primary financial statements (except the statement of shareholders' equity) that are the goal and product of a company's financial accounting records. There has been a review of the classification of items on the balance sheet, the normal order of items presented on an income statement and the breakdown of classifications and items on a statement of cash flows. Going forward the focus will be on management accounting now that the review of financial statements that are the result of financial accounting has been completed.

QUESTIONS

1. What are the primary financial statements that a company would issue following U.S. GAAP?
2. What are the major classifications of items shown on the balance sheet?
3. What is the definition of current assets?
4. What is the definition of current liabilities?
5. What items are typically considered current assets?
6. What items would typically be included in current liabilities?
7. In the sample income statement what line would be the equivalent of earnings before interest and taxes (EBIT)?
8. In the statement of cash flows what are the three classifications of cash flows?
9. What part of the statement of cash flows would creditors, investors and customers generally be most interested in?
10. Explain the differences in dating of the balance sheet, income statement and statement of cash flows.

EXERCISES

1. A company has cash of $10,000, net accounts receivable of $200,000, inventories of $300,000, property, plant and equipment of $500,000 and other assets of $ 250,000. How much does the company have in current assets?
2. Using the same information as in exercise 1 above, what does the company have in total assets?
3. A company has accounts payable of $5,000, accrued expenses of $25,000, current maturities of long term debt of $30,000 and long term debt of $300,000. What is the company's total of current liabilities?
4. Using the information in exercise 3 above, what are the total liabilities of the company?
5. Assume that the information in exercises 1 and 3 relate to the same company at the same date, what is the shareholders' equity in the company.
6. Using the trial balance for XYZ Manufacturing, Inc. in Appendix A, calculate the current assets and current liabilities for the company.
7. Using the trial balance for ABC Hospital Corporation in Appendix A calculate the shareholders equity for the company.

PROBLEMS

1. Using the trial balance for XYZ Manufacturing, Inc. in Appendix A, prepare a balance sheet and income statement for the company.
2. Using the trial balance for Double Bar Ranch in Appendix A, prepare a balance sheet and income statements for the ranch.
3. Using the trial balance for ABC Hospital Corporation in Appendix A, prepare a balance sheet and income statement for the hospital.
4. Using the local hardware store trial balance in Appendix A, prepare a balance sheet and income statement for the store.
5. Comparing the four trial balances in Appendix A, explain any significant differences in the makeup of the current assets of the companies.

CHAPTER 3–BASIC COST TERMINOLOGY AND COST FLOWS

LEARNING OBJECTIVES

1. Identify and give examples of each of the three basic manufacturing cost categories.
2. Describe the basic production process used by manufacturing companies
3. Describe the flow of costs for manufacturing, retail, and service companies and calculate the cost of gold manufactured and cost of goods sold for a manufacturing company
4. Discuss the impact of product costs and period costs on a company's financial statements

INTRODUCTION

All types of organizations incur costs businesses such as manufacturing, retailing and service businesses all incur costs. Non-profit organizations also incur costs as do non-business entities. This chapter will focus on business organizations. Every business organization provides products or services to its customers. Here we will describe the basic differences in business organizations. *Manufacturing companies (*such as automobile companies) take raw materials and make new products from them which are then sold to customers. *Merchandising (retail) companies* (such as Wal-Mart) buy products from manufacturers and the sell them to the final consumer. Merchandising companies would also include a local store such as a hardware store or general purpose store with a variety of products. *Service companies* (such as CPA firms or law firms), by contrast, do not provide a tangible product as their primary business. Additional examples of service firms would include airline companies, hospitals, and automobile repair shops. The service sector is the fastest growing sector of the U.S. economy and employs approximately 75% of the workforce. In addition to the types of organizations described above there are other sectors of the economy to be considered, they will be briefly discussed at appropriate times through the textbook and include agricultural and non-profit (charitable) organizations. In Appendix A, the textbook provides sample trial balances for a manufacturing firm, a retail business, a hospital (service firm) and an agricultural firm. These trial balances will be used throughout the textbook to provide a common point of reference by which to explain the concepts and contrast the types of organizations. It should be noted that some business organizations are a mixture of retail and service in that they sell something tangible but really constitute a service. An example of this type of business would be McDonald's or Kentucky Fried Chicken.

The initial focus will be on manufacturing companies as some of the items to be discussed early in the text relate almost exclusively to manufacturing. In those cases where it is practical we will show a contrast with the other types of business organizations. It might appear simple for companies to determine the costs of producing a product but that cost may vary based upon the reason the company wishes to identify the cost. There are rules for determining the cost of products included in inventory but these rules may vary depending whether the inventory is being valued for inclusion in a set of financial statements in accordance with U.S. GAAP, possibly for a bank, or for inclusion on the company's tax return. For the purpose of making decisions internally the management may want the costs tracked in a different manner that will help them focus on making good decisions or for budgeting purposes.

GENERAL COST CLASSIFICATIONS

Manufacturing costs - most manufacturing companies divide manufacturing costs into three broad categories: direct material, direct labor, and manufacturing overhead. Let's take a look at each of these categories.

Raw materials - the materials that are used in producing the final product are called *raw materials*. This term can be misleading as it could be interpreted to mean unprocessed natural resources like trees or iron ore. In the case of manufacturing the term raw materials is used to mean any material that is used in the final product. It needs to be noted that the finished product of one company could become the raw material for another company. An example of this could be that a lumber mill processes trees that have just been cut and makes lumber out of them, this becomes the final product of the lumber mill. A furniture manufacturing company purchases the lumber and it then becomes a raw material for the production of furniture.

Direct materials are those materials that become an integral part of the finished product and that can be physically and conveniently traced to it. An example of this would be the lumber used to make furniture. Sometimes it isn't worth the effort to trace the cost of relatively insignificant materials to the end products. An example of this would be the glue that is used in the manufacturing of a chair at a furniture factory. The glue would be considered an *indirect material* used in the process.

Direct labor - The term *direct labor* is used for those labor costs that can be easily (i.e. physically and conveniently) traced to the individual unit produced. The labor costs of assembly line workers would be an example of direct labor. Additional examples would include: machinists, carpenters and bricklayers. If labor costs cannot be traced directly to the creation of products or can be traced only at great cost and inconvenience they are considered to be *indirect labor* costs. Indirect labor costs are treated as part of manufacturing overhead and might include such people as janitors, maintenance personnel, and material handlers. The efforts of these workers are necessary to the production of the product but cannot be traced to individual products in any practical manner.

In many industries shifts are taking place in the structure of labor costs. As more sophisticated, automated equipment is being used in the production process it is being run and maintained by skilled indirect workers and is increasingly replacing direct labor. This has caused the percentage of product costs associated with direct labor to drop to below 10% in many industries. In a few companies, direct labor has become such a small portion of the overall cost that these companies no longer track their direct labor costs.

Manufacturing overhead-*Manufacturing overhead* is the third broad category of manufacturing cost. This category includes all items of manufacturing costs that are not direct labor or direct materials. Manufacturing overhead would include such items as indirect labor, indirect materials, repair and maintenance on production equipment, heat and light, depreciation, insurance, and property taxes on manufacturing facilities. The company would also incur depreciation, heat and light, insurance, and property taxes related to the selling and administrative activities of the company, however, these would not be included in manufacturing overhead. Only those costs associated with operating the factory are considered manufacturing overhead. The percentage of sales revenue represented by manufacturing overhead varies greatly among different industries.

Depending upon the individual company, manufacturing overhead may be called *indirect manufacturing costs, factory burden or factory overhead*. All of these terms mean the same thing as manufacturing overhead.

When manufacturing overhead is combined with direct labor it is called *conversion cost*. This term comes from the fact that direct labor and manufacturing overhead are used to convert the raw materials into the final product. If direct materials are combined with direct labor it is called *prime cost*.

NONMANUFACTURING COSTS

Generally, nonmanufacturing costs are broken down into two categories: selling costs, and general and administrative costs.

Selling (marketing) costs include all costs necessary to secure customer orders and get the product delivered to the customer. Sometimes these costs are called order getting and order filling costs. These could include: advertising, attendance at trade shows, sales travel, sales commissions, sales salaries, the cost of the finished goods warehouse and shipping and handling.

General and administrative costs include all costs associated with the general management of the organization. Examples would include: executive salaries, human resource department costs, accounting department costs, secretarial costs and public relations costs.

Nonmanufacturing costs are commonly referred to as selling, general and administrative costs (SG&A).

PRODUCTS COSTS VERSUS PERIOD COSTS

Another way to differentiate costs, in addition to manufacturing and nonmanufacturing costs, is to base the distinction on purpose of the cost. Costs that are put into the product would therefore be classified as *product costs*, while the costs that are not put into the products would be called *period costs* as they are grouped in the financial records by the period they are incurred.

For financial and tax reporting purposes, *product costs* include all costs that are involved with acquiring or making a product. If the company is a manufacturing company these costs would consist of direct materials, direct labor and manufacturing overhead. Product costs are viewed as being attached to the units of product that were produced through the use of the product costs if the firm is in manufacturing. If the firm is in merchandising (retail) then the product costs would include the costs to acquire the product, including freight costs for delivery. When the goods go into inventory awaiting sale to a customer the costs are attached to the units in inventory and would be included in the inventory accounts on the balance sheet. These costs would be removed and then become an expense (typically called cost of goods sold) when the goods are sold to a customer. Since these costs are initially assigned to inventory they are referred to as *inventoriable costs*. It is important to realize that these costs are not necessarily recognized as expenses in the period in which they are incurred.

Period costs are all of the costs that are not included in product costs. These would typically be the selling, general and administrative costs (SG&A). These costs are expensed in the income statement in the period in which they are incurred, using the rules of accrual accounting.

Exhibit 3-1 below depicts the cost flows for the costs we have been discussing.

Exhibit 3-1 - Summary of Cost Flows

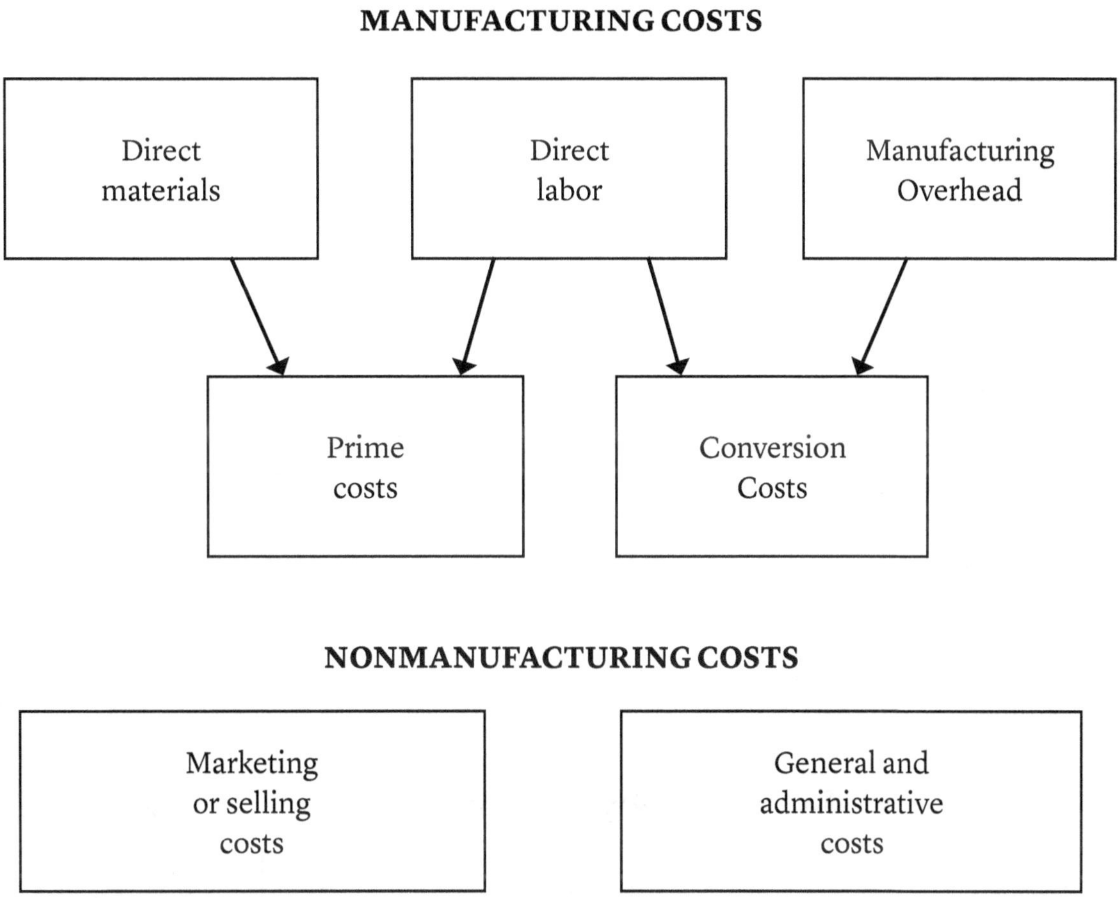

In manufacturing there are typically three classes of inventory, *raw materials, work in process (WIP) and finished goods*. Raw materials inventory consists of the items that were purchased and will be converted to the final product for sale. Work in process inventory is the production that is in process on the factory floor but is not ready for sale to a customer. This inventory would be valued based on the sum of the direct materials put in process, the direct labor used to produce the product to date and the allocation of manufacturing overhead based on production to date. Finished goods consist of the completed product that has not yet been sold to customers. On the balance sheet these three amounts would be added together to represent the inventory line, however, the amounts, by class, would generally be broken down in a footnote to the financial statements in a formal set of financial statements. In the case of a merchandising company there would only be finished goods inventory.

Exhibit 3-2 depicts the cost flows through the inventory accounts in a manufacturing company. Exhibit 3-3 shows how inventory costs flow in a merchandising company.

Exhibit 3-2 -Cost Flows in a Manufacturing Company

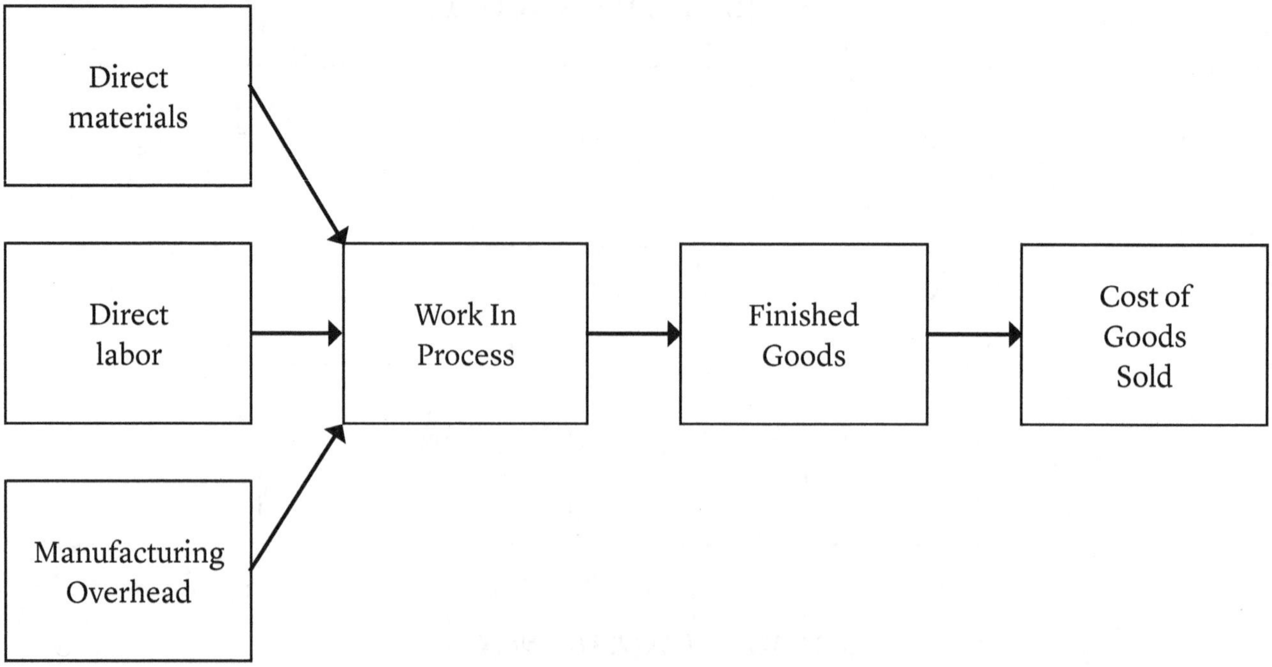

Exhibit 3-3 - Costs Flows in a Merchandising Company

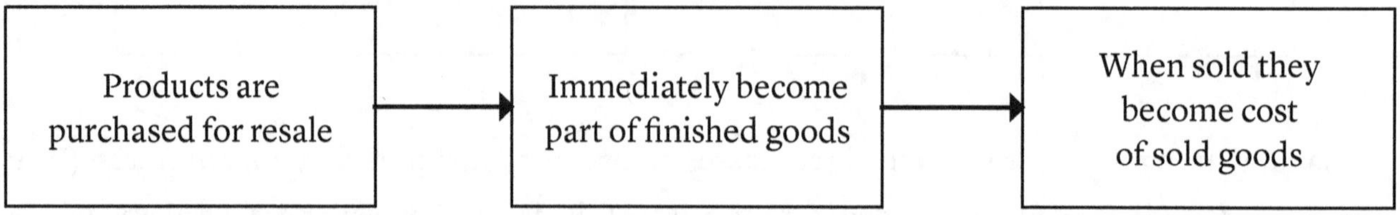

COST OF GOODS MANUFACTURED AND SOLD

In a manufacturing company tracing inventory through the accounts to arrive at the cost of goods sold can be an involved process since there are three types of inventory and a variety of costs. In order to trace these costs through to arrive at the final cost of goods sold for use in the financial statements and on the tax return we have to trace a summary of all costs through for the year of the financial statements or tax return. This is a three step process: the first step is to identify the value of the raw materials used in production during the period, the second step is to combine the direct materials calculated is the first step with the direct labor and manufacturing overhead costs incurred during

the period (this step also accounts for any change in value for work in process during the year) this step gives us the cost of goods manufactured for the year, the final step is to account for the change in finished goods inventory during the year and combine that with the cost of goods manufactured for the year to arrive at the cost of goods sold for the year. The next three exhibits will show this process.

Exhibit 3-4 - Raw Materials Used During the Year

EVERY MANUFACTURING COMPANY
Cost of Raw Materials Used
Year Ending December 31, 20xx

Raw material Inventory, beginning of year	$100,000
Add: raw material purchased during the year	300,000
Raw material available	400,000
Less: raw materials inventory, end of year	50,000
Raw materials used in production	$350,000

Exhibit 3-5 - Cost of Goods Manufactured

EVERY MANUFACTURING COMPANY
Cost of Goods Manufactured
Year Ending December 31, 20xx

Raw materials used in production (from above)	$350,000
Add: Direct labor	70,000
Add: Manufacturing overhead	140,000
Total manufacturing costs	560,000
Add: Beginning work in process inventory	80,000
	640,000
Deduct: ending work in process inventory	90,000
Cost of goods manufactured	$550,000

Exhibit 3-6 – Cost of Goods Sold

EVERY MANUFACTURING COMPANY
Cost of Goods Sold
Year Ending December 31, 20xx

Cost of goods manufactured (from above)	$550,000
Add: beginning finished goods inventory	200,000
Goods available for sale	750,000
Deduct: ending finished goods inventory	225,000
Cost of goods sold	$525,000

To determine the cost of goods sold which will ultimately appear on the income statement and tax return for the entity a manufacturing firm will go through the process shown above to obtain the amount to be reported. The most time consuming part of the process is the preparation of the *schedule of cost of goods manufactured*. This schedule can appear to be complex but generally the information is easily found in the company's computerized accounting system. The schedule of cost of goods manufactured contains the three elements of product costs that we have previously discussed (direct materials, direct labor, and manufacturing overhead). The direct materials are not simply the amount of materials that we purchased during the year, rather the amount purchased during the year has to be adjusted for any change in raw materials inventory during the year. The amount of direct materials used becomes the figure that is brought forward for the calculation of the cost of goods manufactured. The amounts for direct labor and manufacturing overhead are the amounts incurred during the year (using accrual accounting) and need no adjustment before being used in the calculation. The total of these three elements then need to be adjusted by the change in work in process inventory during the year to reach the final number that represents the cost of goods manufactured.

Once the calculation of the cost of goods manufactured is complete, the amount obtained by completing the schedule is then brought forward to be used in the calculation of cost of goods sold. This amount is adjusted by the change in the finished goods inventory from the beginning of the year to the end of the year. Once the cost of goods manufactured is adjusted for the change in finished goods inventory, the calculation of the cost of goods sold is complete. This will provide the amount to be used in the company's financial statements. It will also provide the basis for the amount to be reported in the company's tax return.

For tax purposes certain parts of the information will have to be entered on the company's tax form to make the calculation on the tax form as required. The tax forms that would be used for these calculations depend upon the legal structure for taxes. If the business is a proprietorship, then the calculation will be on Schedule C for Form 1040 of the owner. If the business is a partnership it will be on Form 1065 and a corporation would report the information on Form 1120. Copies of these forms are provided in Appendix C. We will have a more in depth discussion of taxes later in the book.

For a merchandising (retail) company the calculation of the cost of goods sold is much simpler. Since the merchandising company only has a finished goods inventory it is a one step process to calculate the costs of goods sold. The company takes the amount of inventory purchased during the year and adjusts it by the change in finished goods inventory from the beginning of the year to the end of the year.

A service company may have cost of goods sold if part of their service involves selling a product as well as providing a service, such as was mentioned for fast food chains like McDonalds and Kentucky Fried Chicken. In this case the calculation would be the same as those discussed above for the merchandising company. If there are no products involved in the service company's business then there would be no cost of goods sold.

An agricultural company would be likely to have cost of goods sold but the tracing of the costs is more difficult. If the company is a livestock producer the cost of livestock purchased can be traced to the time the purchased livestock is sold. If the livestock is raised it is very difficult to assign costs to the growing of the livestock. Therefore generally a livestock producer would have a very small amount (if any) in the cost of goods sold. If the agricultural company is raising a crop or crops then they would not be likely to have an amount in cost of goods sold as the seed and fertilizer would be expensed in the year used and not included as an inventoriable cost for when the crop was sold.

SUMMARY

In this chapter we have covered the basic classifications of costs, whether they are product costs or period costs. Product costs add value to the product produced while period costs are not related to the production of the product. Product costs flow through the inventory system and are shown on the balance sheet until the product is sold. At that point in time they become a cost that goes on the income statement as cost of goods sold (sometimes called cost of sales or cost of revenue).

KEY TERMS

- direct material
- product costs
- prime costs
- work in process inventory
- direct labor
- period costs
- conversion costs
- finished goods inventory
- manufacturing overhead
- inventoriable costs
- raw materials inventory
- cost of goods sold

QUESTIONS

1. What types of costs would be included in manufacturing overhead?
2. Define prime costs.
3. Define conversion costs
4. Explain the flow of costs through the inventory accounts of a manufacturing firm.
5. Explain how the flow of costs would differ between a manufacturing and a merchandising company.

EXERCISES AND PROBLEMS

3-1. Calculate the total inventory that would be shown on the balance sheet for XYZ Manufacturing based on the trial balance in Appendix A.

3-2. Calculate the total inventory to be shown on the balance sheet of Local Hardware Store based on the trial balance in Appendix A.

3-3. Prepare a schedule of manufacturing overhead for XYZ Manufacturing based on the trial balance in Appendix A.

3.4. Using the information on the trial balance for XYZ Manufacturing, in Appendix A, calculate the raw material purchases during the year if the beginning of the year raw materials inventory was equal to $ 500,000. Assume that material cost of goods sold is equal to raw materials used in production.

3.5. Using the information on the trial balance for XYZ Manufacturing, in Appendix A, calculate the beginning work in process inventory. Assume that cost of goods manufactured is $ 6,319,202.

3.6. Using the information on the trial balance for XYZ Manufacturing, in Appendix A, calculate the beginning finished goods inventory. Assume that cost of goods sold equal $6,433,989 and that cost of goods manufactured equals $6,319,202.

3.7. Identify which items, if any, would be considered raw materials based on the trial balance for ABC Hospital Corporation in Appendix A.

3.8. Calculate direct labor for ABC Hospital Corporation, if any, based on the trial balance in Appendix A.

3.9. Identify and calculate the prime costs for Double Bar Ranch and Cattle Company based on the trial balance in Appendix A.

3.10. Identify the inventory values for: ABC Hospital Corporation, Local Hardware Store, Double Bar Ranch and Cattle Company, and XYZ Manufacturing based on the trial balances in Appendix A. Explain why there would be significant differences in the amount of inventory as a percentage of sales.

CHAPTER 4 – COST BEHAVIOR AND COST TYPES IN BUSINESS

LEARNING OBJECTIVES

1. Understand the difference between variable and fixed costs.
2. Identify and describe semi-variable (mixed) costs
3. Recognize the difference between variable and absorption costing.
4. Recognize the income statement impact difference between variable and absorption costing
5. Identify the benefits of using either variable or absorption costing in decision making.

FIXED AND VARIABLE COSTS

To predict costs and manage them on a day to day basis, managers must identify key activities performed, the resources used in performing these activities, costs of the resources used and the measures of the activities that require the use of resources and thereby drive costs. *To control costs, managers will usually focus on managing the activities that are performed to make, sell and deliver the products or services of the company.* The focus will not necessarily be on the products and services themselves.

To be able to manage costs the cost drivers for each cost must be identified. Along with identifying the cost driver, the relationship, of the cost, to changes in sales and/or production volume must be identified. We will begin by discussing fixed and variable costs.

Fixed costs are those costs that do not change in total due to changes in volume. The focus is on the total fixed costs and not on costs per unit. As volume changes per unit costs will change for the fixed costs but the total costs will not. If we were to focus on costs per unit for the fixed cost we could be led into making decisions based on data that is not relevant. As an example we lease a building for $100,000 per year. If our production volume is 1000 units then our cost per unit would be $100 per unit but if our production volume was 10,000 units then our cost per unit would be $10. We should not base any decisions on the cost per unit for rent because the total amount of the rent will not change based on volume, therefore cost per unit is not relevant to the decision making process.

Variable costs are those costs that that vary, in total, in direct proportion to changes in volume. The variable cost per unit remains constant but the total cost changes with changes in volume. As an example we are producing music CDs, the cost of the CD is $1 per unit, at a production volume of 10,000 units our total cost for the CDs is $10,000, but if the volume increases to 100,000 units our total cost will increase to $100,000. Managers will look at costs per unit for variable costs in making decisions because if they can lower the cost per unit then the total cost will go down proportionally for the variable cost items. In evaluating variable costs the cost per unit is relevant in the decision making process.

In dealing with both fixed and variable costs we are concerned with the relevant range of activity. The *relevant range* is the range of activity levels where the total cost for fixed costs and per unit cost for variable costs will not change. An example of how the relevant range impacts costs is as follows: assume we lease a building for production and due to space limitations our maximum production in the space is 10,000 units per year. As long as our production needs are 10,000 units or less the cost is fixed at the lease of $100,000. If our production needs go to 12,000 units per year we have now gone outside of the relevant range and will have to increase our total fixed costs by leasing additional production space to handle the increased volume. The additional leased production space will increase our total fixed costs now that we are outside of the relevant range. Per unit variable cost will not change within the first 10,000 units as we are within the relevant range. However, once we go outside of the relevant range variable cost per unit could change. This could be caused because labor at the new production facility costs either more or less than at the current production facility. It also could change the cost of our raw materials due to a difference in the shipping costs to the new location.

To summarize fixed costs should be thought of on a total cost basis and variable costs should be thought of on a per unit cost basis.

To determine a company's total costs for any given level of production we can express the total cost function as an equation. The total cost equation can be expressed as:

$$A = Bx + C$$

In this equation A equals the company's total cost and this is obtained by taking B (which represents the variable cost per unit) times x (which represents the production volume) and that sum is added to C (which represents total fixed costs).

Exhibit 4-1 - Summary of Variable and Fixed Cost Behavior

Cost Type	In Total	Per Unit
Fixed cost	Total fixed costs are not affected by changes in volume	Fixed cost per unit changes inversely with changes in volume
Variable cost	Total variable costs change directly in proportion to changes in volume	Variable cost per unit is not affected by changes in volume

We have been discussing fixed and variable costs. The discussion of the costs has been focused on manufacturing as that is the business type where these concepts are most applicable. Generally it is not reasonable to try and apply these concepts in any depth to other types of business organizations. For a service company the primary variable cost would be in labor, but once you hire a full time employee the cost now becomes fixed as the employee will still be paid even if there is not sufficient work but the company's volume in still in the relevant range that requires that employee to be part of the company. In merchandising the variable costs would be the cost of the products sold. In most merchandising companies the product mix is quite varied so this makes it very difficult to trace the variable costs and predict behavior other than as a percentage of sales. In agriculture there are variable costs that can be traced such as feed costs for livestock operations or water costs for irrigation for crop production but they would be hard to trace even as a percentage of sales with any level of predictability. These costs should be looked at for all types of businesses but primarily they will assist decision making in a manufacturing business.

MIXED (SEMI-VARIABLE) COSTS

In addition to costs that fixed and variable, there are costs that have both a fixed and a variable component. The costs are called *mixed (semi-variable) costs.* Examples of this type of cost could include the cost of electricity. With electricity there is a basic cost to have service and have the lights on in the factory (this would be the fixed component) and then are additional charges that are incurred as more equipment is being used or additional shifts are added to meet production needs (this is the variable component). In trying to make decisions regarding mixed costs the managers (or the accounting department) will frequently come up with an equation that will allow the estimation of the total cost for a mixed cost based on the volume of production.

The equation can be estimated by using different mathematical models. The most frequently utilized models are the high-low method and regression. We will discuss both methods starting with the high-low method.

HIGH –LOW METHOD

The high-low method is the simplest mathematical method for estimating the cost equation for a mixed cost. This method is useful when the cost patterns between cost and volumes can be shown as a straight line function and there is a relatively small amount of variance between the points on the line and the cost function line itself. In this case we select only the highest and the lowest points (based on activity level) based on the assumption that both of these points are within the relevant range for the company. Normally there will be several points where data has been recorded, but by selecting only the highest and lowest we simplify the calculation. Once we select the two points we can calculate the cost equation that will represent the line for the mixed cost we are looking at. This equation will be in the same format as the total cost equation that was shown earlier in the chapter. We will illustrate the use of this method based on the data in Exhibit 4-2.

Exhibit 4-2 - Overhead Costs for a Pizza Restaurant

Month	Pizzas	Overhead
1	1200	$7,300
2	3250	$15,600
3	4000	$18,500
4	3500	$16,200
5	2500	$12,650
6	1800	$9,850
7	3200	$15,500
8	2750	$13,500
9	3950	$18,150
10	2600	$12,850
11	3600	$16,950
12	2750	$13,450

In the data presented in Exhibit 4-2 we start out by searching for the highest and lowest levels of activity. The highest level of activity is in month 3 with 4000 pizzas and the lowest level of activity is in month 1 with 1200 pizzas. In using the high low method we subtract the lowest level of activity from the highest level of activity to find the change, in this case the change is 2800 (4000-1200). We then take the overhead costs for the same periods and we subtract the cost for the period with the lowest activity level from the cost for the period with the highest activity level, for this example it amounts to $10,200 ($18,500-7,300).

Once we have these two amounts we can calculate the variable portion of the mixed cost by dividing the change in amount by the change in activity level. This would be $10,200/2,800 or $4 per pizza in our example. Now that we have the variable component of the total cost we can calculate the fixed component. We calculate the fixed component by taking either the lowest or the highest level of activity and multiply the variable cost per unit times the number of units (pizzas) to obtain the total variable cost component. For illustration purposes, we will use the highest activity level and thus we will multiply the 4,000 pizzas times the $4 per pizza of variable costs to obtain the total variable cost portion of the overhead, in this case $16,000. We can then calculate the fixed component of the overhead by subtracting the total variable cost component from the total overhead cost. The fixed overhead component is $2,500 ($18,500-$16,000).

Based on these calculations we come up with our cost equation (total overhead = ($4 x number of pizzas) + $2,500).

This method is very simple and the information provided is accurate enough for decision making purposes if the data that we have is all relatively consistent. If the observed data has large variances in the data then the high-low method would not be appropriate.

REGRESSION ANALYSIS

If there are large variations in the observed data then it becomes necessary to use all observed sets of data to properly calculate the cost function. This most common way to calculate this based on the use of all data points would be to use regression analysis. Regression analysis is based on a complex mathematical formula. However regression analysis can be performed using business calculators or using a spreadsheet program like Excel by Microsoft. The analysis will require the identification of both an *independent* and a *dependent* variable.

In the example shown in Exhibit 4-2 the independent variable is the number of pizzas (the activity level) and the dependent variable is the overhead cost. To perform regression analysis in a spreadsheet we start by entering the data as shown in Exhibit 4-3 below:

Exhibit 4-3 - Data Entered in Spreadsheet

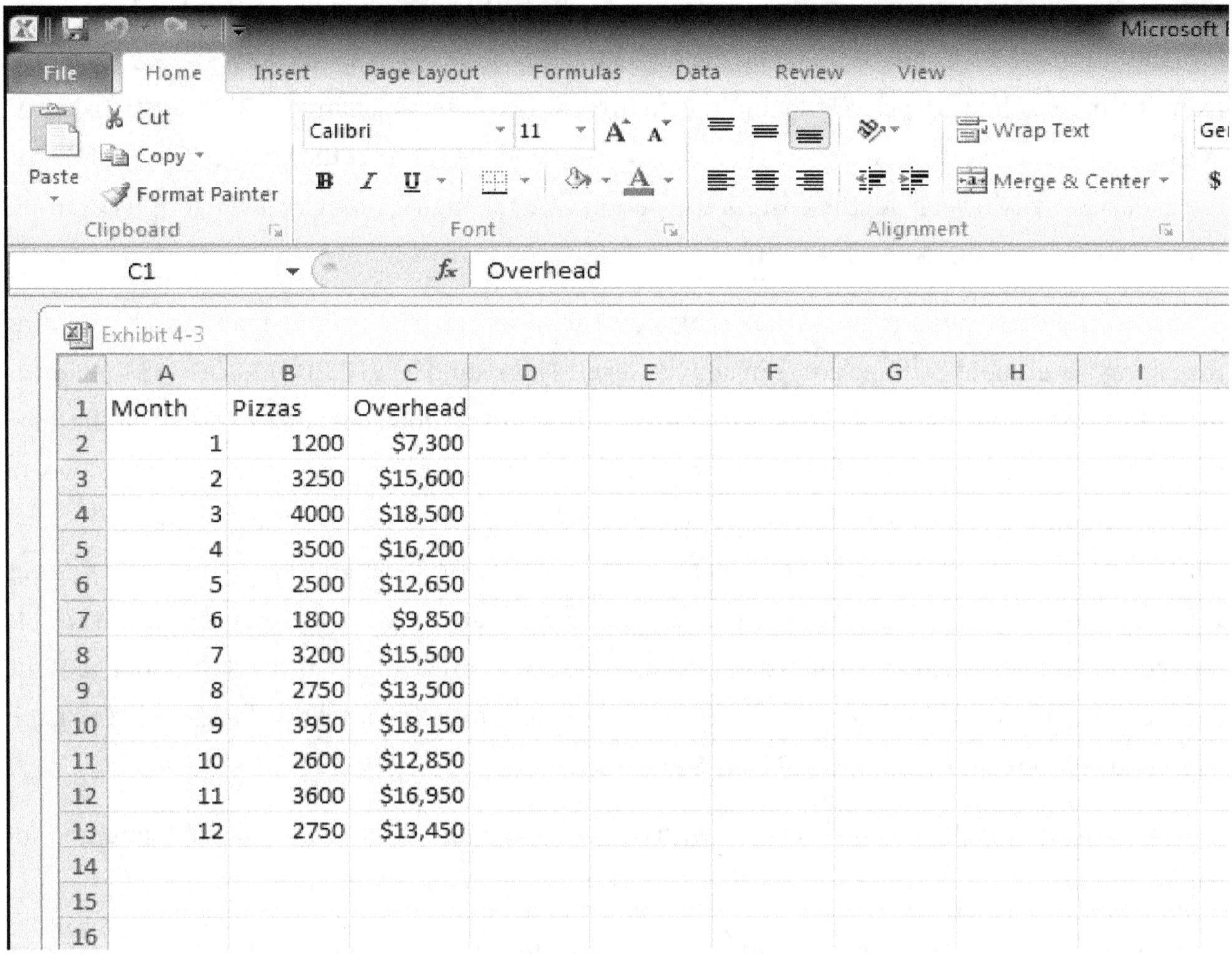

	A	B	C
1	Month	Pizzas	Overhead
2	1	1200	$7,300
3	2	3250	$15,600
4	3	4000	$18,500
5	4	3500	$16,200
6	5	2500	$12,650
7	6	1800	$9,850
8	7	3200	$15,500
9	8	2750	$13,500
10	9	3950	$18,150
11	10	2600	$12,850
12	11	3600	$16,950
13	12	2750	$13,450

Exhibit 4-4 - Regression Analysis

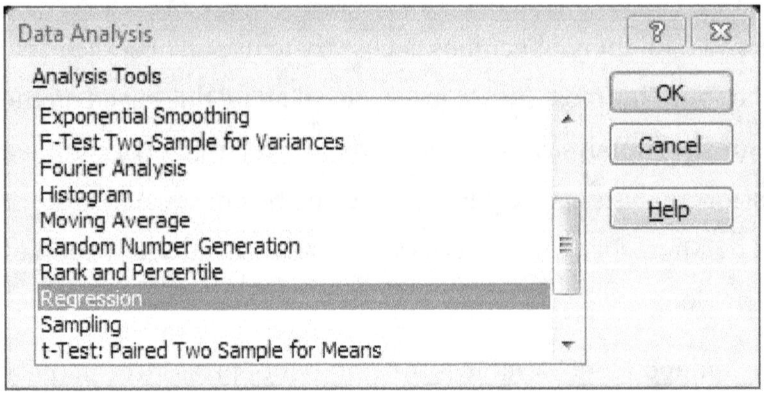

Exhibit 4-5 - Input Ranges

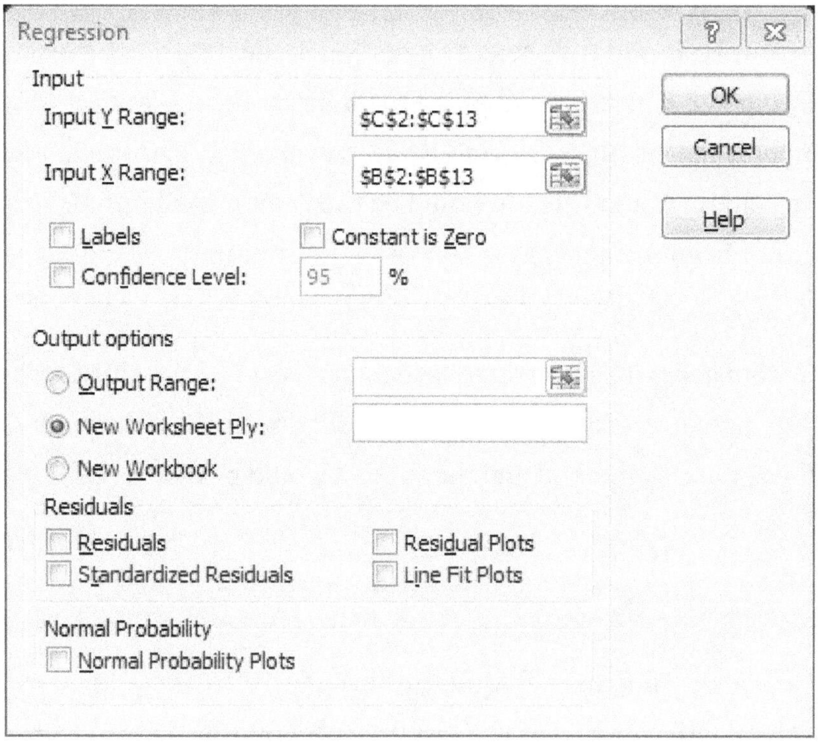

Exhibit 4-6 - Regression Table

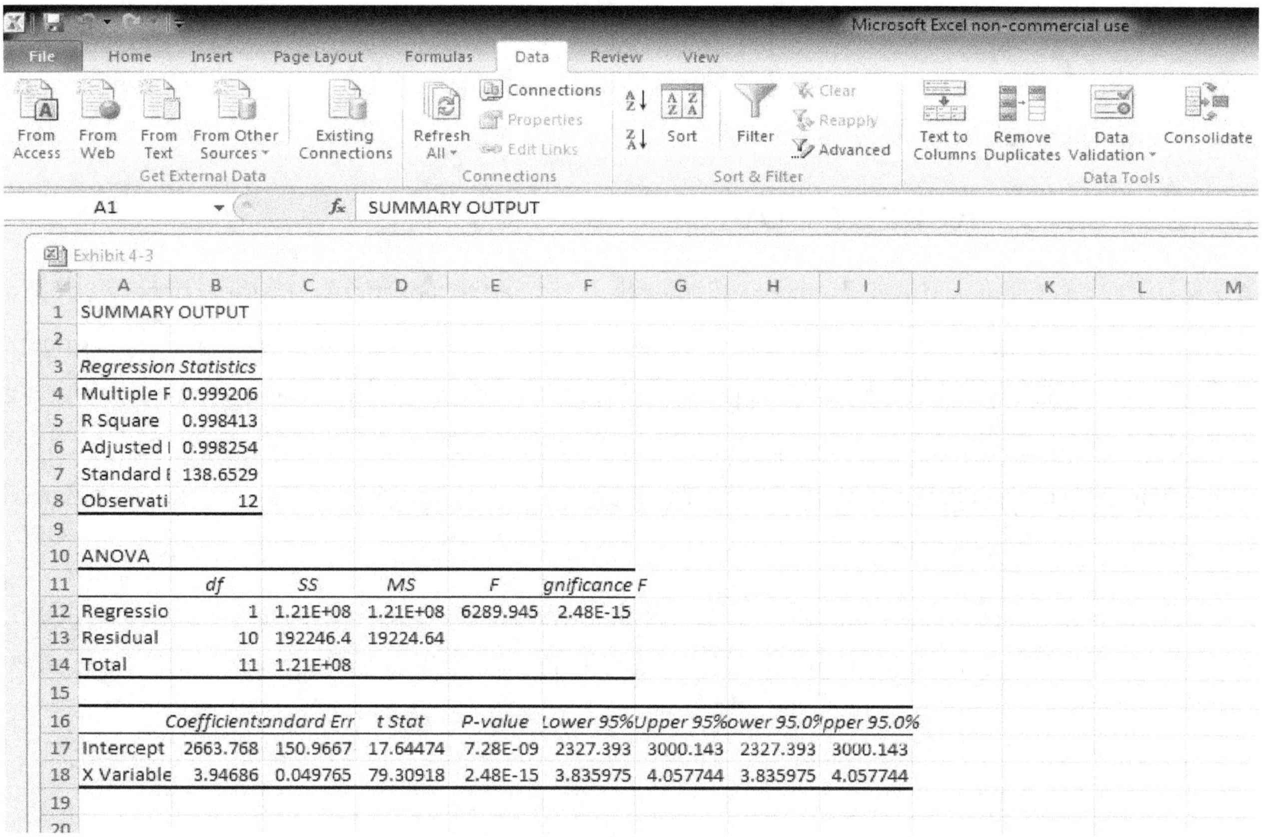
A1 SUMMARY OUTPUT

	A	B	C	D	E	F	G	H	I
1	SUMMARY OUTPUT								
2									
3	*Regression Statistics*								
4	Multiple F	0.999206							
5	R Square	0.998413							
6	Adjusted I	0.998254							
7	Standard E	138.6529							
8	Observati	12							
9									
10	ANOVA								
11		*df*	*SS*	*MS*	*F*	*gnificance F*			
12	Regressio	1	1.21E+08	1.21E+08	6289.945	2.48E-15			
13	Residual	10	192246.4	19224.64					
14	Total	11	1.21E+08						
15									
16		*Coefficient*	*andard Err*	*t Stat*	*P-value*	*Lower 95%*	*Upper 95%*	*ower 95.0%*	*pper 95.0%*
17	Intercept	2663.768	150.9667	17.64474	7.28E-09	2327.393	3000.143	2327.393	3000.143
18	X Variable	3.94686	0.049765	79.30918	2.48E-15	3.835975	4.057744	3.835975	4.057744

Once you have entered the data into a spreadsheet you will then need to perform the regression analysis. To perform the regression analysis you will need to click on the **Data** tab on the Excel toolbar, next you will need to select **Data Analysis** and then select regression in the drop down box (as shown in Exhibit 4-4). A screen will come up where you will need to fill in the Input Y ranges (this is the dependent variable) and the Input X ranges (this is the independent variable). In the example above, Input Y would be the values in column C and Input X would be the values in column B. This is shown in Exhibit 4-5. The final output from the analysis is shown in the summary report that is included as Exhibit 4-6.

While regression analysis provides a more accurate equation for the mixed cost that is being evaluated, it would be costly for a small business to use due to the amount of data to be collected. It is much quicker and less costly to use the High-Low method and therefore it would be more applicable to small business.

STEP COSTS

In addition to fixed variable and mixed costs companies frequently have *step costs.* These are costs that change abruptly at different levels of activity because the resources are only available in large chunks that cannot be divided. Normally the step up in the cost would only be applicable to items that would be considered to be a fixed cost. An example of this would be when a factory adds an additional shift. There is a supervisor needed for the first shift and his/her salary is considered fixed (within the relevant range). Once a second shift is added then a second supervisor is added and thus there is one time large step up in supervisory salaries. This second supervisor would now be considered a fixed cost over the new relevant range of activity.

DIRECT AND INDIRECT COSTS

A *direct cost* is a cost that can easily and conveniently be traced to a particular product or service (cost object). Also it could be easily predicted for a product or service under consideration. This concept goes beyond what we discussed with regards to direct material and direct labor. For example, if a company assigns cost to its various sales offices then the sales manager's salary for any given sales office would be direct cost of that office (e.g. the regional sales manager for the Chicago area would be a direct cost of the Chicago office).

An *indirect cost* is a cost that cannot be easily and conveniently traced to a particular cost object. An example would be a factory that produces multiple products (like Kellogg's cereal). The factory manager's salary would be an indirect cost to a particular variety such as Kellogg's Corn Flakes. To assign the cost to the corn flakes Kellogg's would design and use a cost allocation system.

In a small business direct costs should be traced to the products or services where it is easy to trace. In the case of indirect costs it would not be cost efficient for many small businesses to try and determine a cost allocation system. It would be likely to cost the business more than the information would be worth in decision making to design the system. Therefore, for many small businesses it is better to treat all indirect costs as period costs and not to attempt to allocate these costs.

OVERVIEW OF ABSORPTION AND VARIABLE COSTING

Absorption costing is a system that includes all manufacturing costs, whether variable or fixed, as product costs. Included as product costs would be direct materials, direct labor, variable manufacturing overhead, and fixed manufacturing overhead. This method is required for both financial statement preparation under generally accepted accounting principles (GAAP) and income tax reporting but it may not be the best for decision making purposes. This is also sometimes called *full costing*. As discussed earlier selling, general and administrative expenses (S, G&A) are expensed in the period incurred.

In contrast, under *variable costing* (sometimes called *direct costing*) only those manufacturing costs that vary directly with output are treated as product costs. This means that direct materials, direct labor, and variable manufacturing overhead are treated as product costs but fixed manufacturing overhead is treated as a period cost. As with absorption costing all selling, general and administrative expenses (whether fixed or variable) are treated as period costs under variable costing.

Exhibit 4-7 - Comparison of Absorption and Variable Costing

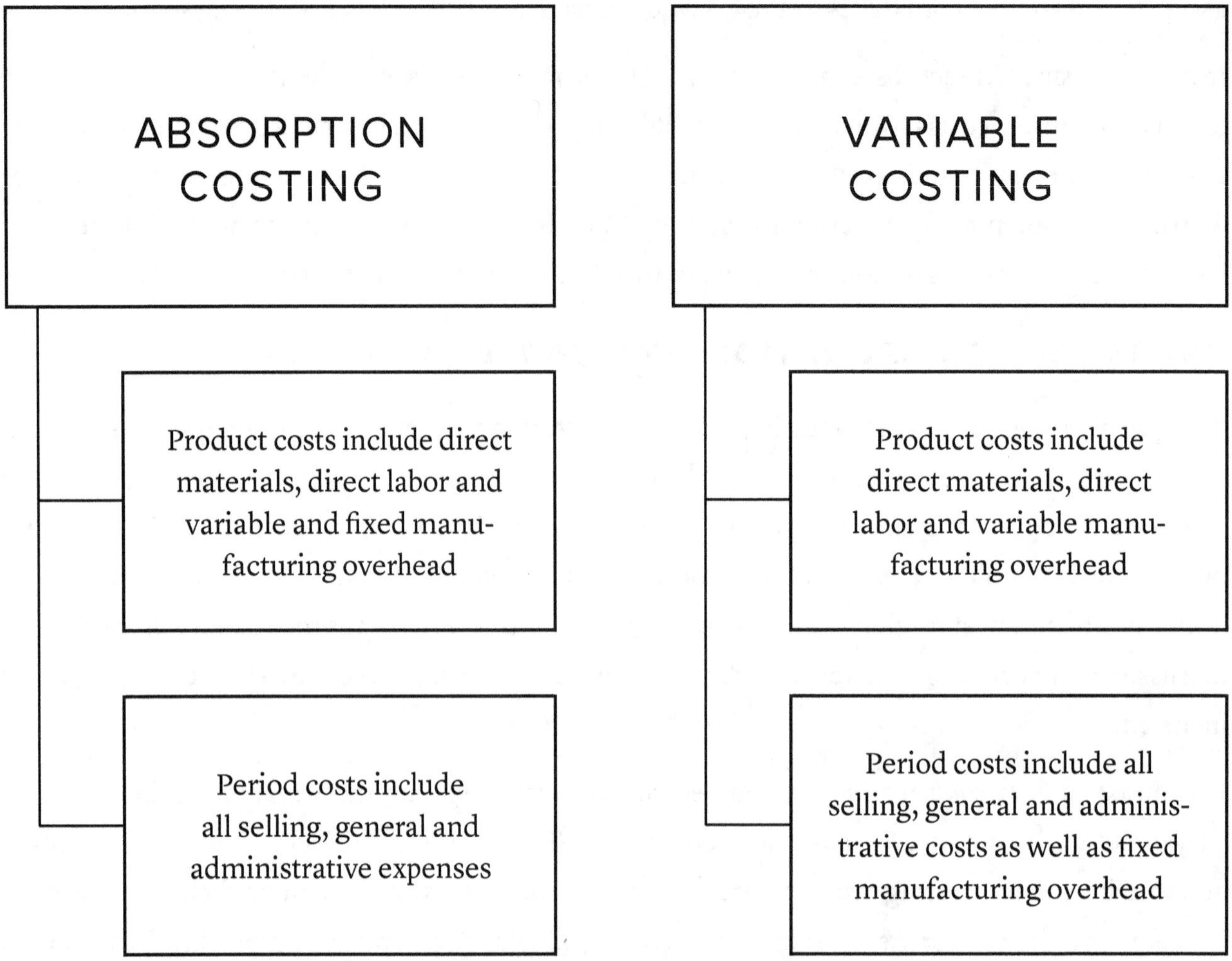

To show the difference in computing unit costs under both absorption and variable costing we will consider Beaver Manufacturing, a small company that manufactures only one product and has the following cost structure.

Number of units produced each year 6,000

Variable costs per unit:

Direct materials $3

Direct labor $4

Variable manufacturing overhead $1

Variable selling and administrative expenses $3

Fixed costs per year:

Fixed manufacturing overhead $30,000

Fixed selling and administrative costs $15,000

We will compute the unit product cost under both absorption and variable costing.

Under absorption costing the unit product cost would be as follows: direct materials of $3, direct labor of $4, variable manufacturing overhead of $1 and fixed manufacturing overhead of $5 ($30,000/6,000 units). This equals a total unit product cost of $13, which is composed of $8 of variable costs and $5 of fixed costs.

Under variable costing the unit product cost would be as follows: direct materials of $3, direct labor of $4 and variable manufacturing overhead of $1 for a total of $8. Under variable costing the fixed manufacturing overhead is considered to be a period cost and therefore is not included in the unit product cost.

Now we will consider an income comparison between the absorption and variable costing approaches. This comparison will use the information above for Beaver Manufacturing and it will also consider the additional information below:

Units in beginning inventory 0

Units produced........ 6,000

Units sold........ 4,000

Units in Ending Inventory 2,000

Selling price per unit $20

Selling and administrative expenses:

Variable cost per unit $3

Fixed per year........ $15,000

As a reminder the unit costs were $13 under absorption costing and $8 under variable costing as calculated earlier. Since there are some units left in inventory at the end of the year some of the fixed manufacturing costs will be left in inventory under absorption costing, and thus are inventoriable costs.

The income statement for *absorption costing* would be as follows:

Sales (4,000 units times $20)	$80,000
Less: Cost of Goods Sold (4,000 units times $13)	52,000
Gross Margin (Gross Profit)	28,000
Less: Selling and Administrative Costs	
(4,000 units times $3 plus $15,000)	27,000
Net Operating Income	$1,000

The income statement under *variable costing* would be as follows:

Sales (4,000 units times $20)	$80,000
Less: Cost of Goods Sold (4,000 units times $8)	32,000
Less: Variable Selling and Administrative Expenses	
(4000 units times $3)	12,000
Contribution Margin (Variable Margin)	36,000
Less: Fixed Manufacturing Overhead	30,000
Less: Fixed Selling and Administrative	15,000
Net Operating Income (Loss)	$(9,000)

The difference in income between the two approaches is due to the fixed manufacturing overhead that would be included in inventory under absorption costing (2,000 units times $5).

This information is very useful for manufacturing businesses of any size. The information becomes very difficult to track for businesses that provide services or are in agriculture. The variable cost information can be tracked by merchandising firms on a percentage basis for the product range as a whole but becomes more difficult to track on an item by item basis since a typically merchandising company sells many different products and some are only sold in small quantities.

This information can be very useful in making management decisions. If a company has the chance for a one-time special order from a new customer, 3000 units for $18 per unit, management can use variable costing to decide if they should accept the order. Assuming the order does not force the Company to operate outside of the relevant range, they could do an analysis similar to the one below.

Sales Price per unit for the special order	$18
Variable costs per unit:	
Direct materials	$3
Direct labor	$4
Variable manufacturing costs	$1
Variable selling and administrative costs	$3
Total Variable cost per unit	$11
Contribution margin per unit	$7

Increase to contribution margin and net operating income if the special order is accepted is $21,000 (3,000 units times $7 per unit contribution margin). Based upon a purely financial assessment the company should accept the special order. The company would need to consider if there are any non-financial reasons to turn the order down.

SUMMARY

In this chapter we have covered the differences between variable and fixed costs. Variable costs (in total) change with activity level but remain constant on a per unit basis. Fixed costs remain constant on a total cost basis but per unit costs change with activity levels. These assume that activity is within the relevant range. We also discussed mixed costs (those that have both a fixed and a variable component). In determining how to estimate the total cost for a mixed cost two methods were discussed for arriving at the cost equation. These methods were the high-low method and regression analysis. Regression analysis is statistically more accurate but for most small businesses the high-low method is accurate enough and is easier to calculate.

Also covered in the chapter were the classifications of costs as direct or indirect. Most of the time direct costs are equivalent to variable costs and indirect costs are equivalent to fixed costs.

Finally, there was a discussion of variable versus absorption costing. Variable costing can be very useful for making management decisions. Companies generally maintain their accounting records based on absorption accounting as this is required for financial statements prepared in accordance with U.S. GAAP and also for income tax reporting purposes.

Below is a summary for the various cost types, assuming the production of a wooden table.

COST ITEM	COST(S) TYPE
Wood used in a table	Variable cost, direct materials, product cost
Labor cost to assemble table	Variable cost, direct labor, product cost
Salary of the factory foreman	Fixed cost, manufacturing overhead, product cost
Cost of production electricity	Variable cost, manufacturing overhead, product
Depreciation of machines	Fixed cost, manufacturing overhead, product cost
Salary of company president	Fixed cost, period cost
Advertising expense	Fixed cost, period cost
Commissions paid	Variable cost, period cost

Below is a summary of the costs that would normally be variable, based upon volume, by company type.

COMPANY TYPE	NORMALLY VARIABLE COSTS
Merchandising company	Cost of goods sold
Manufacturing company	Direct materials, direct labor, and variable manufacturing overhead like supplies
Service company	Supplies, travel
Agricultural company	Feed, water, fertilizer and seeds
All company types	Sales commissions and shipping costs

KEY TERMS

- Variable Cost
- Fixed Cost
- Mixed Cost
- Step Costs
- High- Low Method
- Regression Analysis
- Direct Cost
- Indirect Cost
- Variable Costing
- Absorption Costing

EXERCISES AND PROBLEMS

4.1 - Using the trial balance for XYZ Manufacturing that is included in Appendix A. (a) identify all manufacturing costs (b) classify each cost as variable or fixed and (c) identify if any of the manufacturing costs are mixed.

4.2 - Using the trial balance for Local Hardware Store in Appendix A (a) identify all product related variable costs, if any (b) identify all product related fixed costs, if any and (c) identify any product related mixed costs, if any,

4-3 - Using the trial balance for ABC Hospital Corporation included in Appendix A (a) identify any service related variable costs, (b) identify any service related fixed costs, and (c) identify any service related mixed costs

4-4 - Using the trial balance for Double Bar Ranch included in Appendix A identify any (a) production related variable costs, (b) production related fixed costs, and (c) any production related mixed costs.

4-5 - Using the trial balance for XYZ Manufacturing in Appendix A calculate the average direct material cost per unit and average direct labor cost per unit based the assumptions that there were 55,000 direct labor hours used during the year to make and sell 6,875 units.

4-6 - Using the trial balance for Local Hardware Store determine an appropriate way to forecast direct material costs for products sold.

4-7 -Using the trial balance for ABC Hospital Corporation determine if there are any costs that direct costs for (a) the surgery area and (b) pharmacy.

4-8 - Using the trial balance for Double Bar Ranch determine if there are any direct costs that can be forecast for future periods.

4-9-Company DDD has the following information available:

Selling price per unit $100

Variable cost per unit $45

Fixed costs per year $420,000

Expected sales per year .... 20,000 units

What is the expected operating income for a year?

4-10 – The Hotel in Havre, Montana, has accumulated records of total electrical cost of the hotel. In addition they have collected the number of occupancy-days over the last year. An occupancy day represents a room rented out for one day. This information is presented below:

Month	Occupancy Days	Electrical Costs
January	1,736	$4,127
February	1,904	$4,207
March	2,356	$5,083
April	960	$2,857
May	360	$1,871
June	744	$2,696
July	2,201	$4,580
August	2,377	$5,055
September	840	$2,586
October	135	$1,477
November	695	$2,357
December	1,275	$3,601

Using the information above, calculate the fixed and variable portions of the electrical bill using the High-Low Method.

4-11 – Using the information presented in Problem 4-10 above, calculate the fixed and variable portions of the electrical bill for The Hotel using regression analysis.

4-12 – Joe's Music Store purchases pianos from a large manufacturer and resells them at retail. The average cost per piano, from the manufacturer, is $ 2,500. Joe's sell the pianos for an average price of $3,250. The selling and administrative costs are shown below:

SELLING COSTS:

- Advertising, ... $700 per month
- Sales salaries and commissions, ... $1,000 per month, plus 6% of sales
- Delivery of pianos to customers, ... $25 per piano sold
- Utilities, ... $ 350 per month
- Depreciation of sales facilities and equipment, ... $ 750 per month

ADMINISTRATIVE:

Executive salaries, ... $ 2,500 per month

Insurance, ... $350 per month

Clerical, ... $900 per month, plus $20 per piano sold

Depreciation of office equipment, ... $ 375 per month

During September, Joe's sold and delivered 50 pianos.

1. Prepare an income statement for Joe's, for September. Use the absorption format. Assume that the 50 pianos (at $2,500 each) represents the direct materials cost.

2. Prepare an income statement for September using the variable costing format.

4-13 - Anywhere Hospital is a full service hospital in a small community. It provides emergency, surgical, inpatient and outpatient services. Below is a list of costs incurred by Anywhere Hospital along with a cost object for the cost.

Cost	**Cost object**
Wages of pediatric nurse	The pediatric department
Prescription drugs	A particular patient
Heating the hospital	The pediatric department
Salary of the head of pediatrics	The pediatric department
Lab tests by outside contractor	A particular patient
Supplies used patient care	A particular patient

For each cost shown above, indicate whether it would most likely be a direct or an indirect cost.

4-14 – Below are listed various costs that are found in organizations.

1. Hamburger buns in a McDonald's restaurant
2. Advertising by a dental office
3. Peaches processed and canned by Hunt's
4. Shipping canned peaches from Hunt's factory to customers
5. Insurance on a factory producing clothes
6. Insurance on the corporate headquarters of IBM
7. Salary of a supervisor overseeing production of computers at Lenovo
8. Commissions paid to a door to door salesperson
9. Depreciation of factory lunchroom facilities at a Boeing plant
10. Steering wheels installed in Fords

Required:

a. Classify each cost as being variable or fixed with respect to the number of units produced
b. Classify each as either a period or product cost
c. Classify each as either a direct or an indirect cost.

4-15–Jones Inc. documented the number of units produced as well as maintenance costs for the past five months as follows:

	Number of units	Total overhead costs
October	120,000	$ 6,200
November	170,000	10,000
December	100,000	6,000
January	130,000	8,000
February	140,000	9,000

Jones uses the high/low method of estimating mixed costs.

Required:

a. What is the equation to predict estimated total overhead costs?

b. If the company expects to produce 125,000 units in March, what will be the estimated total overhead costs?

CHAPTER 5 – PROCESS COSTING, JOB ORDER COSTING AND COST ALLOCATION

LEARNING OBJECTIVES

1. Contrast process and job order costing.
2. Show how different business types determine the proper costing method.
3. Recognize issues related to measurement of direct materials and direct labor
4. Recognize issues related to allocation of manufacturing overhead.
5. Understand the allocation of service department costs.
6. Review the direct and step down methods of cost allocation.

PROCESS COSTING

Companies that produce a homogenous product on a continuous basis will generally use *process costing.* Normally this is used by manufacturing companies such as shoe manufacturers, cereal manufacturers, breweries and laundry detergent producers. Process costing is used to accumulate, track and allocate costs to products. These costs are averaged over large numbers of nearly identical products. Companies that use process costing forecast demand and then run the product through the manufacturing process in order to meet the forecast demand.

Rather than accumulate the costs for each product individually, process costing accumulates and tracks costs for each process as products move through production. These costs are then assigned equally to the products that come out of the process. The costs can be grouped in any manner that makes sense given the process of production. They could be grouped by a time frame (e.g. weekly) or they could be grouped by department. For purposes of process costing, a process is defined as the work that is performed on the product. For a cereal manufacturer this would include the making of the flakes, the mixing of the flakes with other items, such as raisins or nuts, and the packaging of the finished mixture.

In a cereal manufacturer costs would be traced for the direct materials used in the process (grain, raisins, or nuts). Direct labor would be traced for the production period. Finally manufacturing overhead would be traced for the period. These costs would be totaled by category and then would be divided by the number of boxes of cereal produced. The packaging could be tracked and allocated or it could be traced directly as the cost per box is known. In a process cost system the cost of direct labor would only include those individuals working directly on the production of the product and would not include supervisors or other personnel, such as maintenance workers, that are not directly working on the product. Those personnel would be part of the manufacturing overhead. In a manufacturing operation the tracing of direct materials and direct labor is relatively easy.

Over a period of time manufacturing companies will be able to use the past history of production to estimate the direct material and direct labor costs related to a product as it will not vary significantly. Over time as prices increase for materials and labor the costs can be changed for the increases by using a percentage increase that matches the percentage of cost increase incurred for the material or labor.

There are other costs associated with labor that can be handled in more than one way depending on the preference of the company. These costs would include fringe benefits, payroll taxes and overtime premiums should overtime be required. These costs could be included in the labor cost to be assigned based on production or they could be included in manufacturing overhead to be allocated to production.

Manufacturing overhead typically is allocated to products. *Allocation* involves finding a logical and consistent method to assign overhead costs to production. The best allocation basis for a given company will be based upon the cost drivers for the company. A *cost driver* for overhead is an activity that causes overhead to be incurred. If the fringe benefit costs, payroll taxes and overtime premium are considered to be some of the components of manufacturing overhead then a logical cost driver for those costs would be direct labor hours and thus would be allocated to the product based on direct labor. Other items of manufacturing overhead, such as equipment depreciation, might be allocated based upon the number of equipment hours used during the time period.

The development of overhead rates for allocation to products produced is based upon the accumulation of costs into *cost pools* and the determination of the appropriate cost driver for each cost pool. Most manufacturing firms that have multiple departments develop a cost pool for each department and then allocate the department cost pool based on the driver for the department. An example of

this would be where a manufacturing firm has a machining department and a finishing department. The cost pool allocation basis for the machining department would most likely be machine hours, while the finishing department would be allocated based on direct labor hours since the finishing activity is a manual process.

In the case of a small manufacturer it would not be unusual to use a single plant wide overhead rate that accounts for all departments. This method would be easier and it requires less time spent on collecting data and requires a less costly computer based accounting system. The increased accuracy that could be provided by the additional investments may well not be worth the additional costs that would be incurred. The most common way to allocate costs when using a single plant wide rate would be based on direct labor hours used in production and thus there would be an hourly rate for manufacturing overhead.

A simple illustration of this follows in Exhibit 5-1.

Exhibit 5-1 - Overhead Allocation Using Direct Labor Hours as the Cost Driver

Sam's Bagel Shop

Cost Item	**Overhead costs per Month**
Depreciation on Bagel Machine	$1,200
Rent	1,500
Utilities	1,000
Miscellaneous	4,000
Total	$7,700
Direct Labor Hours per Month	770
Overhead per direct labor hour	
($7,700 / 770)	$10
Direct labor hours per bagel	
Baking time (10 Minutes)	
Slicing time (2 minutes)	
Allocation for each bagel	
12 minutes (1/5 of an hour)	
(.2 Hours times $10)	$2

It is normal for company managers to want to try and estimate the cost of a product before it is actually produced or before the actual costs are known. For this reason cost estimates are frequently used to obtain a projected cost for an item. The estimate is based on one or multiple pre-determined overhead rates. The pre-determined rate(s) are usually based upon the previous year's actual rates which are adjusted during the budgeting process, thus the pre-determined rate(s) are set based upon expectations set during the budgeting cycle. By using pre-determined rates the manager can estimate the final cost of a product and thus help the sales department set the price for shipment to the customer. The actual costs won't be known until the end of the period. This rate can be used either for long run products or for a special order small run of a given product. This is known as *normal costing*.

Since normal costing involves the use of a pre-determined rate, it means that the amount of manufacturing overhead charged to production will not exactly match the amount of overhead actually incurred. The amount of overhead allocated using a pre-determined rate is generally called overhead applied (also called overhead absorbed). If the amount of overhead allocated to production is more than the overhead incurred then we have a situation where the overhead is overapplied. If the amount allocated is less that the amount incurred then we have overhead that is underapplied. Because of the fact that overhead was applied using the pre-determined rate it will mean that the product cost is being estimated at either more or less than its actual cost. If at the end of the year overhead has been overapplied it would mean that the product actually cost less than estimated and if the overhead is underapplied then the product actually cost more that its estimated cost.

During the year the company had applied overhead of $100,500 based on the use of the pre-determined rate. The journal entry for this would be:

Work in process inventory 100,500

Manufacturing overhead 100,500

The actual expenses are charged to manufacturing overhead as incurred during the year and they total $100,000. As each transaction occurred the entry would as follows (the entry illustrates the total for the year):

Manufacturing overhead 100,000

Cash or accounts payable 100,000

This would leave a credit balance in the manufacturing overhead account of $ 500 at the end of the year. This means that the actual cost was $ 500 less than the estimated cost. Since this is a reduction in the cost of production it would also be a reduction in inventory and cost of goods sold for a proportionate amount.

If the overhead included in work in process inventory at year end represents 10% of the total overhead for the year, overhead included in finished goods inventory represents 30% of the overhead for the year and the overhead included in the cost of goods sold represents 60% of the overhead for the year the overapplied overhead would have to be accounted for proportionately.

This means that $50 (10% of $500) would be taken out of work in process inventory, $150 (30% of $ 500) would be taken out of finished goods inventory and $300 (60% of $500) would be taken out of cost of goods sold. The journal entry would be as follows:

Manufacturing overhead	500	
Work in process inventory		50
Finished goods inventory		150
Cost of goods sold		300

This would bring the manufacturing overhead account to zero at the end of the year after adjustment. If the overhead was underapplied the same process would be used. However, in the case of underapplied overhead the inventory and cost of goods sold accounts would be increased and manufacturing overhead would be decreased since it would contain a debit balance prior to adjustment.

Exhibit 5-2 - Basic Process Costing

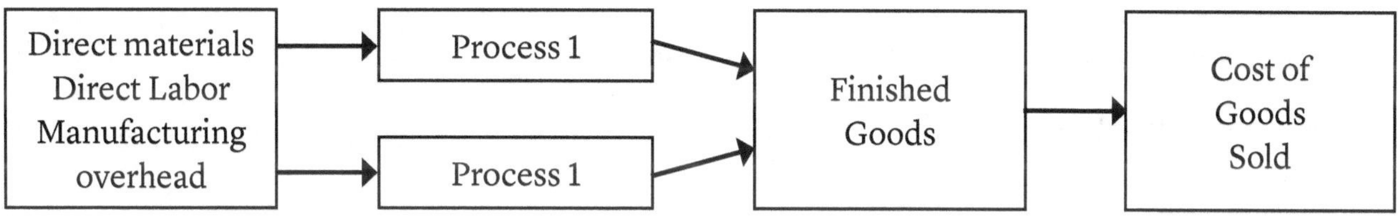

A common calculation done to ensure that we are costing our inventories correctly is the calculation of *equivalent units* completed during the period. This is done to take into account all of the partial units that were completed during the month and all of the units started during the month that are only partially completed. It also considers any units that were started and completed during the month. This measurement shows us that if we had nothing in process at either the beginning or the end of the month how many units we would have been able to start and complete based on the resources used.

To show how this works we have to first look at our beginning work in process inventory. In a cereal factory we could have material in process that would be provide us with 2,000 boxes when finished, the direct materials are 80% complete and the conversion costs (direct labor and manufacturing overhead) are 80% complete. Next we look at how many units were started during the month, for this example we will assume 10,000 boxes. Finally, we look at what is left in process at the end of the month, 3,000 boxes that are 60% complete with regard to direct materials and 60% complete for the conversion costs.

At beginning of the month we had costs in process of $2,000 for materials and $ 1,600 for conversion costs. During the month we incurred $10,000 in direct material cost and $8,400 in conversion costs.

Exhibits 5-3 through 5-6 – Illustrate the calculation of equivalent units, calculation of the equivalent cost per unit and the allocation of costs to the finished units and to work in process using the first-in, first-out method (FIFO). The first-in, first-out method would match the physical flow of the product.

Exhibit 5-3 – Equivalent Units of Production

Equivalent units of production for beginning inventory completed

(2000 units x 20%) 400

Equivalent units started and completed this period

(10,000 units started – 3,000 units in process at end of month) 7,000

Equivalent units in ending work in process

(3,000 units x 60%) 1,800

Total equivalent Units of production 9,200

Exhibit 5-4 – Calculation of Cost per Equivalent Unit

Current period costs

($10,000 + $8,400) $18,400

Equivalent units of production 9,200

Cost per equivalent unit $2

Exhibit 5-5 - Allocating Costs to the Finished Units

Cost of the units completed from the previous month

Costs incurred previously $3,600

Costs to complete the units (400 x $2) 800

Cost of the 7,000 units started and completed

(7,000 x $ 2) $14,000

Total Cost to the Finished Units $18,400

Exhibit 5-6 - Allocating Costs to the Ending Units in Process

Cost of the Units in Process at the end of Month

(1,800 equivalent Units x $2) $3,600

Most small companies use FIFO for valuing their inventories and obtaining their cost of goods sold. The reason for this is that the information is easily obtainable and the calculations are relatively simple. Many large companies use the weighted average method. Some more expensive computer accounting systems will automatically do the calculation for inventory valuation using the weighted average method. Since we are focusing on small business the weighted average method will not be covered.

At this point we will look at these concepts using the data presented in the XYZ Manufacturing trial balance that is in Appendix A. If we total manufacturing overhead from the trial balance we get $3,496,836. During the year there were 56,415 actual direct labor hours used in production. The hourly overhead rate per hour based on actual would be $ 61.98. If the pre-determined overhead rate that was applied during the year was $60.00 per hour, we would have underapplied overhead for the year. This would be calculated as follows: 56,415 (actual hours) times $60.00 (the pre-determined rate) is equal to $3,384,900. We would then subtract the actual from the overhead applied (3,384,900-3,496,836) and would end up with $-111,936. Since the result is negative it means that overhead was underapplied.

This would then be allocated between work in process inventory, finished goods inventory and cost of goods sold to remove the amount under applied from the manufacturing overhead account. The amounts that would be used for the calculation are: finished goods inventory, $545,122, work in process inventory, $286,818, and cost of goods sold, $6,543,071 (calculated by adding cost of goods sold - material, freight in, freight out, direct labor and manufacturing overhead applied as calculated above ($3,384,900)). This would provide the following percentages: finished goods inventory, 7.4%, work in process inventory, 3.9%, and cost of goods sold, 88.7%. Each of these would be multiplied by the $111,936 of manufacturing overhead that is underapplied to calculate the needed journal entry.

The journal entry would be:

Finished goods inventory	$8,283	
Work in process inventory	4,366	
Cost of goods sold	99,287	
Manufacturing overhead		$111,936

JOB ORDER COSTING

While process costing is used only for manufacturing firms, *job order costing* can be used for a variety of firms. It would be applicable to manufacturing firms that produce large custom made products, service firms and other firms such as construction companies. The principles of job order costing would be the same regardless of the industry or firm it is be used for, but the application of the principles might vary in practice. A manufacturing firm that produces large custom order items and a construction company would track the materials and labor by job and add overhead to the job cost based upon a pre-determined rate that would primarily be based on labor,. The pre-determined rate could be an hourly rate based on direct labor hours or could be added based on a percentage of labor. In the case of a service company it is likely that would not be direct materials to add to the job cost. Many times a service company will factor overhead into the hourly rate charged to the job so there would only be entries for direct labor on the job.

We will start by illustrating how a professional service company would track costs by job. We will use a law firm as an example they would have an hourly rate that would be charged to each job based on the experience level of the attorney working on the case. The rate charged might be $ 150.00 per hour which is meant to cover the attorney's salary, benefits, payroll taxes and all company overhead related to the attorney. The client would be billed based on the number of hours of attorney time used and then at the end of the year the law firm would verify whether there was any over or under applied overhead. This would be used as part of the basis for setting the rate for each attorney for the next year.

If we were to look at a hospital they would track things differently. The hospital would set their rates at the beginning of the year based upon their best estimate of usage during the following year. The hospital would also look to set rates differently for the revenue producing departments. The operating room, the emergency room and the various sections of the hospital with beds for patients to stay overnight or for multiple days would be set based upon a rate per hour or per day. These would be based on the cost of supplies used for the patient, nursing salaries, benefits and payroll taxes, overhead for average equipment usage and all other overhead related to the space and its uses. The job cost for the patient would include the amount of time and if used any prescription drugs needed. Prescription drugs would not be included in the hourly rate as there would be too much variation between the patients (this would be the equivalent of direct material for another type of firm). The prescription drug rate charged to the job will be an amount to cover the cost of the drug plus the labor and overhead costs for the pharmacy department. Normally, physicians' salaries would not be included in the hourly or daily rate as most physicians are not employees of the hospital. If they are employees of the hospital, rather than being in private practice, their fees normally would still be charged separately.

For a construction company or a manufacturing firm that makes large custom products, there would be a job card for each project. On the card the direct materials used would be recorded as would the amount of time each worker worked on the project. In addition there would be charges for overhead recorded on the job card based upon a pre-determined rate. These costs would be tracked to see how they are comparing with the quote given to the customer for the job. The quote would have been based on the materials expected to be used, the numbers of direct labor hours, by appropriate personnel, needed to complete the project and the pre-determined overhead rate which usually based upon direct labor hours. At the end of each job the actual use can be compared to the estimates used to quote the job to help the company refine and improve its quoting process. Because these can be tracked at the completion of each job the quoting for future jobs can be corrected on an ongoing basis. By being able to correct on an ongoing basis any amount of over or underapplied overhead should not be significant at year end and therefore should not have any significant impact on income or inventory, if any.

Exhibit 5-7 – Illustration of a Job Cost Card (Bathroom remodel)

5-3	Purchase of bathtub	$300
5-3	Purchase of wall tile	100
5-4	Purchase of lumber and other materials	350
5-5	Purchase of vanity and top	400
5-6	Purchase of flooring	150
5-7	Labor to tear out old fixtures, etc.	200
5-7	Overhead applied based on labor	300
5-10	Labor to install new sub flooring and patch walls	200
5-11	Labor to install new tub and wall board	200
5-12	Labor to begin installation of wall tile	200
5-13	Labor to finish installation of wall tile	200
5-14	Labor to install vanity and complete work	200
5-14	Overhead applied based on labor	1,500
Total costs		$4,300
Amount billed to customer (based on quote)		**$4,500**
Billing in excess of actual costs		**$ 200**

The above would be similar for a manufacturing firm that makes large custom products for its customers. The firm would have quoted the product to the customer and once the customer accepted the quote, work would have begun with the costs being tracked for the individual job within the manufacturing plant.

Either type of firm would track their overhead costs at actual and compare them to the amount they are applying to projects for customers. By tracking this they could refine their quoting process to ensure that there are no significant over or underapplied amounts in overhead at year end.

A hospital would track the costs to be billed to a patient or a patient's insurance in a similar manner. The hospital doesn't have the ability to change rates during a year and thus could have significant amount in either over or underapplied overhead at the end of the year. The hospital doesn't have the ability to change rates during the year because the maximum will be set by government organizations and insurance companies will negotiate other rates (usually lower) for patients that carry their insurance. Below is an example of a patient's account, this patient came into the emergency room and was there for 2 hours, was transferred to the operating room where the surgery took 3 hours and then was transferred to a room within the hospital for a three day stay after surgery. The physicians involved in the patient's care are not employees of the hospital so their bills would be in addition.

Exhibit 5-8 - Illustration of a Patient's Account at a Hospital

6-1	Emergency room (2 hours)	$ 500
6-1	Operating room charges (3 hours)	1.500
6-1	Room charges (semi private room)	800
6-1	Pharmacy charges	250
6-2	Room charges (semi private room)	800
6-2	Pharmacy charges	350
6-3	Room charges (semi private room)	800
6-4	Pharmacy charges	200
Total charges for patient		**$5,200**

The difference you will notice between this job card and the job card in Exhibit 5-6 is that typically a project that a contractor or a custom manufacturing firm would do is quoted and accepted before the work is done so they can check the actual costs against the quote. In the case of a hospital there is no quote and therefore the amount billed will be compared at year end with the costs to see if the rates being charged are sufficient.

In the case of professional service organizations such as: law firms, CPA firms, architectural firms, etc. some of the work may be based on quotes so they could track it like the project is Exhibit 5-7. However, most projects by professional service firms would be more like the hospital where it is based on time and billing rates.

SUMMARY OF PROCESS AND JOB ORDER COSTING

To this point in the chapter we have covered process and job order costing. Process costing is only appropriate for manufacturing firms that are running large quantities of similar products. Job order costing would be appropriate for manufacturing firms that make large custom products, constructions firms, and some service companies. Neither of these methods would have any application for a merchandising firm or for an agricultural production firm.

COST ALLOCATION

The issue of cost allocation becomes important when a business has more than one service department that supports the revenue producing departments. The cost of the service departments ultimately need to be accounted for by the revenue producing departments to ensure that the service department costs are considered when deciding upon pricing of the products or services to the customer. As a general rule service department costs are not an issue with merchandising firms or with professional services firms. Service department costs can be an issue for manufacturing firms and service firms other than professional services, for example a hospital.

We will look at some firms and the types of service departments each firm might have. First, we will consider a manufacturing firm. A manufacturing firm could have the following types of services: materials handling, cafeteria, maintenance and janitorial, human resources, information technology, factory administration and, for some very large manufacturing firms, medical services (company nurse). If we were to look at a hospital it would be likely to have the following service departments: maintenance and janitorial, laundry, food services, human resources, information technology, and hospital administration. A hospital would also be likely to have a cafeteria but normally the cafeteria produces revenue and thus is not a service department. If we were to look at a large hotel there would service departments such as the following: housekeeping, janitorial, laundry, guest services, information technology, and hotel administration.

Since many businesses have service departments there needs to be a systematic approach to ensuring that service department costs are fairly allocated to the revenue producing departments. The first part of developing the system would be to identify the appropriate allocation basis for each service department.

Exhibit 5-9 - Examples of Service Department Allocation Bases

Service Department	Allocation Bases
Cafeteria	Number of meals served
Janitorial services	Square footage
Maintenance	Number of maintenance calls
Laundry	Pounds of laundry
Information technology	Number of computers
Human resources	Number of employees
Factory administration	Total labor hours
Medical facilities	Number of cases handled

The two most common methods for service department cost allocation are the *direct method* and the *sequential method (also called the step down method)*. We will assume the following information for purposes of illustrating the two methods:

We have hotel that has the following services departments: maintenance and janitorial, with an annual cost of $ 200,000, and laundry with an annual cost of $ 50,000. The revenue generating departments are the hotel and the restaurant. The hotel has 435,000 square feet and the restaurant has 10,000 square feet, in addition the laundry department has 5,000 square feet. The hotel uses 90,000 pounds of laundry per year and the restaurant uses 10,000 pounds.

Under the *direct method* the service department costs are allocated directly to the revenue generating departments as follows;

Maintenance and janitorial $ 200,000 allocated to the hotel and restaurant based on square footage. The total square footage to be used under the direct method would be 445,000 square feet (435,000 + 10,000) so the costs allocated to each revenue generating department would be calculated as follows:

Hotel ((435,000/445,000) x $200,000) .... $ 195,506

Restaurant ((10,000/445,000) x $200,000) 4,494

The laundry costs, of $ 50,000 would be allocated as follows:

Hotel ((90,000/100,000) x $50,000) .... $ 45,000

Restaurant ((10,000/100,000) x $50,000) 5,000

Using the *sequential method* service department costs are allocated to all departments using the services, including other service departments. Based on the same information shown above for the direct method the cost allocation would be as follows:

Maintenance and janitorial as allocated using square footage as before but under the sequential method some of the costs will also be allocated to the laundry department based upon the square footage used for laundry. The total square footage would now be 450,000 square feet since we are adding the 5,000 square feet used by the laundry department. The allocation would be calculated as follows:

Hotel ((435,000/450,000) x $200,000) .... $ 193,333

Restaurant ((10,000/450,000) x $200,000) 4,444

Laundry ((5,000/450,000) x $200,000) 2,223

Because some of the maintenance and janitorial costs have been allocated to the laundry department the total laundry department costs to be allocated are now $52,223 ($50,000 + $2,223). The allocations of these costs would be calculated as follows:

Hotel ((90,000/100,000) x $ 52,223).. $ 47,001

Restaurant ((10,000/100,000) x $ 52,223) 5,222

The differences in calculations between the direct and the sequential methods will end with different amounts allocated to the hotel and to the restaurant under each method. Under the direct method the hotel will end up with total allocations of $ 240,506 ($195,506 + $ 45,000) while under the sequential method the hotel will end up with total allocations of $ 240,334 ($ 193,333 + $ 47,001). The restaurant allocation also will vary under the methods with the total allocation being $ 9,494 ($4,494 + $5,000) under the direct method and $ 9,666 ($4,444 + $5,222) under the sequential method.

There has only been a small amount of discussion regarding cost allocation. The discussion of cost allocation has been limited because it is primarily an issue for large businesses and the focus of this book is on small business. It has been covered so that a small business person would have a basis for reference should it become a significant issue for a given small business.

SUMMARY

In this chapter we have discussed process costing, which is generally only applicable to manufacturing firms that are producing large quantities of similar (homogeneous) products. Job order costing has applications for more business types that process costing. Job order costing can be used for manufacturing firms making large custom order products, construction companies, and a variety of service type businesses. Neither of these costing methods would be applicable for merchandising or agricultural production firms.

We briefly covered cost allocation using both the direct and the sequential methods. This was covered for reference purposes and cost allocation is not normally an issue in small business but can be a significant issue for large businesses.

KEY TERMS

- process costing
- job order costing
- normal costing
- overapplied overhead
- underapplied overhead
- equivalent units
- first in, first out (FIFO)
- cost allocation
- direct method
- sequential (step down) method

EXERCISES AND PROBLEMS

5-1. Describe the differences between process costing and job order costing.

5-2. Describe the process that would lead to a company having overapplied manufacturing overhead.

5-3. Prepare a journal entry to adjust underapplied manufacturing overhead assuming the following information: the ending work in process inventory is $350,000, the ending finished goods inventory is $450,000, the cost of goods sold for the year is $2,400,000, and the amount of underapplied overhead is $16,000.

5-4. Calculate the equivalent units of production assuming the following information: the beginning work in process inventory had 5,000 units that were 60% complete, during the month there were 15,000 started in process, and at the end of the month there were 7,000 units in process that are 70% complete. The company uses the first in, first out method.

5-5. George, Inc. manufactures a product that goes through two production processes. The schedule below shows the information for the first process for the month June.

Unit information:

Work in Process, June 1 (materials 100% complete;	
conversion costs 40% complete)	5,000
Started in production	180,000
Total units to be accounted for	185,000
Units accounted for:	
Transferred to the next process	175,000
Work in process, June 30 (materials 100% complete;	
conversion costs 30% complete)	10,000
Total units accounted for	185,000

Costs in the beginning work in process inventory of the first process were materials, $1,500; and conversion cost, $4,000. Costs added during the month were: materials, $54,000; and conversion cost, $348,000.

Using the first in first out method prepare:

a. A computation of equivalent units for the month for the first process.

b. Compute the costs per equivalent unit for the month for the first process.

5-6. Easy Bakery, Inc. makes premium cake mixes that go through two processing departments, blending and packaging. The following information was recorded in the blending department during September:

Production data:

Units in process, Sept. 1, (materials 100% complete; conversion 30% complete)	10,000
Units started in production	170,000
Units in process, Sept. 30, (materials 100% complete: conversion 40% complete)	20,000

Cost data:

Work in process inventory, September 1:	
Materials cost	$ 8,500
Conversion cost	4,900
Total cost in beginning inventory	$13,400
Cost added during the month:	
Materials cost	139,400
Conversion cost	244,200
Total cost added during the month	383,600
Total Cost	$ 397,000

All materials are added at the beginning of work in the blending department. The company uses the FIFO method.

Prepare a production report that includes the following information:

a. The number of units completed and transferred to the packaging department

b. A calculation of the equivalent units for month

c. The cost per equivalent unit for the month.

5-7. The Western Montana Beverage Company manufactures flavored bottled water. They use a process costing system. Raw material and conversion costs are incurred at the same rate during the manufacturing process. Data for the mixing department for October are as follows:

Work in process, Oct. 1, (80% complete)— 5,000 units —$60,000 production cost

Started during the month—90,000 units—$1,002,500 production cost

Work in process, Oct. 31 (40% complete) 10,000 units

Western Montana uses the first in, first out method to calculate equivalent units.

Required:

a. How many units were completed in October?

b. How many units were started and completed in October?

c. How many equivalent units were completed in October?

d. What is the cost per equivalent unit?

e. What is the cost in ending work in process?

5-8. The University of the Northwest uses job cost records for many of its research projects. The reason the University uses job costing is that some of it research projects are sponsored by the federal government and they need a basis to justify requests for reimbursement of costs.

The following information relates to a research project in the engineering school:

- January 3 Direct materials, various supplies $ 925
- January 6 Direct materials, various materials $780
- January 3-7 Direct labor, research associates 110 hours
- January 3-7 Direct labor, research assistants 200 hours

Research associates receive $30 per hour, while assistants receive $18 per hour. The overhead rate is 75% of direct labor cost.

a. Create a job cost record and post all of the data to the project cost record.

b. Calculate total project costs through January 7.

5-9. Beaver Construction Company has contracted to build a small office building for a local law firm. Beaver use the job order costing system and has a pre-determined overhead rate that is equal to 80% of direct labor costs. To date Beaver Construction has incurred the following costs on the project:

Materials cost	$10,500
Electrical sub-contract cost	8,000
Plumbing sub-contract cost	9,200
Carpenter labor	240 hours at $25 per hour
General labor	400 hours at $18 per hour
Supervisor labor	80 hours at $35 per hour

a. Create a job cost record and post the cost to the record.

b. Calculate total project costs to date.

c. Assume the project is 25% complete as to costs and the contract price for the job is $250,000. Calculate the expected profit on the job.

5-10. Creole Countertops produces custom countertops, for residential use, that are sold nationwide. The company adds overhead, to projects, at a rate of $ 8.00 per direct labor hour. The company accumulates overhead costs in a separate manufacturing overhead account and uses normal costing to assign overhead. The following data provides details of the company's activity during the first half of the year:

	Jan. 1	June 30
Direct materials inventory	$ 59,600	$ 60,500
Work in process inventory	$ 44,000	$ 43,000
Finished goods inventory	$ 24,250	$ 23,000
Production data:		
Direct materials purchased	$157,500	
Direct labor costs ($15/hr.)	$300,000	

a. Calculate the cost of direct materials used during the period.

b. Calculate the cost of goods manufactured during the period.

c. Calculate the cost of goods sold during the period. Assume there is no over or under applied manufacturing overhead.

d. If the actual overhead incurred by Creole for the six months was $ 152,500. Calculate the over or under applied manufacturing overhead for the six months.

5-11. Seiling Hospital has a Radiology Department that provides X-ray services to the hospital's three revenue producing departments. The variable costs of the Radiology Department are allocated to the revenue producing departments on the basis of the number of X-rays provided to each department. Budgeted and actual data relating to the cost of X-rays taken last year are as follows:

	Variable Costs	
	Budgeted	Actual
Radiology Department	$19 per X-ray	$20.50 per X-ray

The budgeted and actual number of X-rays provided for each department last year was:

	Pediatrics	OB care	General Hospital
Budgeted number of X-rays	7,000	4,500	12,500
Actual number of X-rays Taken	7,200	3,500	11,500

Determine the amount of radiology Department variable cost that should have been allocated to each of the three revenue producing departments at the end of last year using the direct method of allocation.

5-12. Refer to Seiling Hospital in Problem 5-10. In addition to the Radiology Department, the hospital also has a Janitorial Services Department that provides services to all other departments in the hospital. The fixed costs of the service departments are allocated using the following bases:

Department	**Basis for Allocation**
Janitorial Services	Square feet of space occupied
	Radiology Department 6,000 sq. ft.
	Pediatrics 25,000 sq. ft.
	OB Care 22,000 sq. ft
	General Hospital 97,000 sq. ft.
Radiology Department	Long run average X-rays per year
	Pediatrics 9.000 X-rays
	OB Care 5,500 X-rays
	General Hospital 15,500 X-rays.

The budgeted and actual fixed costs in the two service departments are as follows:

	Janitorial Services	Radiology
Budgeted fixed costs	$450,000	$600,000
Actual fixed costs	$444,000	$606,000

a. Show the allocation of the budgeted fixed costs for the two service departments using the sequential (step down) method.

b. Show the allocation of the actual fixed costs for the two service department using the sequential (step down) method.

CHAPTER 6 – COST-VOLUME-PROFIT ANALYSIS

LEARNING OBJECTIVES:

1. Use the contribution margin ratio to compute changes in contribution margin and net income resulting from changes in sales volume.
2. Analyze what if decisions using CVP analysis
3. Compute a company's break-even point in unit sales and sales dollars
4. Calculate the level of sales needed to achieve a desired net profit before and after income tax

CONTRIBUTION MARGIN

Traditional financial reporting focuses on function in calculating the cost of goods sold. The difference between sales and the cost of goods is the traditional measure of *gross profit*. In the traditional measurement cost of goods sold includes both variable costs (such as direct labor and direct materials) and fixed costs (such as depreciation and property taxes). Because cost of goods sold has both unit level costs (variable costs) and facility level costs (fixed costs) it makes it difficult to predict the changes in cost of goods sold when production increases or decreases.

On the other hand the contribution margin income statement is arranged by behavior rather than by function. This means that the contribution margin income statement focuses on the unit level (variable) costs so that changes in total contribution margin can be calculated relatively easily when production increases or decreases. Since the facility level (fixed) costs do not change within the relevant range they are considered after the total contribution margin before determining net income. In Exhibit 6-1 a traditional income statement is shown and in Exhibit 6-2 a contribution margin income statement is shown, both use the same data based on production and sales of 100 units.

Exhibit 6-1 - Traditional Income Statement

Sales	$1,500
Less: Cost of goods sold	
Variable costs	$400
Fixed costs	200
Total Cost of goods sold	600
Gross Profit	900
Less: S, G & A costs	
Variable costs	$100
Fixed costs	200
Total S, G & A costs	300
Net Income	$600

Exhibit 6-2 Contribution Margin Income Statement

Sales	$1,500
Less: Variable costs	
Manufacturing costs	$400
S, G & A Costs	100
Total Variable Costs	500
Contribution Margin	1,000
Less: Fixed costs	
Manufacturing costs	$200
S, G & A costs	200
Total Fixed Costs	400
Net Income	$600

While the data used in Exhibits 6-1 and 6-2 end up with the same net income based on the 100 units, it should be noted that the difference in approach will help us in determining the impact on changes in the level of production. In the traditional income statement it is difficult to quickly see how changes in production level will impact the net income. However, the contribution margin format allows us to quickly determine the change to net income based on changes in level of production and sales.

In Exhibit 6-2 we can quickly determine that the total variable cost for each unit is $5 (total variable costs of $ 500 divided by the 100 units). This means that each unit of change in production and sales will cause net income to change in the same direction by $10. *This is the contribution margin per unit* and is calculated by taking the selling price per unit of $ 15 ($1,500/100 units) and subtracting the variable costs of $ 5 per unit. Thus, if volume increases by 10 units, net income will increase by $100 and if volume decreases by 10 units then net income will decrease by $ 100.

The contribution margin income statement can also be shown using percentages. The *contribution margin ratio* is calculated by dividing the contribution margin, in dollars, by sales dollars. Exhibit 6-3 shows the same information (in summary form) as Exhibit 6-2 but also with percentages for sales, variable costs and contribution margin.

Exhibit 6-3 - Contribution Margin Income Statement with Percentages

	Total	**Percentage**
Sales	$1,500	100
Less: Variable costs	500	33.3
Contribution margin	1,000	66.7
Less: Fixed costs	400	
Net income	$600	

By calculating the contribution margin ratio (percentage) we can quickly determine any change in net income caused by changes in production and sales volume. This is done by multiplying the change in sales by the contribution margin ratio to determine the change in net income. In our example the change in sales of 10 units caused a change in sales dollars of $150 ($15 per unit times 10 units). We would multiply the $150 change in sales dollars by the 66.7% to arrive at a change in net income of $100.

Using the contribution margin ratio would be especially useful for small businesses as it is easy to calculate the ratio and it is easy to calculate how changes in volume will affect the net income of the company. It is also very useful for merchandising companies as the percentage can be calculated as a whole for the business. This makes it simpler for the merchandising firm to estimate how volume changes will affect net income given the current product mix of sales. The business does not need to estimate the margin for each product and then take volume by product to determine how changes in volume will impact the net income of the business. In our example, the company is making a profit and our analysis talks about how the profit would change based on change in sales volume. Next we will discuss using the contribution margin to analyze other opportunities.

WHAT IF APPLICATIONS FOR CONTRIBUTION MARGIN

Suppose a company is not making a profit or if the profit level is not enough to ensure that the business will be able to remain in business. In this case the business managers have to consider options to increase the company's profitability. The management has several potential options to increase the profitability. The most common options could include (1) increase price, (2) reduce the variable costs of manufacturing, (3) increase sales through a change in the sales commission structure (this would increase the variable selling costs per unit), and (4) increasing sales through product improvements and advertising the product improvements.

For purposes of this analysis we are going to assume that the company has competitors for this product's sales and therefore the price is set at the market price and increasing the price is not a viable option. We will now analyze the other options. For the purposes of analysis we will continue with the same company as shown in Exhibits 6-1 to 6-3.

The first option we will analyze is reducing variable manufacturing costs per unit. In the data previously shown we had variable manufacturing costs of $4 per unit ($400 divided by 100 units). If we could reduce the variable manufacturing costs to $3.75 per unit the contribution margin income statement would be as shown in Exhibit 6-4.

Exhibit 6-4 - Contribution Margin Income Statement (reduced variable manufacturing costs)

Sales	$1,500
Less: Variable costs	
Manufacturing costs	$375
S, G & A Costs	100
Total Variable Costs	475
Contribution Margin	1,025

Less: Fixed costs	
Manufacturing costs	$200
S, G & A costs	200
Total Fixed Costs	400
Net Income	$625

As the exhibit shows the reduction in variable manufacturing costs causes the net income to increase even though there has been no increase in sales volume. The reduction in variable manufacturing costs is positive for the company as long as it doesn't cause a decline in product quality.

The second option would be to change the sales commission structure. The purpose in changing the sales commission structure would be to cause the sales agents outside of the company to push the company's product more since it would now have a better commission than the competitors' products. Since this move would increase variable selling expenses the only way the company could offset the increase would be through increased sales volume. For purposes of this example we are going to assume that by increasing the sales commission from $1 per unit to $ 1.50 per unit the company will experience a 30% increase in sales volume (sales would now be 130 units). Exhibit 6-5 shows how this would impact the income statement.

Exhibit 6-5 - Contribution Income Statement (increased volume and sales commissions)

Sales (130 units times $15)	$1,950
Less: Variable costs	
Manufacturing costs	$520
S, G & A Costs	195
Total Variable Costs	7159
Contribution Margin	1,235
Less: Fixed costs	
Manufacturing costs	$200
S, G & A costs	200
Total Fixed Costs	400
Net Income	$835

In calculating the new income statement we have to multiply all of the variable costs by the new sales volume. Thus we have $520 of variable manufacturing costs (130 units times $4 per unit) and $ 195 of variable selling costs (130 units times $1.50 per unit). This option shows that we could increase the total profit even though we increased the variable costs since the volume of sales units also increased.

The third option we are going to explore is making product improvements and increasing advertising expenditures to tell customers about the product improvements. We will charge slightly more for the product due to the improvements but there will be no changes in any variable costs. It is estimated that the product improvements will increase sales units by 30%, thus bringing sales to 130 units. The new sales price will be $ 17.50 per unit and the increase in advertising costs will be $250.

The new income statement is shown in Exhibit 6-6 below.

Exhibit 6-6 - Contribution Income Statement
(Product Improvements and Increased Advertising)

Sales (130 units times $17.50)	$2,275
Less: Variable costs	
Manufacturing costs	$520
S, G & A Costs	130
Total Variable Costs	650
Contribution Margin	1,675
Less: Fixed costs	
Manufacturing costs	$200
S, G & A costs	450
Total Fixed Costs	650
Net Income	$1,025

The variable costs shown in Exhibit 6-6 are based on the original variable costs of $4 per unit for manufacturing variable costs and $1 per unit for variable S, G & A costs.

Each of these alternatives has been considered independently of the other options. In a normal business situation a combined strategy using parts of each of the options would also be considered. We

are not going to cover that here as there would be too many potential possibilities in combining the stand alone options presented above. Any of these options could be viable for a small business.

BREAK-EVEN ANALYSIS

It is useful for many businesses, but especially for small businesses to know the numbers of sales units or the dollar amount of sales that are necessary for the business to break even. The *break-even point* is the level of sales where the contribution margin, in total, just covers the fixed expenses of the businesses and therefore net income is zero. A question that comes to mind at this point is, "Why would a company want to just break even?" The answer is that a company is not just interested in breaking even but that the analysis serves as a starting point for evaluation. By knowing the break-even point, the business owner can make a determination if the business makes any sense to pursue. If the break-even point is very high the owner can quickly realize that the business is not viable and therefore not waste time and money pursuing it. If the break-even point is reasonable given the nature of the business, then the business owner can look at other analyses using the same concept. We will cover additional analyses later in the chapter. The break-even point can be calculated in either unit sales or dollar sales.

To calculate the break-even point in units we take the total fixed costs and we divide that by the contribution margin per unit. Using the information that was presented in Exhibit 6-2 the calculation would be as follows: sales price per unit of $15 minus variable costs per units of $5 give us a contribution margin per unit of $10. The total fixed costs of $400 would then be divided by the $10 contribution margin per unit and we would arrive at a break-even point of 40 units.

To calculate the break-even point in dollars we would divide the total fixed costs by the contribution margin ratio. In Exhibit 6-3 we calculated the contribution margin ratio as 66.7%. We would take the total fixed costs of $400 and divide it by 66.67% (.6667). This would give us a break-even point in dollars of $ 600.

After doing both calculations we can double check the calculations to make sure we have done them correctly. The way to double check would be to take the break-even point in units and multiply the number of units by the selling price per unit to see if it equals the break-even point in dollars. In this example the break-even point is 40 units; if we multiply that by the selling price per unit of $15 we get an amount of $600 which equals the break-even point in dollars. Since the numbers agree we know that the calculations are correct.

TARGET NET INCOME (PROFIT)

Now we can expand on the use of break-even analysis to include the idea of a target amount for the net income (profit) of the business. By using the same procedures as we used to determine the number of units or the amount of sales dollars needed to break-even we can calculate the unit or dollar sales needed to achieve a desired level of net income.

Based on the information shown in Exhibit 6-2 above we can estimate the increased sales in units and dollars needed to raise the net income from $600 per month as shown in Exhibit 6-2 to $2,000 per month, which is the level of income that the owner feels is the minimum acceptable level. We have previously calculated that the contribution margin per unit is $10 ($15 selling prices minus $5 of total variable costs). By subtracting the current level of net income from the desired level of net income we can calculate the additional amount of profit needed. In this case the additional profit needed to reach the targeted net income level desired by the owner we would subtract the current level of $ 600 from the desired level of $ 2,000 per month and determine that we need to increase net income by $1,400 per month. We would then divide the $1,400 per month by the contribution margin of $10 per unit and come up with an additional 140 units per month needed to reach the targeted net income.

We could also calculate the additional sales dollars needed to reach the targeted net income level by the use of the contribution margin ratio. This would be done by dividing the $1,400 of additional income desired by the contribution margin ratio of 66.67% (.6667).This would yield a result of additional monthly sales dollars needed of $ 2,100.

Here we would double check our calculations to make sure that we have correctly calculated the amounts. This is done by multiplying the additional units needed by the sales price per unit to see if the amount matches the sales dollars we calculated. In this case there were an additional 140 units needed and when multiplied by the $ 15 per unit selling price the result is additional sales dollars needed of $ 2,100 which is the same as we calculated using the contribution margin ratio. This confirms that our calculations are correct. Exhibit 6-7 shows the new contribution margin income statement that reflects achieving the targeted net income level.

Exhibit 6-7 – Contribution Income Statement with Targeted Net Income Achieved

Sales (240 units times $15)	$3,600
Less: Variable costs	
Manufacturing costs	$960
S, G & A Costs	240
Total Variable Costs	1,200
Contribution Margin	2,400
Less: Fixed costs	
Manufacturing costs	$200
S, G & A costs	200
Total Fixed Costs	400
Net Income	$2,000

This procedure is relatively simple to use and can be calculated fairly easily by managers or owners for any size business. The easiest calculation to use for evaluation purposes is the contribution margin ratio as it does not require data for each individual item sold by the company. This is especially helpful for a merchandising firm.

We have been considering the break-even point and targeted net income without considering income taxes. Now we need to consider *targeted net income* on an after tax basis. We will use the same data as we have been using for all of the calculations so far and will add in the tax issue. We will assume that the company has an income tax rate of 20% and that the targeted net income that the owner wants ($2,000 per month) is based on after tax income. We now have to calculate the sales level needed to provide the targeted net income on an after tax basis. To do this we would take the after tax targeted net income and divide it by the after tax rate of the income. We get the after tax rate of the income by subtracting the tax rate from 100%. In this case the after tax rate would be 80% (100% - 20%). If we divide the $ 2,000 by the 80% we arrive at a new targeted net income of $ 2,500 before tax.

To reach this level the business will need to increase sales above the amount calculated before to cover the taxes. For this calculation we are going to use the contribution margin ratio to calculate our new sales level. The net income needs to increase by $500 per month ($2,500–$2,000) to cover the taxes and provide the desired level of after tax net income. When we divide the additional $500 by the contribution margin ratio of 66.67% we determine that an additional $750 of sales is needed per month. We can quickly calculate the additional unit sales required by dividing the $750 by the $15 per unit selling price, thus we need 50 additional units of sales per month to cover the taxes of the business. Exhibit 6-8 shows the new income statement.

Exhibit 6-8 - Contribution Income Statement with After Tax Targeted Net Income

Sales (290 units times $15)	$4,350
Less: Variable costs	
Manufacturing costs	$1,160
S, G & A Costs	290
Total Variable Costs	1,450
Contribution Margin	2,900
Less: Fixed costs	
Manufacturing costs	$200
S, G & A costs	200
Total Fixed Costs	400
Net Income before taxes	2,500
Income taxes	500
Net Income	$2,000

We have now finished our discussion of break-even and targeted net income,

MARGIN OF SAFETY

The *margin of safety* is the excess of budgeted (or actual) sales dollars over the break-even point. This shows the amount by which the sales can drop before losses would begin to be incurred: The higher the margin of safety, the lower the risk of not breaking even. In our original example as shown in Exhibits 6-1 and 6-2 the margin of safety was $ 900 dollars in sales ($600 of net income divided by the contribution margin ratio of 66.67%).

A business owner could apply this concept to his targeted net income to see how much sales could decline before the targeted net income could not be met.

OPERATING LEVERAGE

Operating leverage is a measure of the proportion of fixed costs in a company's cost structure. This is used as an indicator of how sensitive profit is to changes in sales volume.

Operating leverage is computed by dividing the total contribution margin by net income. The higher the level of fixed costs in relation to variable costs the higher the degree of operating leverage. If operating leverage is high then net income will be very sensitive to changes in sales volume. This means that a small percentage increase or decrease in sales dollars will result in a large percentage increase or decrease in net income. A company with high variable costs in relation to fixed costs will have a low level of operating leverage and will not be as sensitive to changes in sales volume.

Based on the information that was presented in Exhibit 6-2 the company's operating leverage would be 1.667 ($1,000 of total contribution margin divided by net income of $600). This is a moderate level of operating leverage. Using the information shown in Exhibit 6-7, the company has a lower level of operating leverage. In this case the level of operating leverage is 1.2 ($2,400 of total contribution margin divided by $2,000 of net income). The company is in an even better position at this level of operating leverage.

SUMMARY

In this chapter we have discussed the differences between the traditional income statement and the contribution margin income statement. The difference relates to how the costs are shown to arrive at net income. The contribution margin income statement focuses on behavior while the traditional income statement focuses on function. We also discussed contribution margin per unit and the contribution margin ratio and how these concepts can be used in analyzing the operations of a business.

After this discussion of contribution margin per unit and contribution margin ratio the chapter discussed how these measures could be used to calculate the break-even point. From there the concept of target net income was introduced and the use of the same measures was discussed with regards to target net income on a before tax basis and on an after tax basis.

The chapter concluded with brief discussions of margin of safety and operating leverage.

KEY TERMS

- Gross profit
- contribution margin per unit
- contribution margin ratio
- Break-even point
- target net income
- margin of safety
- Operating leverage

EXERCISES AND PROBLEMS

6-1. George Brown started a lawn mowing service during the summer. He currently prices his service at $ 30 per lawn. He estimates variable expenses for gasoline and other items total $ 18 per yard.

If he were to increase his price to $36 per yard, how many fewer yards could he mow and maintain the same net income?

6-2. Last year, Stony Corporation had a contribution margin of 35%. This year, fixed expenses are expected to remain constant at $125,000. Sales are expected to be $600,000, which is 10% higher than last year.

How much would net income increase for the company be if the contribution margin ratio were to increase to 38%?

6-3. Smith Company has current sales of $700,000 and variable costs of $420,000. The company's fixed costs are $250,000. Based upon a market survey it is anticipated that a $15,000 increase in advertising would increase sales by 5%.

Should the company increase advertising expenditures by $15,000? What will be the impact on Smith's net income?

6-4. Two medical schools friends, Joe and Don, opened a concierge medicine business after medical school. They decided to set their annual fee per patient at $4,000. They have variable expenses that total 10% of revenue and fixed expenses that total $20,000 per year. They set their salaries at $125,000 each.

Calculate the number of patients their business needs to break-even.

6-5. Sheila's Sensational Seafood Restaurant was opened 10 years ago. The restaurant is only open Friday through Monday and only serves dinner. The business has had a decline in recent months and this has Sheila concerned. Last month the restaurant broke even. Upon analyzing the business Sheila saw that the restaurant served 1,200 meals during the month. The variable cost per meal is $9 and the total fixed costs for the business were $30,000.

What was the average selling price per meal during the month?

6-6. Harbor Millwork current sells its bathroom cabinets for $200 each. The cabinets have variable costs of $100 and the company's annual fixed costs are $100,000. The company's tax rate is 25%.

Calculate the number of cabinets the company would need to sell to make an after tax profit of $30,000.

6-7. Last month MS Enterprises sold 50,000 units of their product, total sales were $250,000, total variable costs were $150,000 and total fixed expenses were $75,000.

1. What is the company's contribution margin ratio?
2. Estimate the change in the company's net income if sales were to increase by $10,000.

6-8. Monaco Products has a single product whose selling price is $16 and whose variable cost is $12. The company's monthly fixed expenses are $4,400.

1. Solve for the company's break-even point in sales units using the contribution margin per unit method.
2. Solve for the company's break-even point in dollars using the contribution margin ratio.

6-9. Loner Corporation has a single product whose selling price is $150 and whose variable costs are $100 per unit. The monthly fixed expense of Loner is $60,000.

1. Using the contribution margin per unit method calculate the unit sales needed for Loner to make a target net income of $20,000. Ignore income taxes.
2. Using the contribution margin ratio method calculate the dollar sales needed for Loner to make a target net income of $25,000. Ignore income taxes.

6-10. Neander Corporation is a distributer of surf boards used at resort hotels. Details from the budget for next month follow.

Selling price	$200 per unit
Variable expenses	$100 per unit
Fixed expense	$7,500 per month
Unit sales	150 units per month

1. Calculate the company's margin of safety.
2. Calculate the margin of safety as a percentage of sales.

6-11. Using the information from the XYZ Manufacturing trial balance in Appendix A. Assume that annual sales in units are 7,000 units.

1. Calculate the break-even point in unit sales using the contribution margin per unit method.
2. Calculate the break-even point in dollars using the contribution margin ratio method.

3. Calculate the level of dollar sales needed to create a target net income of $500,000. Ignore income taxes.

6-12. Using the information from the Local Hardware Store trial balance in Appendix A. Assume that 60% of the cost of goods sold is variable and 40% are fixed.

Calculate the break-even point in dollar sales using the contribution margin ratio method.

6-13. Morgan Hastings started his company three years ago. Since he was in grade school he has been fascinated by neon signs. Due to this fascination his company produces neon signs. He is considering introducing a new custom sign that he believes will satisfy an unfulfilled demand. Based upon his research into the potential market for the sign he feels that the company will sell 8,000 of these signs annually. The expected sales price is $75 per unit, and the variable costs will be $30 per unit. The company's annual fixed costs are $270,000.

1. How many signs must be sold to break-even?
2. How many signs must be sold to earn a target net income of $22,500?
3. What would be the company's profit be if they sold 8,000 signs?
4. What would be the break-even point if the sales price decreased by 10%? Round your answer to the next higher number.

6-14. Our Fine Feathered Friends Inc. distributes wooden birdhouses that sell for $20 per unit. Variable costs are $6 per unit, and total fixed costs are $210,000 per year.

4. What is the product's contribution margin ratio?
5. Use the contribution margin ratio to calculate the break-even point in sales dollars.
6. If the company experiences a change in demand and total sales increase by $60,000 during the next year. How much should net income increase by assuming no change in fixed expenses? Ignore income taxes.

6-15. Joe Smith recently opened a pub in the university district. Because of licensing restrictions the only liquor Joe can serve is beer. The average price of a glass of beer is $3.00 and the average cost to Joe is $2.00. Joe hired a bartender and a waitress at $3,000 and $2,000 per month, respectively. Joe's fixed operating costs, not including the bartender and waitress are $5,000 per month.

Joe currently sells no food but is considering selling hamburgers during the lunch to increase trade as the lunch hour sales are quite small. It will also allow him to be more competitive with other local bars that offer food during the lunch hour.

Joe would like to sell the hamburgers for $1.30 each in order to be attractive to customers. He will be able to buy buns for $1.20 per dozen and ground beef for $3.00 per pound. Each pound of ground beef will make six hamburgers. Other ingredients will cost .10 per hamburger. Joe will need to hire a part time cook at $1,200 per month and other additional fixed costs will be $300 per month.

1. If Joe sells only beer, how many glasses of beer does he need to sell eachmonth to make a profit of $2,000 per month?
2. Suppose that Joe decides to sell hamburgers. How many hamburgers does Joe need to sell each month to break even on the hamburgers? Assume there is no effect on beer sales.
3. The main reason for adding hamburgers is to attract additional customers. Suppose that each month there are 2,400 extra customers at lunch time and that each extra customer buys one hamburger and additional beer sales average 1.5 glasses per each additional customer. Compute the added profit (or loss) generated by the extra customers.
4. Joe could offer a higher quality hamburger if he spends 50% more on the ingredients. The higher quality hamburgers would sell for $ 2.00. If half of the 2,400 customers purchased the higher quality hamburger how much would offering the higher quality hamburger add to Joe's net income? Assume all other facts are the same as in item 3.

CHAPTER 7 – RELEVANT COSTS FOR DECISION MAKING

LEARNING OBJECTIVES

1. Identify relevant costs and benefits in a decision process
2. Analyze pricing for a special order
3. Prepare a make or buy analysis
4. Analyze a decision involving scarce or limited resources
5. Prepare an analysis on whether to sell a product or process it further

RELEVANT COSTS

Relevant costs for making a decision are those costs (or revenues) that differ between alternatives that are being considered. This concept means that cost and revenues that are not different between alternatives are irrelevant. In analyzing the alternatives we are only interested in future costs and revenues for each alternative, past costs and revenues are irrelevant. For example, if you trying to decide whether to go out for dinner or to fix dinner at home, there would be relevant costs for each alternative. The main cost that would differ between the alternatives is the cost of the food. For this example we will say that the food costs $5 if you eat in and $8 if you eat out. These costs are relevant because they differ between the alternatives and therefore they are avoidable.

An *avoidable cost* is a cost that can be eliminated in whole or in part by choosing one alternative over the other. In this case by choosing the alternative of going out to eat you would avoid the cost of food for eating at home ($5). By choosing to eat at home you would avoid the cost of eating out ($8). Therefore, both the cost of eating at home and the cost of eating out are avoidable. Avoidable costs are relevant costs while unavoidable costs are irrelevant. In this example the cost of your home would be unavoidable regardless of your decision about where to eat as you would still have the cost of the home in either circumstance, therefore the cost of your home would be irrelevant.

Some broad categories of costs are never relevant, two of these are:

1. Sunk costs (costs incurred in the past)
2. Future costs that do not differ between the alternatives.

In discussing relevant costs there are other terms that can be used interchangeably. These would be *relevant cost, incremental cost, differential cost and avoidable cost*. To identify the costs that are relevant (avoidable) in a particular decision situation, the following steps should be followed:

1. Eliminate the costs and benefits that do not differ between the alternatives. These irrelevant costs would be those identified in the broad categories listed above.
2. Use the remaining costs and benefits that differ between the alternatives in making the decision. The costs that remain are the relevant (avoidable) costs.

It should be stated at this point that costs that are relevant for one decision may not be relevant for a different decision situation. Basically this means that the decision maker will need different costs for different purposes. As an example, if we take the example above about whether to eat out or to eat at home, the relevant costs in that example would have no relevance regarding a decision on whether to drive or to fly to San Diego.

In making a decision managers use a decision model. A *decision model* is any method used for making a choice. Exhibit 7-1 depicts the decision process.

Exhibit 7-1 – Decision Process

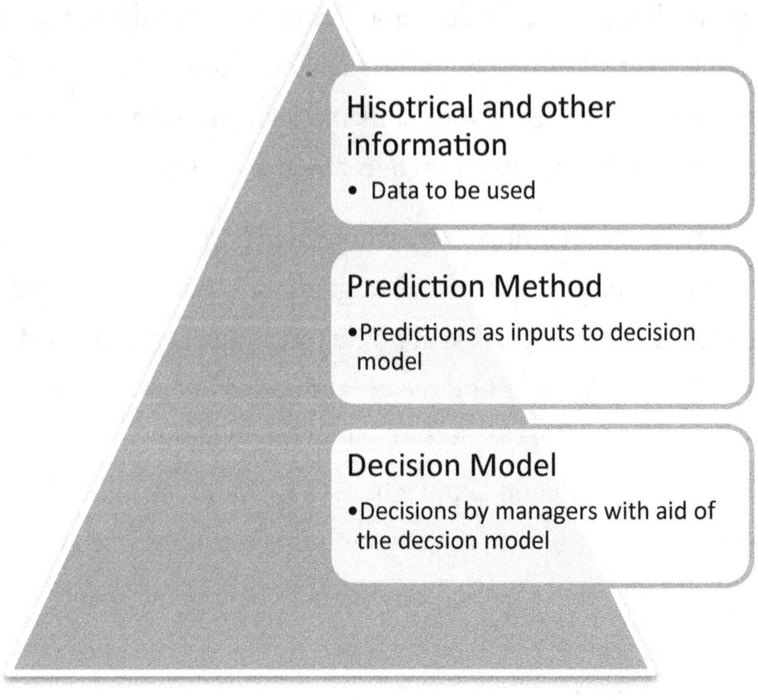

In the best of all worlds, decision making information would be both relevant and predictably accurate. In the real world such information can be either too difficult or too expensive to obtain. This problem leads to the use of estimates and accountants, in providing information to managers, are often forced to choose between information that is more relevant or information that is more accurate.

Accuracy is not important if the information is irrelevant. Just because information is very precise it is not necessarily information that should be used since it may not be relevant. Information that is imprecise but relevant can still be useful. A common type of information that may be imprecise but is still useful in decision making is the sales prediction for a new product. While it is likely that the sales prediction will vary from the actual sales should the product be offered, the sales prediction may be useful in deciding whether to make the product. The relevant information need to have some degree of accuracy but does not have to be precise. In the example of sales prediction for the new product, if the prediction is within 10-15% of what the future is likely to show then it will still have relevance even though it is not exact.

The degree to which information is relevant or precise may depend on the degree to which it is quantitative or qualitative. Qualitative aspects are those for which measurement in terms of dollars and cents is difficult and imprecise; while quantitative aspects are those where measurement in dollars and cents is easy and fairly precise. In making business decisions more data based on quantitative aspects than on qualitative aspects makes the decision easier and more straight forward. However, no decision should be made entirely on the quantitative aspects as qualitative aspects are important in decision making even though they are more subjective. Sometimes the qualitative aspects will outweigh the quantitative aspects of a business decision. Take an example where a manufacturing company could install a machine that would save labor and the labor savings would pay for the machine in a short period of time. The quantitative aspects show that the investment should be made. However, if the manufacturing company provides most of the jobs in a community and the installation of the labor saving equipment would lead to laying off members of the community who will not be able to find another job in the community. At his point the business may decide to forego the installation of the equipment because of the qualitative factor of how it would affect the community.

Finally let us look at one final example of relevant costs with regards to quantitative information. Previously, it was mentioned that a potential decision could whether to drive to San Diego or to fly to San Diego.

The costs that would be different between the two options are as follows:

Driving	
Gasoline (50 gallons at $3.50 per gallon)	$ 175.00
Maintenances and repairs (1,000 miles at $.06 per mile)	60.00
Hotel stay (1 extra evening)	250.00
Meals (1 extra day)	50.00
Total Cost	$ 535.00
Flying	
Cost of airfare	$ 425.00
Rental car (1 day)	75.00
Total Cost	$ 500.00

Based on this analysis the decision would be to fly if decided upon purely quantitative factors.

The use of relevant information in decision making is applicable for any type or size of business. Most large companies have a very in depth and formalized approach to evaluating alternatives. Small companies can use this type of analysis in a less formalized structure to help them make good business decisions.

SPECIAL ORDER DECISIONS

Deciding whether to accept a special order is a decision about pricing. Special order decisions are usually short -term decisions where management must decide what price would be appropriate for the special order. Special orders are orders placed by customers that are different from those placed in the ordinary course of business. An example could be a one-time order placed by a new customer, a foreign customer or even a competitor. The decision is only applicable if the company has excess capacity at the point in time the special order would be received and manufactured, in the case of a manufacturing firm.

Special order pricing decisions are also the possible with non-manufacturing companies. Take an example of a CPA firm that has staff that is underutilized during the summer, would the firm consider discounting an audit fee for a company that had a fiscal year end of June 30. The audit could be done in July or August, when most CPA firms have their slowest time of year. It is also the time of year when new employees that have just completed their college work are starting on the job. The special priced audit could be used for training of the new employees before the busy season hits.

A common place where special pricing can occur is with airlines seats that are on flights that are relatively empty. The airlines price their seats according to time of year and destination. They also have different prices if the passenger stays over a Saturday night, as this helps them with filling airplanes that frequently are under filled. An example of airline pricing would be a flight from Detroit to London, in the summer the flight could cost the passenger $1,500 for a standard economy seat, but in January or February a passenger could get the same seat for $1,000. This is because the flights during the winter typically have a lower number of passengers and the airline is hoping to attract passengers during the slow time of year.

Let's look at a special order decision for a manufacturing company. Creature Comfort Seat Covers manufacturers seat covers for tour buses, passenger buses and personal cars and trucks. Creature Comfort is offered a special order from a tour bus line for 100,000 seat covers for $27 per seat (the normal selling price is $40 per unit). Creature Comfort's total manufacturing cost per seat cover is $30 of which $5 are fixed costs. All selling, general and administrative costs are fixed. The normal annual volume of seat covers is 1 million units. Should Creature Comfort accept if they have the capacity to produce the covers without it affecting their normal customer orders? Exhibits 7-2 and 7-3 show the analysis using the contribution approach.

Exhibit 7-2 – Contribution Income Statement without the Special Order

Sales	$40,000,000
Less: Variable expenses	
Manufacturing	25,000,000
Selling and administrative	0
Total variable expenses	25,000,000
Contribution margin	15,000,000
Less: Fixed expenses	
Manufacturing	6,000,000
Selling and administrative	8,000,000
Total fixed expenses	14,000,000
Operating income	$ 1,000,000

Now we will show the income statement with the special order.

Exhibit 7-3 – Contribution Income Statement with the Special Order

Sales	$42,700,000
Less: Variable expenses	
Manufacturing	27,500,000
Selling and administrative	0
Total variable expenses	27,500,000
Contribution margin	15,200,000
Less: Fixed expenses	
Manufacturing	6,000,000
Selling and administrative	8,000,000
Total fixed expenses	14,000,000
Operating income	$ 1,200,000

Based on the analysis presented in Exhibits 7-2 and 7-3, the company should accept the special order based upon a quantitative analysis. The company could choose to decline the order if there are qualitative reasons that outweigh the quantitative analysis.

MAKE OR BUY DECISIONS

When preparing an analysis of outsourcing and *make or buy decisions* an in-depth analysis of relevant quantitative and qualitative aspects need to be considered. The make or buy decision is a short-term decision regarding the purchasing of components used in manufacturing from another company rather than producing the components internally. It is also a decision about whether producing the parts internally is a good use of capacity not currently in use.

If a company chooses to produce its own components then the company will be vertically integrated. *Vertical integration* occurs when a company is involved in multiple levels of the value chain. In an extreme circumstance the company that is vertically integrated would control the original source of raw material, the material that is ready for manufacture, the manufacture of the item for sale and a retail or wholesale business that sells the final good. This could be a company owning a mine that produces copper, the copper ore is then smelted into copper ingot that can be used for the production of copper tubing which the company makes at their manufacturing facility, finally the company would own a wholesale distribution company that sells the copper tubing to plumbers for use in the plumbing of businesses and homes.

Let's look at an example of the make or buy decision.

The Fly By Fishing Company makes fishing equipment for avid fishermen. They currently make their both their fly fishing rods and their spin casting rods. They have the opportunity to purchase the spin cast rods from another manufacturer under a private label agreement. The spin casting rods would be made to look identical to the current Fly By rods including the use of their logo so the customer would notice no difference. The company produces 10,000 rods per year and the cost data related to the manufacturing costs is shown below:

	Total Costs	Per Unit
Direct materials	$ 400,000	$40
Direct labor	500,000	50
Variable manufacturing costs	250,000	25
Fixed manufacturing costs	450,000	45
Total cost	$1,600,000	$160

If the company purchases the rods from the other manufacturer the cost per rod will be $120.00 per rod. The quantitative analysis follows in Exhibits 7-4 and 7-5.

Exhibit 7-4 - Rods Purchased from Other Manufacturer

	Cost to Make (per unit)	Cost to Buy (per unit)
Direct Materials	$40	
Direct Labor	50	
Variable manufacturing	25	
Fixed manufacturing	45	$45
Purchase price		120
Total cost	**$160**	**$165**

Exhibit 7-4 compares the price to purchase the rods with the price to make the rods and based on the assumption that none of the fixed manufacturing costs would be eliminated the quantitative analysis shows that it would be better for Fly By to continue to manufacture the spin casting rods. Upon further analysis of Fly By's operation it is determined that if the spin casting rods are purchased from the other manufacturer that one supervisor (part of the fixed manufacturing costs) would no longer be needed. The cost related to the supervisor is $60,000 per year. Because this fixed cost would be eliminated it now becomes a relevant cost, a new analysis showing this change is shown in Exhibit 7-5.

Exhibit 7-5 -Rods Purchased from Other Manufacturer - Some Fixed Manufacturing Costs Eliminated

	Cost to Make (per unit)	Cost to Buy (per unit)
Direct Materials	$40	
Direct Labor	50	
Variable manufacturing	25	
Fixed manufacturing	45	$39
Purchase price		120
Total cost	**$160**	**$159**

The analysis in Exhibit 7-5 shows that with the elimination of some fixed manufacturing costs that it would now make sense based upon the quantitative analysis to purchase the rods rather than make them. At this point the company would need to determine whether the $1 cost savings per rod is worth making the change given the qualitative factors that may be involved.

RESOURCE UTILIZATION DECISIONS

A company has a *constraint* when a limited resource of some type restricts the company's ability to provide a good or service. When the company faces a constraint then the managers are faced with a *resource utilization decision*. Since the company is unable to fully satisfy demand the managers must decide how the constrained resource should be used. In this case managers should emphasize the product that will make the largest contribution per unit of the constrained resource. A constraint can also be referred to as a *limiting factor or scarce resource*. Limiting factors could include labor hours, machine hours, or a scarce raw material. Most of the time, the limiting factor will be labor hours or machine hours so we will focus on those limiting factors.

As an example let's discuss a shoe company that makes athletic shoes. The company has a limiting factor of machine hours. The factory is limited to a maximum of 15,000 hours of machine time. The company can make 15 pairs of its basketball shoe or 10 pairs of its cross training shoe in one hour of machine time. Unit data for the two shoes follow:

	Basketball	Cross training
Selling price per pair	$100	$150
Variable costs per pair	75	105
Contribution margin per pair	25	45
Contribution margin ratio	25%	30%

A retailer approaches the shoe manufacturer and wants it to fill a special order of 1,000 pairs of shoes of either type. The manufacturer will need to determine which shoe would provide more profit for the company. If the company has sufficient capacity to produce either shoe, the limiting factor becomes demand. In that case the shoe company would choose to produce the cross training shoe for the special order as each pair adds a contribution margin of $45 while the basketball shoe only adds $25 per pair of contribution margin, Thus the total contribution margins added for the cross training shoes would be $45,000, and would be $25,000 for the basketball shoes. The company would be better off by $20,000 if they chose to produce the cross training shoes.

If the company has enough demand to use and exceed the capacity of their machines, then the limiting factor becomes machine time. In that case the analysis will change due to the change in the limiting factor.

The new analysis will focus on machine hours to determine the added contribution margin per machine hour. The data on this analysis is presented below:

	Basketball	Cross training
Pairs per machine hour	15	10
Contribution margin per pair	$25	$45
Total hours to produce 1,000 pairs	66.7	100

In this case the total contribution margin that would be contributed by the basketball shoes of $25,000 would be divided by the number of hours to produce the shoes of 66.7 and we would arrive at a contribution per machine hour of $375. The total contribution margin of $45,000 for the cross training shoes would be divided by the 100 hours of machine time to arrive at a contribution per machine hour of $450. Using machine hours as the limiting does not change the decision in this case as it would still be better to produce cross training shoes for the special order. However, in some cases the change in the limiting factor would change the decision.

Analyzing which product is best due to limiting factors is applicable to virtually all businesses. In the case of a service company the most common limiting factor would be labor hours available to perform the work. In the case of a merchandising company the most common limiting factor would shelf space for product combined with floor space for holding shelves or product that cannot be put on shelves. In the case of an agricultural production company the most common limiting factor would be acreage.

SELL OR PROCESS FURTHER

The decision whether to sell a product or process further is another common business decision that is faced by managers of manufacturing firms. A good example would furniture manufacturers. They have several options for how they sell their furniture: (a) assembled and finished, this how the average consumer would see it on the showroom floor of the furniture store; (b) unassembled and finished, this is a very common way to see furniture in a big box store, the consumer takes the furniture home in a box and assembles it at home (Sauder is a large company that does business this way); (c) unassembled and unfinished, the consumer assembles the furniture at home and then finishes it with the finish they desire; and (d) assembled and unfinished, the consumer gets the furniture they want already assembled but gets to finish it the way they prefer.

Each of these options provides the product with a different cost structure as each additional process performed at the manufacturing facility adds to the cost. The incremental costs added for each additional process would be the relevant costs for decision making purposes as all costs to that point are the same between the alternatives. The only future costs that differ between the final states of the product are the additional processing costs. For purposes of analysis data is presented below regarding the manufacture of desks.

	Assembled Finished	Unassembled Finished	Unassembled Unfinished	Assembled Unfinished
Sales price	$275	$225	$200	$250
Cost to Produce	200	170	155	185
Contribution Margin per Unit	75	55	45	65

The data above shows that there can be significant incremental revenue by processing the furniture further but there are also some significant incremental costs. Based on the data above that it would

appear that the best way for the company to do business would be to assemble and finish all of the furniture it produces.

This simple analysis could cause us to make the wrong decision based on the total contribution margin for the company. Assuming the company can sell all of the desks they produce, we would have to consider production capacity for each stage of completion. If the company's daily production capacity based upon the stage of completion as follows, we would need to consider this information as well:

	Assembled Finished	Unassembled Finished	Unassembled Unfinished	Assembled Unfinished
Daily Production Capacity In Units	90	125	140	110

The analysis once this additional information is added looks like this:

	Assembled Finished	Unassembled Finished	Unassembled Unfinished	Assembled Unfinished
Contribution Margin Per unit	$75	$55	$45	$65
Daily Production	90	125	140	110
Daily Contribution Margin	$6,750	$6,875	$6,300	$7,150

Once the production capacity is considered, another relevant piece of information, is added the decision changes and would lead the managers to think that furniture that is assembled but unfinished would be the best way for the company to proceed. In normal business practice the decision is not usually an all or nothing proposition and the most likely outcome would be to manufacture a mixture of the different stages of completion depending upon what market segment the company was trying to attract to its products.

Probably the industry that constantly adjusts the product mix based on stage of production the most frequently is the oil refining business. Out of a 42 gallon barrel of oil the refinery gets approximately the following mix: gasoline, 22 gallons: diesel 7 gallons; heating oil, 1.5 gallons; jet fuel, 5.5 gallons; LPG gas, 1.5 gallons; miscellaneous (including petrochemicals), 4.5 gallons. Each of these items come out of the refining process at different stages and by taking more out of production earlier the product mix can be changed and is changed based on the time of year.

SUMMARY

In this chapter we have discussed relevant costs and benefits that a company uses in the decision making process. These costs and benefits are defined as those future costs and benefits that differ between the alternatives. We used those concepts to illustrate how they might be used in deciding whether or not to accept a special order. Next, we applied the concept to a make or buy decision that a company could face. Then consideration was given to how the relevant costs would affect a decision involving the allocation of scarce or limited resources. Finally, an example was presented where relevant information would be applied to decide whether to sell a product at one point in the production process or process further and sell later in the process.

KEY TERMS

- Relevant cost
- avoidable cost
- unavoidable cost
- differential cost
- Decision model
- make or buy decision
- constraint
- limiting factor
- Vertical integration
- resource utilization decision
- Sell or process further decision
- scarce resource

EXERCISES AND PROBLEMS

7-1. Robert Jones, Inc. sells a patio table with umbrella for $125 per unit. The production of the table causes the company to incur the following costs: direct materials, $45; direct labor, $25; variable overhead, $20; and fixed overhead $10. The company has received a special order for the tables for 75 units. The company has sufficient capacity to produce the tables. The order would require temporary storage costs of $250.

1. Should the company accept the order at $100 per unit?
2. If the company requires a minimum profit of $875 on any special order, what should the selling price be?

7-2. Mary Lou, Inc. uses 10,000 pieces of a component in the production of their product each year. Currently, the component is purchased from an outside supplier at $12 per unit. The company has had idle capacity for some time now and expects to continue to have idle capacity in the future. If Mary Lou were to manufacture the component in their facility, they would have the following costs associated with the production:

Direct materials	$3 per unit
Direct labor	$3 per unit
Variable overhead	$2 per unit
Fixed overhead per unit	$2 per unit

The manufacture of the component would have no effect on fixed overhead.

If Mary Lou were to make the product in house what impact would, if any, the production have on the net income of Mary Lou?

7-3. Wild Ride, Inc. produces ski videos in two lengths on separate DVD's. The company can sell their entire output of either product. The relevant data for the two products is as follows:

	Short Version	Long Version
Selling Price	$15	$30
Variable costs per DVD	$3	$5
Machine hours per unit	2	5

Total fixed overhead is $250,000. The company only has 100,000 hours of machine time available. The machine time is a constraint for the company and therefore management must decide which DVD to produce to maximize the company's profit.

Which product should Wild Ride produce to maximize profit?

7-4. JJ Toys manufactured 1,000 robots that were defective. The manufacturing costs related to the toy robots were:

Direct materials	$40
Direct labor	$30
Variable overhead	$10
Fixed overhead	$20

The robots normally sell for $140 per unit. The company could rework the robots which would cost: direct materials $20; direct labor $10; variable overhead $5 and fixed overhead $15. The alternative is for the company to sell the robots "as is" for a selling price of $95.

1. Which alternative will maximize profits or minimize loss for the company?
2. Are there any qualitative factors that the company should consider in addition to the quantitative factors?

7-5. Tory, Inc. manufactures a variety of engines for use in farm tractors. The company has always produced all of the components for its engines. An outside supplier has offered to sell the company one type of piston for a cost of $20. To evaluate this option the company has gathered the information below, relating to the costs of producing the piston internally:

	Per Unit	Annually (20,000 Units)
Direct materials	$9	$180,000
Direct labor	5	100,000
Variable overhead	2	40,000
Fixed overhead, traceable	2	40,000
Fixed overhead, allocated	5	100,000
Total Cost	$23	$460,000

1. Assuming that the company has no alternative use for the facilities currently being used should the pistons be purchased from the outside supplier?
2. Suppose that company could use the facilities to produce a new product and the total contribution margin of the new product would $100,000. Should the company buy the pistons from the outside supplier in this case?

7-6. Antelope, Inc. manufactures 25,000 units of product A-6 each year for use in its production process. The cost per unit for the company to produce the product, at the current level of production is as follows:

Direct materials	$ 4.25
Direct labor	9.00
Variable overhead	6.00
Fixed overhead	2.75
Total cost per unit	$ 22.00

An outside supplier has offered to Antelope 25,000 units per year of A-6 for $20 per unit. If Antelope accepts the offer the facilities currently being used to produce A-6 could be leased to another company for $50,000 per year.

1. Calculate the increase or decrease in Antelope's net profit if they accept the offer from the outside supplier.
2. Calculate the increase or decrease in the company's net income if the offer from the outside supplier was $23 per unit and the company accepted the offer.

7-7. Underground Products, Inc. produces several products from I ton of didanium, a material that is mined. The material and processing costs total $75,000 per ton, one-third of which is allocated to product S-3. 5,000 units of product S-3 can be made from each ton of didanium. The units can be sold at the split-off point for $10 each, or processed further at a total cost of $10,000 and then be sold for $13 each.

Should S-3 be sold at the split-off point or be processed further and then sold?

7-8. An administrator at Parkview Hospital is considering how to use space made available when the outpatient clinic moved to another building. The choices that have identified are as follows:

a. Use the space to expand the laboratory testing area. Expected additional annual revenue from use of the space would be $350,000 and additional increased costs would be $310,000.
b. Use the space to expand the eye clinic. Increased revenue would be $450,000 and increased costs would be $425,000
c. The gift shop is run by an independent retailer who would like to have the additional space and has offered additional rent of $15,000 per year.

Based upon the data above, prepare a table showing the impact on the net income, of the hospital, of each option.

7-9. A petrochemical factory produces two products, F and G, as a result of a joint process. Both products are sold to other manufacturers as ingredients in their products. Product F sells at the split off point for $50 per gallon; G sells for $.35 per gallon data for January follows:

Joint processing costs $2,000,000

Gallons produced and sold:

F 5,000,000

G 3,000,000

Suppose that the 3,000,000 gallons of G could have been processed further into H at an additional cost of $180,000. The H output would be sold for $.42 per gallon. F will always be sold at the split-off point.

Should product G be processed further into H and sold as H?

7-10. A growing corporation in a large city has offered a local 200-room hotel a 1-year contract to rent 40 rooms at reduced rates of $55 per room instead of the regular $90 per room. The corporation will sign the contract for 365-day occupancy because its visiting manufacturing and marketing personnel are virtually certain to use all the space each night.

Each room occupied has a variable cost of $15 per night (for cleaning, laundry, etc.).

The hotel manager is reluctant to sign the agreement as she expects the occupancy rate to be 85% for the year. If she signs the agreement the remaining 160 rooms would be expected to have a 95% occupancy rate.

1. Compute the total contribution margin, for the year, without the contract.
2. Compute the total contribution margin, for the year, with the contract.
3. Is the contract profitable for the hotel?
4. Compute the lowest room rate the manager should be willing to accept for the contract. This should be based on the point where the total contribution margin is the same with or without the contract.

7-11.Western Montana Corp. produces two products, cigars and chewing tobacco, from a joint process involving the processing of tobacco leaves. Joint costs are $75,000 for this process, and yield 2,500 pounds of cigars and 5,000 pounds of chewing tobacco. Cigars sell for $80 per pound, and chewing tobacco sells for$20 per pound. Cigars require $80,000 in separate costs, while chewing tobacco requires $50,000 in separate costs. Chewing tobacco can be produced further for $25,000 in additional separate costs into a premium, flavored chewing tobacco that would sell for $30 per pound.

1. Should Western process the chewing tobacco further into the premium chewing tobacco?

7-12. Big Sky Meat Producers, Inc. is a processor of beef in southwestern Montana. The company has a large supply of T-bone steaks on hand and is trying to decide whether to sell the T- bone steaks the way they are or to produce them further into filet mignon and New York strip.If the T-bone is sold as originally cut the company has prepared the following analysis for a 1 pound T-bone.

Selling price ($3.00 per pound)	$3.00
Joint costs incurred to this point	2.50
Profit per pound	$ .50

Big Sky has the option of processing the T-bones further into filet mignon and New York strip steaks cutting one side of the T-bone yields one, 6 ounce filet mignon and cutting the other side yields one, 8 ounce New York strip. The cost of processing the T-bone into these steaks is $.50 per pound. The filet mignon can be sold for $4.50 per pound and the New York strip can be sold for $3.60 per pound.

1. Determine the profit or (loss) from producing the T-bones into the filet mignon and New York strip steaks.
2. Would you recommend selling the product as T-bones or as filet mignon and New York strip?

7-13. Larry Johnson, Inc. has the following cost structure in its budget for the upcoming year:

Sales (20,000 units at $30)	$600,000
Manufacturing costs	
Variable	$11 per unit
Fixed	$180,000
Marketing and administrative costs	
Variable	$4 per unit
Fixed	$20,000

1. What is the expected level of profit?
2. Should the company accept a special order at $20 per unit if variable marketing expenses associated with the special order are $2 per unit instead of the normal variable selling expenses per unit? What would be the impact on profits if the company accepted the special order? Assume that this order is in addition to the 20,000 units in the budget
3. What is the lowest price the company should be willing to accept for a 2,000 piece special order assuming there are no variable marketing costs for the units produced

for the order, and the company requires a minimum profit of $1,000 on all special orders? (The selling price should be rounded up to the next even dollar)

7-14. Trek Specialties produces two sizes of backpacks: one for people between 5 and 6 feet tall and one for people over six feet tall. Both backpacks are using the same machine in the processing of the backpack. It takes 20 minutes of machine time to make the smaller backpack and 30 minutes of machine time to make the larger backpack. The data concerning the two sizes follow:

	Small	Large
Sales price (per unit)	$150	$200
Direct materials	60	80
Direct labor	30	40
Variable overhead	15	20
Contribution margin	$ 45	$ 60

Machine time is limited to 5,000 hours per year. The company can sell its entire output of either size but due to other manufacturing constraints they cannot use more than 75% of the available machine time for either product.

1. Calculate the product mix that would provide the greatest total contribution margin for the company.
2. Assume that the limitation on machine time is 60% for either product; calculate the maximum total contribution margin the company could make.

7-15. Refer to the information presented in the trial balance for XYZ Manufacturing, in Appendix A, calculate the variable cost per unit assuming 7,000 units on annual basis. There should be costs for direct materials, direct labor and variable overhead. Based on your calculation of these variable costs, determine whether XYZ should accept a special order for 800 units at $1,200 per unit.

CHAPTER 8 – CAPITAL BUDGETING DECISIONS

LEARNING OBJECTIVES

1. Evaluate capital budgeting (investment) decisions using the payback method and discuss its limitations
2. Evaluate capital budgeting decisions using the Net Present Value (NPV) method.
3. Evaluate capital budgeting decisions using the Internal Rate of Return (IRR) method.
4. Evaluate the impact of taxes on capital investment decisions.

INTRODUCTION TO CAPITAL BUDGETING

Capital budgeting (investment) decisions are made by all sizes and types of organizations and involve the purchase of new equipment, machinery or facilities. These types of decisions are made by any organization that carries on any type of business, whether for profit or not for profit, privately owned, publicly owned, or governmental organizations. The process for business organizations is designed to ensure that the investment makes economic sense for the organization. In the case of governmental organizations, they will not necessarily use these techniques as they are concerned with providing a service for the citizens and not about earning a return on the funds invested in the capital item. When we talk about *capital investments* we are talking about large cost items that have lives of several years. The techniques that we will discuss in the chapter can be used to make screening *decisions or preference decisions. Screening decisions* relate to whether a proposed investment passes a preset hurdle. *Preference decisions* relate to selecting from among several competing investments that have passed the screening decision.

Capital investments may be considered for a variety of reasons, these may include: necessary repair or replacement of key equipment or facilities, upgrade of current equipment or facilities (usually to enable cost savings), equipment to allow production of a new product or other valid business reasons.

To determine if the proposed investments are a good investment the return has to be measured based on the same value as the expenditure made at the beginning. Because capital investments involve large amounts of money and last for several years we have to analyze the costs and benefits of the investments based on the time value of money. The focus of the *time value of money* is on cash flows, not on accounting income. Accounting income and cash flows quite often are not the same thing. The concept of the time value of money is related to the fact that business (or individuals) would rather have $1 today than $1 in three years. This is because there is an expectation that $1 in the future will not purchase as much as it will today because of inflation. In addition to the loss in purchasing power businesses feel they need to have a return on the money invested for it to be a good investment. Therefore when determining the appropriate rate for discounting cash flows from the investment, businesses combine both the inflation factor and the return factor. The concept of *discounted cash flows* means that future cash flows are brought back to the equivalent amount of money today based upon the pre-determined rate of return. The methods we will discuss in the chapter are methods for determining the return based on the discounted cash flows from the future. The only exception to using discounted cash flows that we will discuss is the payback method.

PAYBACK METHOD

Generally companies use the payback method only as an initial screening calculation to see if it makes sense to do more in depth financial analysis on a proposed investment. Large companies frequently have an initial payback screening level of five years. This means that if the undiscounted cash flows will return the initial investment within five years then the project is worth further analysis, if not the project is given no further consideration. Most small and medium size businesses have a shorter payback period for their initial screening (usually two or three years). Some small businesses use payback as the only measure for evaluation capital investment decisions.

The *payback method* is very simple and easy to calculate if the expected future cash flows are an anticipated amount that won't change over the life of the investment. As an example, assume a company is evaluating a proposed investment where the initial cash outflow is $52,125 and the annual cash inflow the project will provide is $12,000 per year. To calculate the payback period, in years, we divide the outflow of $52,125 by the annual inflow of $12,000 and we arrive at a payback period of 4.34 years. This project might meet the initial screening requirement for many large businesses but probably would not meet the criteria for most small and medium size businesses unless there were other factors to consider.

The calculation of payback becomes complicated if the cash inflows are not the same each year. In this case we have to calculate the number of years by going through a step by step procedure. The procedure is not difficult but it takes a little more time than if the cash inflows were the same each year.

Let's assume we have an initial investment of $150,000 and our cash inflows are $30,000 per year for the first 3 years and are $35,000 per year for years 4-8. The calculation procedure would be to subtract each full year until the investment remaining is less than a full year's inflow and then we would calculate what portion of that year would be needed. Given the information provided above the calculation would look like this.

Cash Outflow	$150,000
Year 1 cash inflow	(30,000)
Amount remaining	120,000
Year 2 cash inflow	(30,000)
Amount remaining	90,000
Year 3 cash inflow	(30,000)
Amount remaining	60,000
Year 4 cash inflow	(35,000)
Amount remaining	25,000

Since the amount remaining is less than the cash inflow for year 5 we will have to calculate what portion of a year is needed to arrive at our final calculation for payback. The calculation is the amount remaining divided by the amount of cash inflow for the next year.

In this case it is $25,000/$35,000 or .714. We add this to the number of full years' cash inflows used (in this case 4) and we arrive at a payback period of 4.714 years.

This concludes the discussion of how to calculate the payback period. The payback method has a limitation in its use, as it does not take into account the time value of money. The method could be modified to take into account the time value of money so that we could arrive at a discounted payback period, but doing that causes the method to lose its simplicity and its use as an initial simple screening method. We will not cover the discounted payback method here as it would not be a simple method for small business to use.

NET PRESENT VALUE

The net *present value (NPV)* method is the widest used method for evaluating capital investment decisions as nearly 94% of large corporations use it as at least one of the methods for screening decisions. Historically, it has also been the widest used method for making preferences decisions. The use of the method requires that the company choose a *discount rate* to apply to the screening process. Usually the rate chosen by the company would be its minimum required rate of return which will approximate the company's weighted average cost of capital, for the last dollar of capital employed, plus a small return above the cost of capital. The weighted average cost of capital is an average of the rates the company has to pay to borrow funds, either through the issuance of bonds or through bank loans, or to issue additional stock to raise the funds for investment.

In using the method the company compares the value in today's dollars of the future cash inflows, after discounting the inflows for the discount rate and then subtracting the cash outflow that is required at the beginning or during the project. There are several tools that can be used to calculate the net present value of an investment. The first tool is the use of present value tables such as those in Appendix B. If we take the example from above where the company was going to spend $52,125 dollars on a project and was going to get annual return that is a constant amount, of $12,000 per year. We now add the fact that the investment is expected to last for 8 years and the company's desired return is 12%. With these facts we can use the tables in Appendix B to calculate the NPV. To determine the present value of the cash inflows we would go to the table for the present value of an annuity. The term *annuity* means a stream of even payments.

We go to the column for 12% and we go down the column until we reach the row for 8 years and we find a value (called an interest factor) of 4.9676. We multiply this by the amount of the annual cash inflows of $ 12,000 and we would arrive at the present value of the cash inflows, $59,611.20. We would then take this amount and subtract the original cash outflow from it to arrive at the net present value of the project, in this case $59,811.20–$52,125 = $7,486.20. The screening use of the NPV method is that any project that has a positive net present value will be considered. If a project has a negative net present value then the project would normally not be considered.

The next way we can calculate the net present value of a project is through the use of a financial calculator. Each model of financial calculator may have a slightly different way of entering the data, but they will all require that you enter the cash outflow at the beginning as a negative number (usually done by pressing the+/- key before entering the amount) and all of the cash inflows as positive

numbers. The calculator will require that you enter the discount rate as an interest rate and then you can follow the calculator's instruction book on how to compute NPV.

The third method that can used for calculating the net present value is to use a spreadsheet like Excel that has financial calculations built in for use. To use Excel for this calculation you will need to select the formulas area from the toolbar, then you select NPV, This will bring up an entry screen for you to enter the interest rate as a decimal, therefore 12% would be entered as .12 and the data related to the cash inflows the screen is shown below:

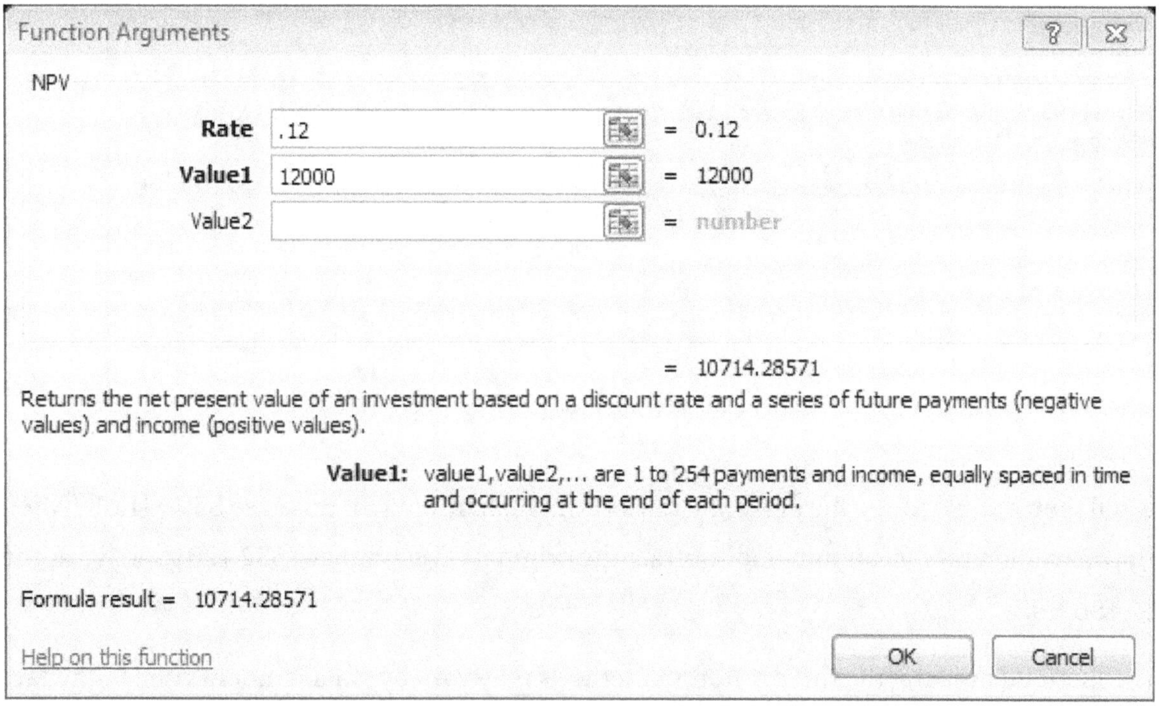

On this screen you would enter all cash inflow values, in our example there would be 8 entries as shown below:

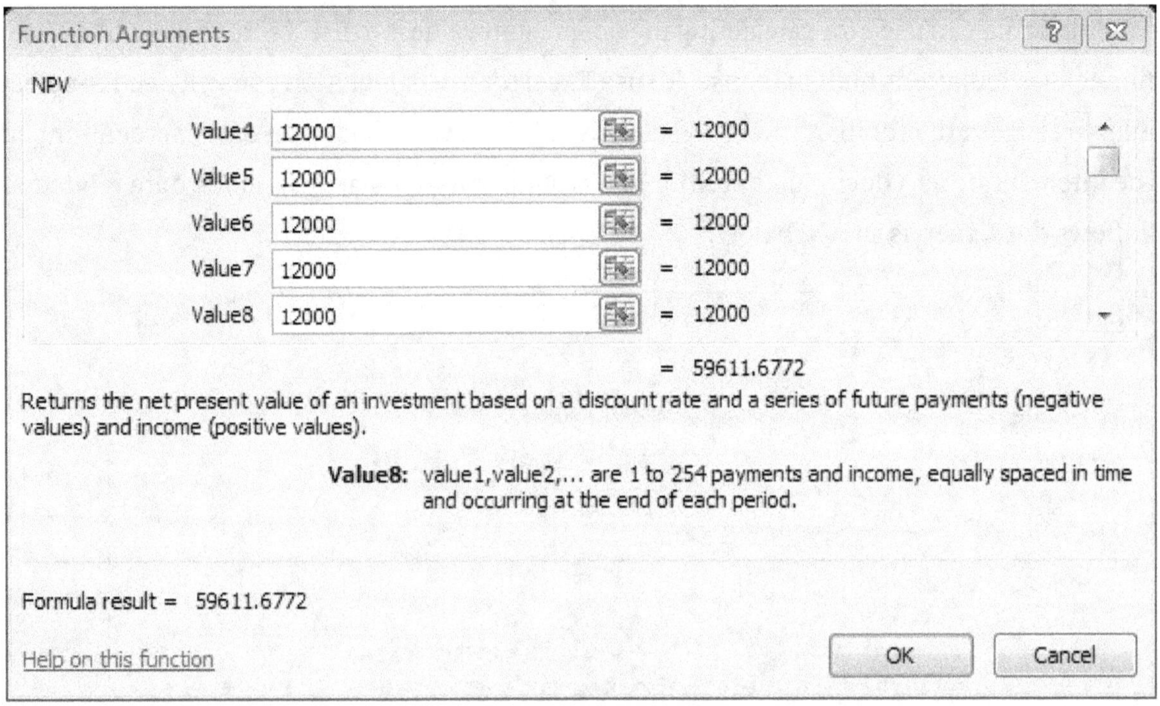

Here you will then be able to see the present values of the cash inflows, in this case $59,611.68 (when rounded), you would use this amount and subtract the original investment of $52,125 to arrive at the NPV of $7,486.68.

The values obtained by using the three different methods may vary by small amounts due to the fact that the table, the calculator and Excel will probably use a different number of decimal points in the interest factor that they calculate.

All three of these methods can also be used when calculating the NPV for a project with uneven cash flows. The second example we used during the discussion of payback required us to have an initial cash outflow of $ 150,000 and cash inflows of $30,000 per year for the first three years and cash inflows of $35,000 for years 4-8. If we again assume a required return of 12%, the solution using Excel would look like this:

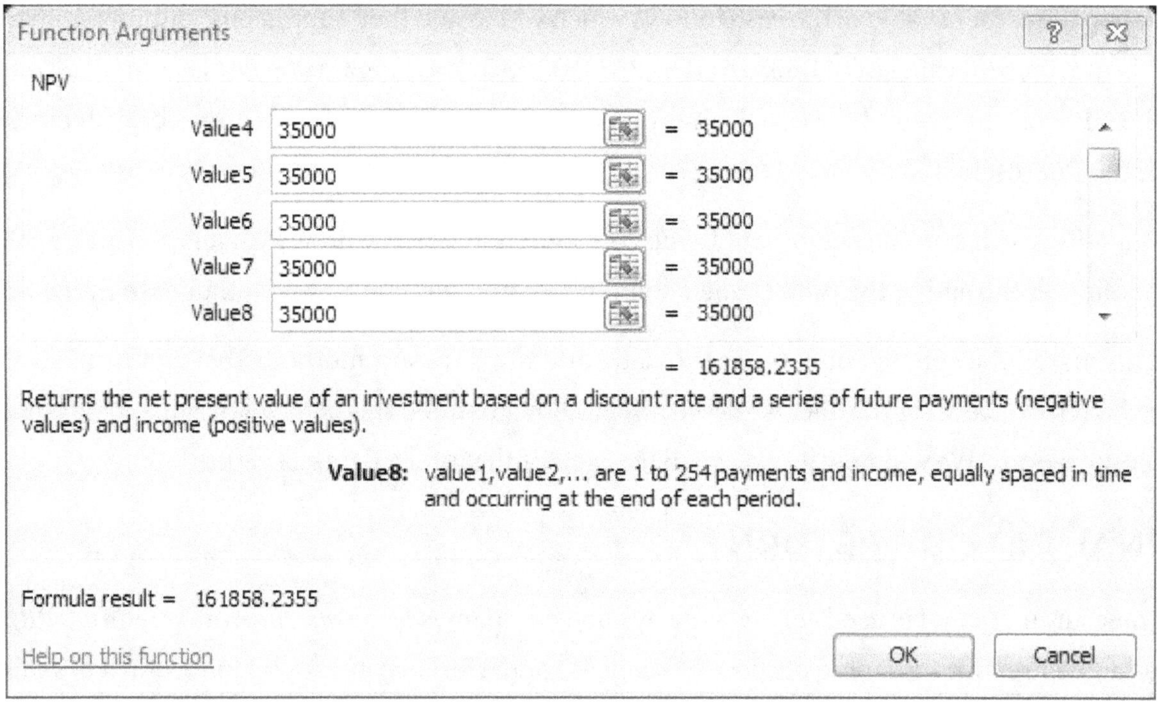

Here we see that the present value of the cash inflows is $ 161,858.24, when we subtract the cash outflow of $150,000 we end up with a positive NPV of $11,858.24, which means that the project would be considered further.

There would be no difference in how the data would be entered into a financial calculator if you compared it to the first example. The method for using the present value tables would be different when you have uneven cash inflows. Now each inflow would have to be multiplied by the interest factor for the appropriate year from the present value of an amount of $1 table in Appendix B. This process becomes more involved and at this point it would generally take less time to use either the financial calculator or the application in Excel. The calculation using the tables is shown below.

Year	Cash Inflow	Interest Factor	Calculated Amount
1	30000	0.8929	26787.00
2	30000	0.7972	23916.00
3	30000	0.7118	21354.00
4	35000	0.6355	22242.50
5	35000	0.5674	19859.00
6	35000	0.5066	17731.00
7	35000	0.4523	15830.50
8	35000	0.4038	14133.00
			161853.00

This gives you the present value of the cash inflows which you would then subtract the outflow from to arrive at the net present value of $11,853.00 (161,853.00 – 150,000). Again you notice a small difference in the NPV value amount between the methods due to the difference in the number of decimal places for the interest factor.

If there is a *salvage value* on the equipment being considered under any project that is considered to be a cash inflow at the end of the project and should be treated the same as any other cash inflow.

We have discussed the concept of net present value and the different methods that can be used to calculate the NPV once all of the data is known. As previously stated this is the widest used measure by large corporations. We will now move to a discussion of the internal rate of return.

INTERNAL RATE OF RETURN

Another measurement that is used very heavily by large companies is the *internal rate of return (IRR)*. This also can be used for screening purposes as well as for preference purposes. In recent years this has started being the preferred measure of the CEOs for many large corporations. The major reason for this being preferred is that it is easier to understand that a project has an IRR of 15%, if that is the case, than the project has a net present value of $25,000, if that is the case. Because it is easier for the CEOs to understand this measure, it is also easier for them to explain it to their respective boards of directors. If you take all sizes of companies the NPV method is still the most used but the IRR method is rapidly catching up.

The internal rate of return is the actual return earned by the investment. The internal rate of return represents the discount rate at which the investment would return a NPV of zero ($0). This means that the present value of all cash inflows would be exactly equal to the present value of all cash flows at that rate of return. The present value tables can be used to calculate the IRR but for most situations it is inconvenient and time consuming. In the case of the first example we have be following through this discussion, the use of the tables is relatively easy. To use the tables you would take the payback period and by going across the table (present value of an annuity) for the 8 year row and you would find the 4.34 factor at the 16% column. Thus, the IRR for this investment is 16%.

The second example we have been following had a payback period of 4.714 years. In looking at the table and going across the 8 year row we do not see that interest factor in the table. This means that the IRR is not an even percentage amount and we would have to calculate the IRR by using the two closest amounts and extrapolating to find the actual rate. This takes more time and is subject to a greater risk of error than using either a financial calculator or the IRR function in Excel.

In using a financial calculator to calculate IRR you will need to enter all of the cash flow data. The outflows will have to be shown as negative amounts and the inflows will have to be shown as positive amounts. Once the cash flow data has all been entered you can solve for the IRR. The exact procedure, for entering the data and calculating the IRR, will vary by the calculator model.

In using Excel to solve for the IRR you will need to enter the cash flow data starting in cell A2 (cell A1 is reserved and will cause a calculation error if used). Once the data has been entered select the formulas option from the toolbar and then the financial option from the formulas toolbar. This will bring up a menu as discussed before and from that menu you will choose IRR. This will than bring up an entry screen and you will need to enter the range of data on this screen (you can leave the guess field blank). This will give the IRR which will be shown on the screen in the same location as it was on the NPV screen in Excel. The screen is shown below for the first example we have been following through this chapter.

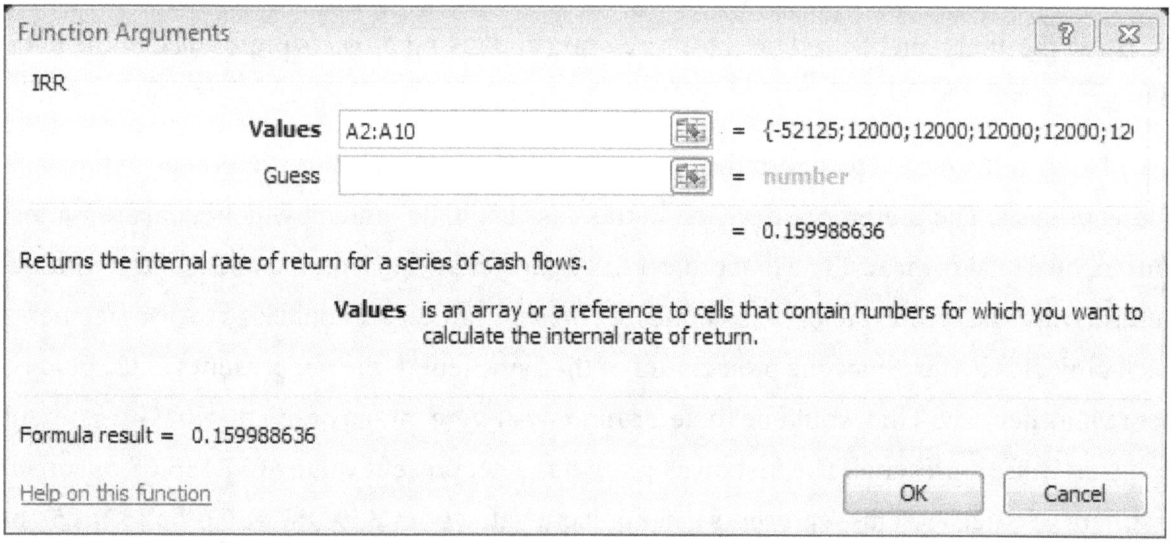

This shows a value of .159988636 this would be rounded to an IRR of 16%.

We will show the result for the second example we have been using throughout this chapter.

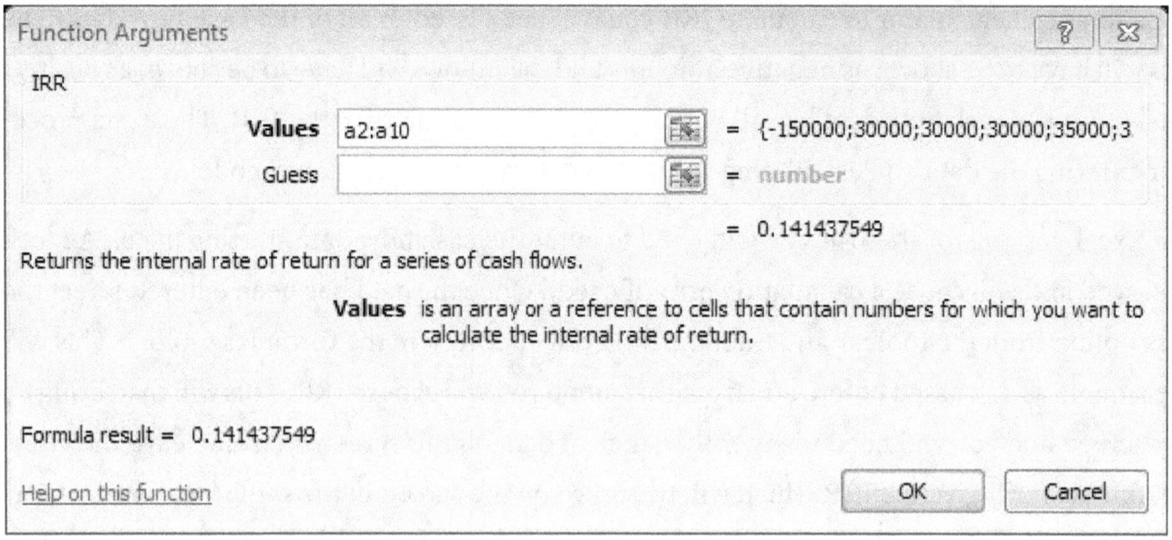

This returns a value of .141437549 which means that the IRR is 14.14%.

We have now discussed the three main ways that companies evaluate capital budgeting (investment) projects. These methods can be used both for screening and giving projects preference in the decision making process.

Now we will look at the results to determine which project should be given a preference in the decision making process. The preference decision in this case could depend on which measure is most important to the decision maker. The first project has a shorter payback period and a better internal rate of return, while the second project has a better net present value. This could lead to disagreements over which project is better. Since the projects are of the same length the net present value could be looked at in another way. That would be to determine what percentage of the original investment the net present value represents. The first investment has a net present value of $7,486.68 on an initial investment of $ 52,125. This represents a net present value of 14.36% ($7,486.69 / $52,125), of the original investment. The second investment has a net present value of $11,858.24 on an initial investment of $ 150,000. This represents a net present value of 7.91% of the original investment. Based upon this it would appear that the correct decision would be the first investment proposal as it has a higher IRR, a shorter payback period, and a net present value that is a higher percentage of the original investment.

We have covered the three most common measures that business uses in making decisions about capital investments. All of these measurements are used by more than two-thirds of all large corporations. Which measure is most important in decision making depends upon the management of the company.

A large percentage of small businesses only use the payback period and set a shorter payback period as being acceptable. It is common for large corporations to continue to look at any project that has a payback of five years or less. Many small businesses won't accept payback period that is more than two years except in extreme circumstances. The reason for this is that most small businesses can't afford to tie up their funds as long before getting them returned on a non-discounted basis.

INCOME TAX EFFECTS ON CAPITAL INVESTMENT EVALUATION

To this point we have been evaluating capital investment opportunities and have been ignoring the effect income taxes could have on an investment decision. To properly evaluate the capital investment proposals we need to consider the effect income taxes could have on the proposals.

Income taxes will have an effect on the proposal because since these are capital projects they will need to be depreciated over a period of years for income tax purposes (as well as for financial statement purposes). For purposes of analysis we are going to assume that the items in the projects meet the criteria to be depreciated over a seven year life according to IRS guidelines. Under the tax laws these items would qualify for depreciation using the Modified Accelerated Cost Recovery System (MACRS) which would allow for a larger deduction in the early years in use and a smaller deduction in the later years. For the purposes of our calculations we will use the optional straight line depreciation method since it is easier.

First we will look at the impact that income taxes will have on the first investment we have been using throughout the chapter. The original cost is $52,125. When we divide the original cost by the seven years we get annual depreciation of $7,446.43. If we assume that the company's tax rate is 30% then the depreciation deduction would save us approximately $2,234 in taxes each year, this becomes an additional cash inflow. The second way that taxes will impact the decision is on the original calculation of cash inflows. The basis for the cash inflows is either a cost savings or an increase in revenue. In either case the cash inflows represent an increase in taxable income that will be subject to taxes. In the first example we have been following the annual cash inflows were $12,000 per year. When we apply the 30% tax rate to the additional income that the project would provide we come up with a tax cost of $3,600 per year.

Now that we have calculated a tax benefit from the project as well as a tax cost for the project we have to adjust the calculation of annual cash inflows to reflect the impact of income taxes. Our new cash inflows would be the cash inflows originally calculated less the tax cost for those inflows plus the tax savings for the depreciation benefit. In this case the calculation would be $12,000–$3,600 + $2,234

= $ 10,634. To evaluate the project on an after tax basis we would now need to recalculate the payback period, the NPV and the IRR using the new annual cash inflow amount.

Payback would be calculated as $52,125 / $10,634, which would give us a payback period of 4.90 years where previously it had been 4.34 years. If the company's policy to continue to evaluate any project that has a payback of less than 5 years, this would still be a potentially acceptable project.

Next we would have to recalculate the net present value. If we use the tables for this calculation we would have $10,634 X 4.9676 = $52,825.46 as the present value of the cash inflows. When we subtract the original investment of $52,125 we would have a positive net present value of $700.46 where it was originally calculated as $7,486.68. Since the net present value is still positive it means that the project is still a potential investment to be made.

Now we calculate the net present value using Excel and then we will calculate the IRR using Excel.

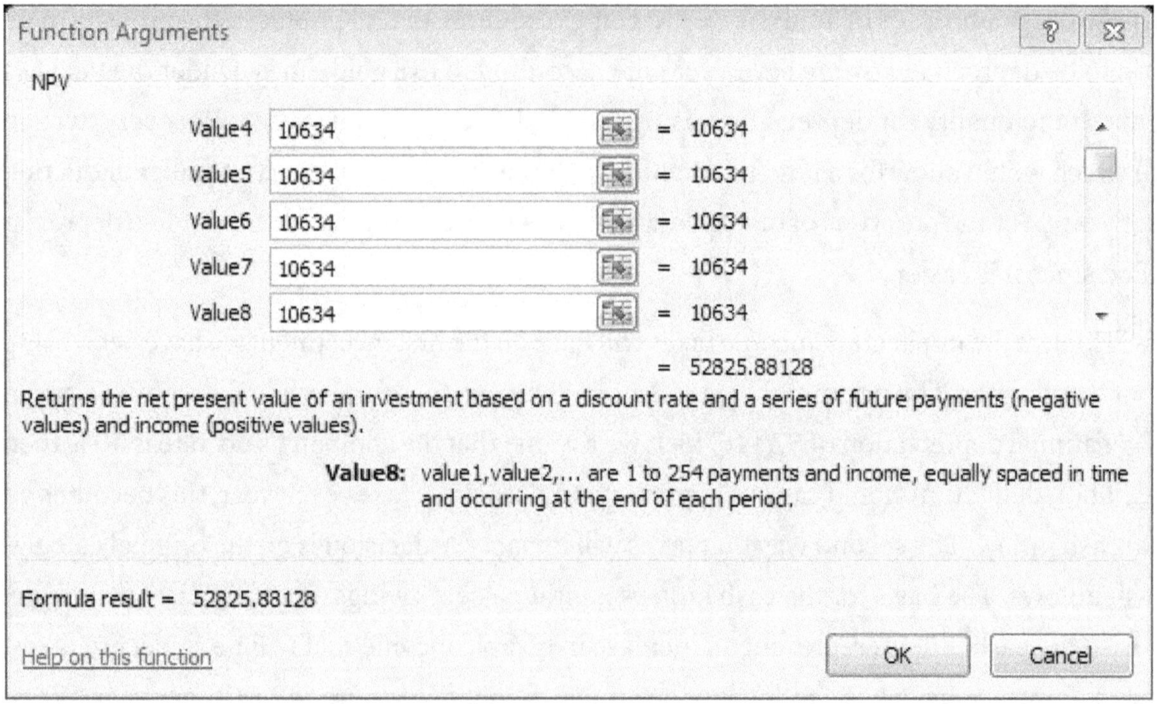

In using Excel for the calculation we come up with a present value of the cash inflows of $52,825.88, which means that we show a positive net present value using Excel as well.

We would expect to show a positive net present from Excel since we had already calculated it using the tables and the difference between the two methods is usually only a minor amount.

We will now use Excel to calculate the IRR. The Excel calculation is shown below:

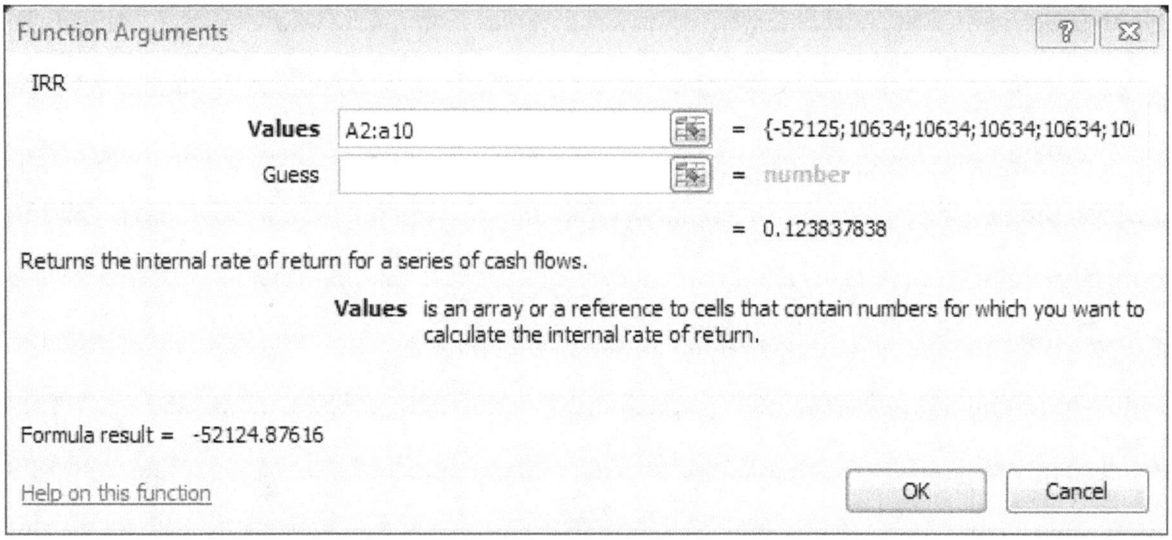

We had previously calculated the IRR on this project it had been 16%, now it is showing and IRR of 12.38% as a result of taking taxes into account. This is a significant reduction in IRR and depending upon the company's minimum acceptable level of IRR this project could be eliminated from consideration after accounting for the impact of income taxes on the investment.

Now we will consider the income tax effect on the second proposal. The project had an initial investment of $150,000. We going to assume that this is also property that would fit in the 7 year category for taxes and we are going to assume straight line depreciation of $21,428 ($150,000 / 7) per year. Based on the assumed 30% tax rate this would create tax savings of $6,428 per year. Using the 30% tax rate we would have tax costs of $9,000 ($30,000 X 30%) per year for the first three years and $10,500 ($35,000 X 30%) for years 4-8. Our new net cash inflows would be $27,428 ($30,000-$9,000 + $6,428) for the first three years and $30,928 for years 4 - 8.

Using these new cash inflow amounts we will first calculate payback as follows:

Original investment	$150,000
Year 1 cash inflow	27,428
Amount remaining	122,572
Year 2 cash inflow	27,428
Amount remaining	95,145
Year 3 cash inflow	27,428
Amount remaining	67,717
Year 4 cash inflow	30,928
Amount remaining	36,789
Year 5 cash inflow	30,928
Amount remaining	5,861

At his point we would stop our analysis of this project because we have a payback period greater than five years and the company's policy would not allow further consideration. This project has failed the first of the screening decision models.

The tax impact on the second project has changed it from being in consideration to being eliminated from consideration. This shows the importance of considering the impact of taxes on investment decisions. The first project would remain in consideration after all of the screening calculations have been done but the calculations after the impact of taxes have made it so the second project would not continue to be considered since it does not meet the payback requirement.

SUMMARY

We have looked at the concepts of payback period, net present value, and internal rate of return and have shown various tools that can be used to calculate these screening measurements. We also discussed how management might use these screening measurements in assigning the preference level for the decision making process. Finally we discussed the impact of income taxes on the analysis of the payback period, net present value and the internal rate of return. In one case the consideration of income tax effects eliminated a project from consideration.

KEY TERMS

- Capital investments
- Time value of money
- Net present value
- Interest factor
- screening decisions
- discounted cash flow
- discount rate
- salvage value
- preference decisions
- payback method
- annuity
- internal rate of return

EXERCISES AND PROBLEMS

8-1. Bunjee Corporation will receive $300 per year for each of the next five years and an additional $1,000 at the end of the fifth year. The total payments are $2,500. Assuming an interest rate of 10% what is the NPV of the payments?

8-2. Silver Star Restaurant is planning to open a new location.
Their current plans show the following cash flows:

	Outflows	**Inflows**
Initial Investment	$185,000	$ 0
End of year 1	$150,000	$200,000
End of year 2	$200,000	$250,000
End of year 3	$275,000	$325,000
End of year 4	$300,000	$375,000
End of year 5	$300,000	$400,000

Assuming the company has a desired rate of return of 14%; calculate the NPV of the investment in the new location.

8-3. Zumalt Company is considering an investment in a machine that costs $36,048 and will deliver cash inflows through cost savings of $10,000 per year for 5 years. The company's cost of capital is 10%. Ignore income taxes.

1. Compute the NPV based on the company's cost of capital of 10%.
2. Assume the company has a minimum desired return of 12%. Compute the NPV based on 12%.
3. Compute the project's IRR.

8-4. Based on the information in exercise 8-3, assume the project has an IRS depreciation period of 5 years and that Zumalt's tax rate is 25%.

1. Calculate the company's after tax cash inflows for the 5 years.
2. Calculate the NPV of the new cash inflows using the company's cost of capital of 10%.
3. Calculate the IRR of the project.

8-5. George's Bake Shoppe is investigating the purchase of a new donut making machine that would cost $18,600. The new machine would allow the company to reduce labor costs $3,800 per year. In addition, the new machine would allow George to offer a new style of donut. George has estimated that the new style of donut would have annual sales of 1,000 dozen. He has also estimated that the new style of donut would have a contribution margin of $1.20 per dozen. The machine will have a useful life of six years.

1. Calculate the total annual cash inflows that should be used for making the investment decision.
2. Calculate the IRR for the donut making machine.
3. Calculate the NPV of the machine using 8%, 10% and 12%.

8-6. The Company is considering four investment proposals. The information related to the four proposals is presented below:

	A	B	C	D
Initial investment	$90,000	$100,000	$70,000	$120,000
Annual cash inflows	25,000	18,000	15,000	35,000
Life of the project	5 years	7 years	6 years	6 years

Assume a desired rate of return of 12%. Ignore income taxes.

1. Calculate the net present value of each project
2. Calculate the IRR for each project.
3. If the company uses NPV as the criteria for selecting a project, rank the projects in order of preference.
4. If the company uses IRR as the primary selection criteria, would the order of preference change?

8-7. Management of Under Water Corporation is considering an investment with the following cash flows:

	Investment	Cash Inflows
Year 1	$15,000	$1,000
Year 2	$ 6,000	$2,000
Year 3		$3,000
Year 4		$4,000
Year 5		$5,000
Year 6		$6,000
Year 7		$5,500
Year 8		$4,000
Year 9		$2,500
Year 10		$1,000

1. Calculate the payback period for the project.
2. Assuming an 8% cost of capital, compute the NPV for the project. Ignore income taxes.

8-8.You just won the state lottery in the amount of $1.6 million. You have two options in how you can receive the cash: cash today of $1.1 million dollars or 20 annual payments of $90,000 each.

1. Assuming an annual rate of return of 4%, which payment option would be better?

8-9. Susanne Taylor frequently purchases stocks and bonds for investment. She has set a goal of a minimum return of 14% on each investment. She purchased 200 shares of stock in a company 3 years ago for $13,000. She recently sold the stock for $16,000. For each of the 3 years she owned the stock she received a dividend of $425.

1. Using the net present value method determine if she made 14% on this investment. Ignore income taxes.
2. Calculate the IRR on this investment.

8-10. XYZ Manufacturing is considering investing in a new piece of equipment. The equipment will cost $ 450,000. By purchasing the new piece of equipment the company will be able to increase sales of one product by an amount that will add $75,000 to the total contribution margin for each of the next 5 years. In addition the piece of equipment will reduce costs for other products by $30,000 per year for the next 10 years. The equipment has an estimated use period of 10 years. Ignore income taxes in all calculations.

1. Calculate the net present value of the investment assuming a cost of capital of 12%.
2. Calculate the IRR of the investment.

8-11. A wheat farmer is considering the purchase of a combine. The combine would cost $700,000 but the farmer would be able to make payments of $80,000 per year for ten years (including interest). The combine would last for 15 years and would save the farmer $70,000 per year for each year the combine lasts. Ignore income taxes.

1. Calculate the net present value of the investment using a cost of capital of 10%.

8-12. Max Brown owns a cattle ranch. Max has accumulated $100,000 that he can reinvest in the business. He is considering two possible uses of the funds. The first option would to purchase a cattle hauler for $75,000. The cattle hauler would last for 10 years and would save Max $12,500 per year in cattle hauling costs. The second option is purchase additional land for $100,000 that can be used for grazing or for growing hay for cattle feed. Max has estimated that the land would provide savings on feed costs of $15,000 per year for the next 15 years. Max has not estimated any savings beyond 15 years as things are not predictable beyond that point.

1. Calculate the net present value for each option using a cost of capital rate of 12%.
2. Calculate the IRR for each option.
3. Recalculate the net present value for option 2 assuming that at the end of 15 years, Max retires and sell the land he purchased for $100,000. Still use the 12% cost of capital.
4. What would the IRR be for the land purchase based on the additional information presented in requirement 3?

8-13. ABC Hospital Corporation is considering purchasing an MRI machine to fulfill a need that is currently not covered in the community. The MRI machine will cost $750,000 to purchase. The hospital estimates that there will be 1,000 uses of the MRI per year and that each use will add $125 of contribution margin. The machine is expected to last 10 years. Ignore income taxes.

1. Calculate the payback period for the machine.
2. Calculate the net present value for the MRI machine assuming a cost of capital of 10%.
3. Calculate the IRR for the MRI machine.
4. Are there any qualitative factors that should be considered by the hospital management in making the decision?

5. Would your answer to number 4 be different if the hospital is a community owned not for profit hospital?

8-14.The Great Law Corporation is evaluating the purchase of new office equipment for its law practice. The initial investment required would be $50,000. The equipment would be depreciated using a straight line for taxes and would have a tax life of 5 years. The before tax annual cash flow, for the five years, will be $15,000. The Corporation has a tax rate of 30% and the desired after-tax rate of return is 16%.

1. Calculate the net present value of the investment.
2. Calculate the IRR on the investment.
3. Should the investment be made? Why or why not?

8-15. Samuel is about to invest $1,000. He is very cautious and would like to have help evaluating two different options. Also, in keeping with his cautious nature he wants the projects evaluated using different rates of return. The rates he would like you to use in the calculations are 8%, 10% and 12%. The two projects shown have expected cash inflows as shown below:

Year	Project 1	Project 2
1	$550	$350
2	650	550
3	600	750
4	600	750

1. Calculate the net present value for each project using each of the 3 rates of return and indicate which project(s) would be acceptable under each rate of return.
2. Calculate the payback period on each project.
3. Make a recommendation to Samuel regarding which investment he should make. Explain you reason(s) for the recommendation.

8-16. Mabel Putter is the owner of a golf course on the edge of a large city. She is considering installing lighting so that the course can be operated at night. She purchased the course the course last year for $450,000. Her receipts from the operation of the golf course for the past season were $140,000 and her total expenses were $86,000

The required investment to light the course would be $100,000. The lighting system will require 400 lamps of 850 watts each and will run an average of 4 hours per day during the 28 week golfing season. The cost of electricity is .08 per kilowatt hour. Because of a variety of reasons it is expected that the lights will be used for only 130 days during the season or a total of 520 hours.

The changes in operating revenue and expenses that will happen as a result of the lighting project are as follows:

Based on 130 nights of operation per year:

Revenues will increase by $450 per night for the first two years and will be $275 per night for years 3-5.

Labor costs will be $68 per night of operation.

Annual cost of light bulbs will be $1,500 per year.

Other lighting maintenance costs will be 3.5% of the original installation cost.

At the end of 5 years it is estimated that the light equipment will have a salvage value of 30% of the original installation cost.

Ms. Putter feels that she needs at least a 10% return on her investment for the project to be worthwhile.

Calculate the net present value of the project to see if it meets the desired 10% return.

8-17. Suppose the Amalgamated Corporation is planning to buy new equipment to expand production of its most popular product. The information related to the possible purchase of the new equipment is:

Cash cost of new equipment	$400,000
Estimated life in years	10 years
Salvage value in 10 years	$ 45,000
Incremental revenue per year	$350,000
Incremental expenses per year	$185,000

(does not include depreciation)

Assume the company has a tax rate of 40%. All revenues and expenses, other than depreciation, are in cash. Assume that the company depreciates the equipment on a 10 year life for tax purposes and uses the straight line method. Also assume that depreciation is calculated based on original cost less the salvage value. The company requires a 14% return on its projects.

1. Compute depreciation per year
2. Compute anticipated net cash inflows (after-tax), from the project, per year.

3. Compute the payback period. Use the after tax cash inflows.
4. Calculate NPV on the project. Use after tax cash inflows.
5. Calculate IRR on the project. Use after tax cash inflows.

8-18. The Fast Freight Company has been offered an eight year contract to haul waste for a nuclear power plant. This contract would be new business for the company and would require that the company purchase several specially designed trucks at a total cost of $400,000 if they accept the contract. Other information to be considered as part of the analysis is below:

Net annual receipts (before taxes)	$110,000
Major repair cost on the trucks after 4 years	$50,000
Salvage value of the trucks in 8 years	$20,000

The company depreciates the trucks using the straight line method, with a depreciation period of 5 years, and assumes no salvage value for tax purposes. The company has a 30% tax rate and requires a 15% after tax return on all equipment purposes.

1. Calculate the net present value of the contract.
2. Should the company accept the contract? Why or why not?

CHAPTER 9 – BUDGETS AND THEIR USES IN PLANNING AND DECISION MAKING

LEARNING OBJECTIVES:

1. Understand the purpose of budgeting
2. Prepare a sales budget
3. Prepare a production budget
4. Prepare a direct materials budget
5. Prepare a direct labor budget
6. Prepare a manufacturing overhead budget
7. Prepare a selling and administrative expense budget
8. Prepare a cash budget
9. Prepare a budgeted income statement
10. Prepare a budgeted balance sheet

UNDERSTANDING THE PURPOSE OF BUDGETING

Budgets are financial plans that deal with operating a business over a specified period of time. All businesses budget to have a basis for running the business in future periods. Individuals should budget so they don't end up getting in financial difficulty. Budgets often are viewed by people as meaning setting limitations on spending. The real purpose of budgeting is to create a plan whereby based upon the expected sales the company does not overspend. A proper budget formalizes the planning process, allowing managers to take steps to avoid problems or to take advantage of opportunities. Budgets are a comprehensive financial overview that should be used to help coordinate financial and operational activities. Managers use budgets as they go through their *planning, operating and control* activities.

Planning is the cornerstone of good management and requires the development of goals and objectives for the organization which in turn set the parameters for the financial plan which is represented by the budget. Operating activities involve the day-to-day decision making activities that take place within an organization. Control involves ensuring that the planning and operating activities are meeting the goals and objectives developed by the organization.

The advantages of budgets:

1. Budgeting makes managers think ahead as they have to formalize their planning activities.
2. Budgets provide managers with an opportunity to evaluate existing activities and consider opportunities for improvement or for new activities.
3. Budgeting helps managers in communicating and coordinating activities across the organization.
4. Budgeting provides benchmarks to help managers evaluate ongoing performance.

In the budgeting process managers must be involved in setting the budgets for their departments. In the best situation, the managers should provide a budget for their department based upon the organization's goals and sales plan for the upcoming year. If the departmental budget cannot be accepted as submitted then there is a discussion with the departmental manager and any changes are agreed upon with the manager. This is an important step as managers need to feel responsible for their budget. If the budget is assigned to the department manager they generally do not "buy-in" and therefore do not feel responsibility for the plan. Assigning budgets to department managers without their input is the biggest mistake that can be made in the budgeting process.

Different companies use different budgeting techniques. The most common way budgets are done is basing the budget on the assumption that the business activities that are currently being done will continue to be done and the next year's plan is based on changes in the level of those activities. The budget will also take into account any planned improvement in how those activities are completed. Some companies have chosen to use a *zero-base budget*. This method means that the budget starts from a zero base, which is essentially considering the business as a startup business every year. There is no assumption regarding activities to be carried on during the year. The managers instead have to evaluate the budgeted sales by product and decide which activities will be used to meet the sales budget. This means that they have to identify each activity that will be needed and then plan the budget for the activity. Zero-base budgeting is more time consuming than the traditional model and in use has not been shown to provide significantly better planning, operating and controlling activities within

the businesses that have used it. The major benefit to zero-base budgeting is the ongoing evaluation of the activities to be performed in meeting the organization's goals and objectives.

THE MASTER BUDGET

The purpose of budgeting is so a company can have a master budget that can be used for the purposes of planning, operating and controlling the organization. Below are diagrams showing the master budget process for a manufacturing company and a merchandising company.

Exhibit 9-1 - The Master Budget Process for a Manufacturing Company

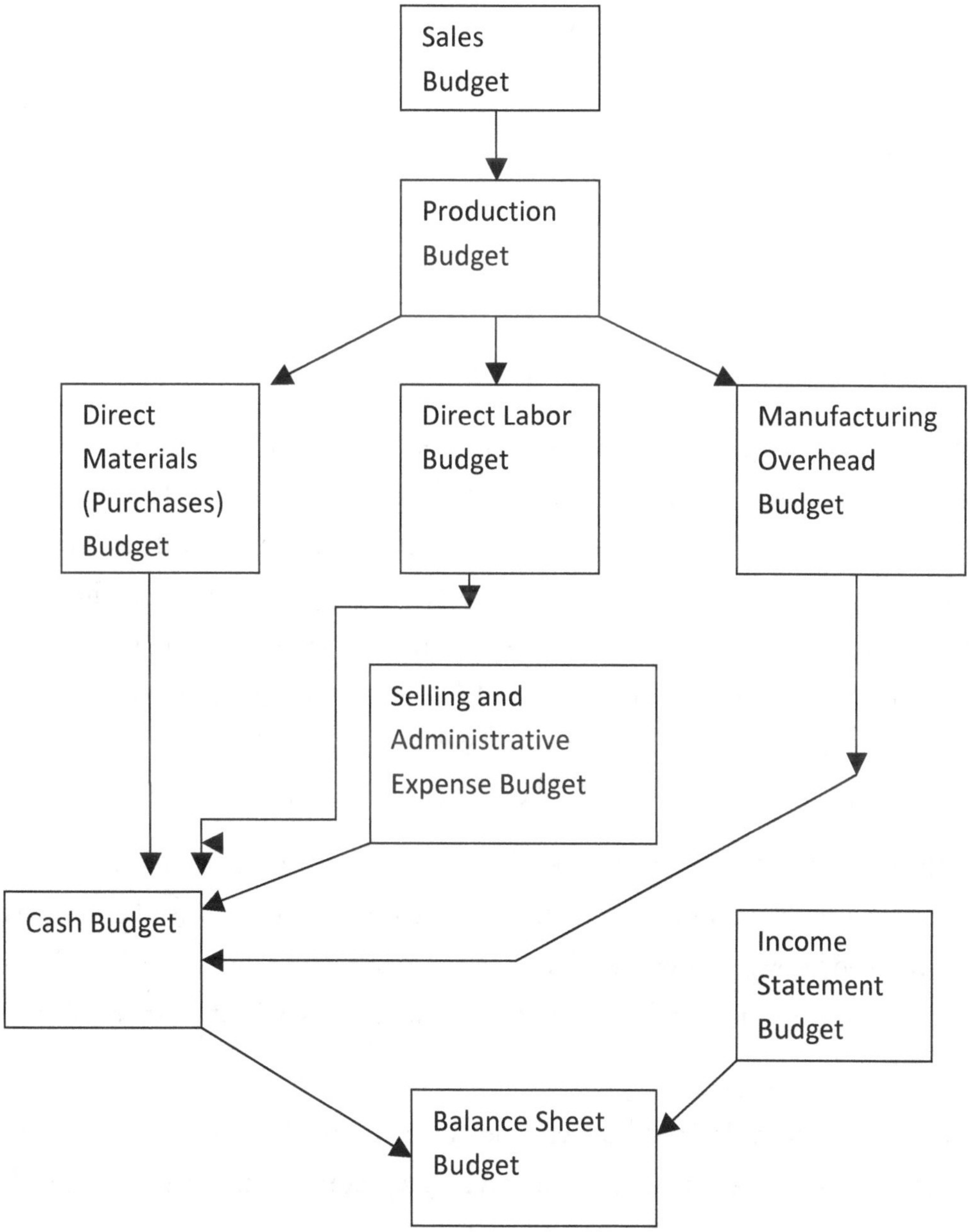

Exhibit 9-2 - Master Budget Process for a Merchandising Firm

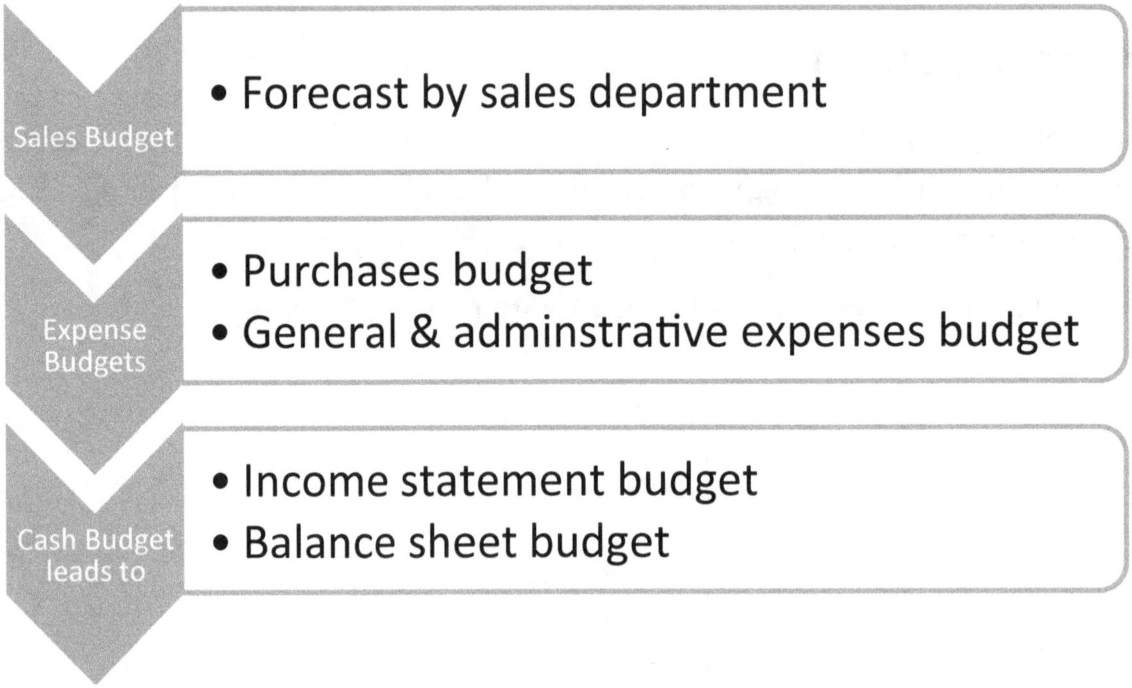

PREPARATION OF A SALES BUDGET

The starting point for the budgeting process has to be the preparation of the sales budget. The sales budget will drive several other parts of the budget. Budgets for direct materials (which drive the purchases budget); direct labor and all other variable manufacturing expenses will be driven by the sales budget. In the case of merchandising companies the sales budget will drive the purchases budget and the labor budget. In the case of service companies the sales budget will drive the budget for professional personnel to deliver the anticipated sales level. In the case of agricultural production the sales budget will have an impact on the variable costs if the production activity is related to the raising of livestock as the sales budget will drive the number of head of livestock needed.

The setting of the sales budget can be arrived at by using a variety of methods. The most common methods are either to use the current year actual and plan on an increase based upon the economic forecasts in general and knowing how change in the economy affects the company or by polling key customers to determine how they think the economy in their areas will affect their sales for the next year.

By using the general economy the company can look at economic forecasts and relate that to their industry. Over a period of time the company can develop a predictive model that would allow, as an example that if the economy increases by 2% then their business will grow by 4%. The use of the general economy will have to be adjusted for any changes to the company's product line or sales area.

The use of polling of customers may provide a better starting point than the general economy since individual regions of the sales area may do better or worse than the economy has a whole. Also, if the company is bringing out new products the company could get a better feel on how the new products will affect sales by discussing the new products with their larger customers in key regions.

Either of these sale forecasting methods would work for businesses than are in manufacturing, merchandising or the service industries, with some exceptions. As an example, a hospital may not be able to use these methods as the growth of the economy does not necessarily affect the hospital's revenue and there would not be any large key customers to poll. A hospital would be forced to look at how much third parties will allow the prices for services to increase. The third parties would be insurance companies and the government (Medicare and Medicaid).

The most difficult area for planning sales is in the agricultural production industry. If a farmer is producing crops the weather will play a large role in production levels of the crop. Also, the farmer has a difficult time predicting the price per bushel of the crop produced since it varies by the amount of the crop available. The farmer can forecast sales by using the last five years average crop production and looking at futures prices for the time of year he would be planning to sell his crops. Futures prices on commodities are set, by investors, based on the best estimates of crop production and demand for the future. The rancher raising livestock would have the same types of problems in forecasting sales as the farmer. However, the rancher has the ability to control the quantity he wishes to sell. The rancher also could use futures prices to estimate the selling price for the livestock.

Once the company has prepared the sales budget then the budgeting process can proceed to forecasting the costs of meeting the sales budget.

PRODUCTION BUDGET

Once the sales budget is complete the company will need to prepare a production budget. The production budget can be prepared based off the number of units in the sales budget, if units are forecast in the sales budget, or off the sales dollars in the budget. The production budget will be based on the number of units to be produced during the year or if the driver for production is not units, because the product is all manufactured to custom order specification, then the dollar amount to be produced.

To arrive at the production budget we must start with the budgeted sales and add the desired ending inventory to arrive at the total amount we need available for a combination of customer shipments and a safe level of inventory. From the total amount we need available we subtract the beginning of the year inventory to arrive at our production budget. The inventory to be used in this calculation is the finished goods inventory.

As an example, Good Guys Manufacturing has a sales budget of 5,000 units. The sales department has convinced management that the minimum level of inventory at the end of the year should be 800 units. The inventory level at the beginning of the year is 600 units. The calculation of the production budget would be as follows:

Sales budget (units)	5,000
Desired ending inventory (units)	800
Units needed to meet budget	5,800
Beginning inventory (units)	(600)
Production required(units)	5,200

The production budget drives the needs for: direct materials (and thus the purchases budget), the direct labor budget, and the variable manufacturing budget. The production budget can have an impact on the fixed manufacturing overhead budget based on the required numbers it will take to produce the production budget.

DIRECT MATERIALS (PURCHASES) BUDGET

The purchases budget will be based on the amount of materials required to produce the quantity in the production budget. The calculation of the purchases budget begins with the materials required per unit of production. Continuing with Good Guys Manufacturing, the amount of material required for each unit of production is $100. This would mean that $520,000 (5,200 units X $100) of direct material would be required for production.

To calculate the purchases budget we add the desired end of the year raw materials inventory to the production requirement to obtain our total direct materials availability requirements. From the total availability requirements we subtract the beginning raw materials inventory to arrive at our purchases budget. If we assume that Good Guys desires the ending raw materials inventory to be $45.000 and we assume that the beginning of the year raw materials inventory was $55,000, we would have the following calculation of the purchases budget:

Direct materials for use in production	$520,000
Desired ending raw materials inventory	45,000
Direct material available	565,000
Beginning raw material inventory	(55,000)
Purchases budget	$510,000

With the completion of the purchases budget we will move on to the direct labor budget.

DIRECT LABOR BUDGET

The direct labor budget will be based on the production budget and will be calculated by multiplying the required number of units times the labor cost per unit. This is one of the easier budgets to calculate in a simple manufacturing process. It can be one of the most difficult to calculate in a complex manufacturing process, especially if the product is custom made to order. For the purposes of our example with Good Guys we will assume a simple manufacturing process where the direct labor is easy to calculate. The company needs to produce 5,200 units and the direct labor required per unit is $200.

The direct labor budget calculated to this point is $1,040,000. This is not the final step in calculating the direct labor budget as we need to know how many production workers will be required and the direct labor budget may require adjustment based on the number of production workers.

Here we will calculate the number of workers required and make an adjustment to the budget, if required. For purpose of our example the average production worker at Good Guys is paid $32,000 per year. If we divide the $1,040,000 for labor required by the $32,000 per employee we arrive at 32.5 employees required. The company will either have to have 33 production workers or use overtime to cover the extra production time needed. We will assume that the cost is the same whether it is 33 employees or the use of overtime. With the need for 33 production workers the direct labor cost now becomes $1,056,000 ($32,000 X 33).

Now we will consider the manufacturing overhead budget.

MANUFACTURING OVERHEAD BUDGET

The manufacturing overhead budget has two components: the variable overhead budget, and the fixed overhead budget. The variable overhead budget is based on the production like the direct materials and direct labor budgets were. It can be calculated by using the same procedure as for direct labor but will not usually require any adjustment of the initial calculation. In the example we have been using of Good Guys the variable overhead cost per unit is $125. We would calculate the total variable overhead required by multiplying the cost per unit times the number of units in the production budget. In this case we multiple $125 times the 5,200 units to arrive at the total variable overhead cost for the budget of $650,000.

The fixed portion of the manufacturing overhead budget would be made up of items that do not vary based on the production budget. These would include: depreciation, property taxes, supervisor salaries and benefits, and facility rental. For Good Guys we will assume the budgeted amount to be $450,000, not including depreciation. Depreciation will be a non-cash expense of $125.000.

We have completed the manufacturing part of the budget. We now need to budget the selling and administrative expenses.

SELLING AND ADMINISTRATIVE EXPENSES

Generally selling and administrative expenses are similar to the fixed manufacturing overhead in that they do not change significantly based on the level of sales. In the case of Good Guys this is true except for sales commissions. Sales commissions are variable with the level of sales and in this case are equal to 1% of sales. The portion of the Selling and administrative expenses that do not change with the level of sales are $1,250,000 for budgeting purposes. This would include: executive, selling, and support salaries and benefits, cost of operating the computer system, office supplies expenses and travel expenses for the salespeople, among other expenses.

We have now finished the expense side of the budget and need to prepare the cash budget.

CASH BUDGET

In creating the cash budget we have to consider all of the expenses items previously calculated and we also have to consider the dollar amount of sales budgeted. In the case of Good Guys we are going to assume that the product sells for $900 per unit and therefore total sales for the year will be $4,680,000.

The first step in preparing the cash budget is to calculate the cash collections for the year. This is done by taking the accounts receivable at the beginning of the year and adding it to the sales amount and then subtracting the estimated accounts receivable at the end of the year to arrive at the estimated cash collections. We will assume that Goods Guys had $350,000 in accounts receivable at the beginning of the year and will have $390,000 in accounts receivable at the end of the year. The calculation of cash collections follows:

Accounts receivable, beginning	$ 350,000
Sales during the year	4,680,000
Potential cash collections	5,030,000
Account receivable, ending	(390,000)
Cash collections during the year	$4,640,000

We now have to calculate the cash expenditures during the year. We will first sum all of the amounts we calculated. This is shown below:

Purchases budget	$ 510,000
Direct labor budget	1,056,000
Variable overhead budget	650,000
Fixed overhead budget	450,000
Selling and administrative expenses	1,250,000
Sales commissions ($4,680,000 X 1%)	46,800
Total budgeted expenses	$3,916,000

To calculate the actual cash disbursements required we have add the beginning of the year accounts payable and accrued expenses to the budgeted expenses and then subtract the estimated ending of the year accounts payable and accrued expenses. We will assume that Good Guys had accounts payable and accrued expenses of $45,000 at the beginning of the year and will have $60,000 at the end of the year. The calculation of budgeted cash disbursements follows:

Total budgeted expenses	$3,916,000
Accounts payable, beginning of year	45,000
Potential cash disbursements	3,961,000
Accounts payable, ending	(60,000)
Cash disbursements for the year	$3,901,000

We can now put together the annual cash budget, however, we have to consider if the company is planning to spend any funds on capital investments. We will assume that the company is going to spend $ 350,000 on capital investments. With this the cash budget is as follows:

Cash collections	$4,640,000
Cash disbursements	(3,901,000)
Net cash flow from operations	739,000
Capital investments	(350,000)
Net cash flow for the year	$ 389,000

To this point we have been dealing with everything on an annual basis. In fact businesses prepare their budgets based on a monthly budget that rolls up to total the annual budgets. The processes are similar for all of the areas discussed, except the cash budget, if we apply the budgeting principles on a monthly basis. The amounts for all variable expenses can be easily calculated on a monthly basis based upon the sales budget by month. The fixed expenses would be assumed to occur evenly over the year and therefore could be divided by 12 to arrive at the monthly amounts. A company would normally plan which months there would be expenditures for capital investments.

The monthly cash budget becomes more complicated because now we are dealing with the timing of the collections and the disbursements. Companies will build history as to when the cash can be expected to be collected from sales and when the budgeted expenses will have to be paid. In the case of Good Guys they have determined that their cash collection model is as follows:

10% of the monthly sales will be in cash. 75% will be collected in the month following the month of sale and the final 15% will be collected in the second month following the month of sale. To illustrate how this would affect the monthly calculation we will assume the monthly sales for the first quarter are budgeted as follows:

January	$360,000
February	$400,000
March	$420,000

To calculate the cash collection for March we would have apply the percentages previously determined to the sales for the first quarter. This would be done as follows:

March sales, 10% in cash (10% X 420,000)	$ 42,000
February sales, 75% month following, (75% X $400,000)	300,000
January sales, 15% 2nd month following (15% X$360,000)	54,000
Total cash collections for March	$396,000

Next we would need to calculate the cash disbursements for March. We will assume that fixed costs are evenly spread over the 12 months. Our fixed cost disbursement would be fixed overhead $37,500 ($450,000 / 12), and our fixed selling and administrative expenses would be $104,167 ($1,250,000 / 12, rounded). Good Guys also keeps the direct labor personnel on evenly throughout the year and just increases or decreases inventory based on the sales for the month. The cost for direct labor would be $88,000 ($1,056,000 / 12). Variable overhead is assumed to be expended evenly throughout the year and would be $54,167 ($650,000 / 12, rounded). Purchases are paid for in the month following the purchase and sales commissions are paid in the month following the sale. Purchases are equal to 10.49% of sales and sales commissions are equal to 1% of sales. Good Guys plans to spend $50,000 on capital investments in March. With this information we can now calculate the cash disbursements budget for March as follows:

Purchases (Feb sales of $400,000 x 10.49%)	$ 41,960
Direct labor	88,000
Variable overhead	54,167
Fixed overhead	37,500
Selling and administrative	104,167
Commissions (Feb. sales $400,000 x 1%)	4,000
Capital Investments	50,000
Total cash disbursements for March	$ 378,834

We can now show the cash budget for March as follows:

Budgeted cash collections	$396,000
Budgeted cash disbursements	(378,834)
Net cash flow for March	$ 17,166

This completes the discussion of the cash budget.

BUDGETED INCOME STATEMENT

The income statement also would be budgeted on a monthly basis that would roll up to the total for the year. We will start by preparing a budgeted income statement for the year based on the information presented in the different budget pieces prepared so far. The annual income statement would be as follows:

Sales (annual)	$4,680,000
Cost of goods sold:	
Direct materials (not purchases	$ 520,000
Direct labor	1,056,000
Variable manufacturing overhead	650,000
Fixed manufacturing overhead (includes cash expenses and depreciation)	575,000
	(2,801,000)
Gross Profit	1,879,000
Selling and administrative expenses ($1,250,000 + $46,800)	(1,296,800)
Net income	$ 582,200

Now that we have completed the annual income statement, we will now show an income statement for the month of March

Sales	$420,000
Cost of goods sold:	
Direct materials (11.11% of sales)	$ 46,662
Direct labor (22.56% of sales)	94,769
Variable overhead (13.89 % of sales)	58,333
Fixed overhead ($575,000 /12)	47,917
	(247,681)
Gross Profit	172,319
Selling and administrative expenses ($104,167 + $4,200)	(108,367)
Net Income	$ 63,952

In the example we have been using in the budgeting section we have been ignoring any income tax effects. If we were to consider income taxes the calculations for cash flow and net income would change by the amount of income taxes. In the case of cash flows income taxes would only be shown in the months where payments would be required, but on the income statement the income tax expense would be shown in every month.

BUDGETED BALANCE SHEET

We now have to prepare the budgeted balance sheet. Normally, this would be prepared only for the end of the year. In a few cases the balance sheet may need to be budgeted on a monthly basis but for our purposes we are not going to prepare a monthly balance sheet. The balance sheet would be based on several pieces of data we have already used as well as some that we have not discussed before. The items we have discussed include the ending finished goods inventory (800 units) which we will value at $540 per unit for a total value of $432,000. Our ending work in process inventory will be $20,000. We have also stated that our ending raw materials inventory will be $45,000 and our ending accounts receivable balance will be $390,000. In our budgeting process we have stated that we will have capital investments of $350,000, this amount will have to be added to the beginning of the year balance in fixed assets (property, plant and equipment) of $650,000. We have also discussed that depreciation expense will be $125,000 for the year; this is added to the beginning of the year balance of $400,000. The last asset we have track is cash. The beginning balance was $50,000 and the end of the year balance will be increased by the net cash flow of $389,000.

On the other half of the balance sheet the only liability the company has is the ending balance of $60,000 in accounts payable and accrued liabilities. The stockholders' equity section has common stock of $10,000 at par value and additional paid-in-capital of $190,000. The beginning retained earnings in the business were $958,800 and the net income for the year is $582,200 as previously shown on the budgeted income statement.

With the asset, liability and equity values now established we can prepare the budgeted balance sheet as shown below:

ASSETS

Cash		$439,000
Accounts receivable		390,000
Inventories:		
Raw materials	$ 45,000	
Work in process	20,000	
Finished goods	432,000	497,000
Property, plant & equipment	1,000,000	
Less: accumulated depreciation	(575,000)	425,000
Total Assets		$1,801,000

LIABILITIES AND STOCKHOLDERS' EQUITY

Accounts payable and accrued liabilities	$ 60,000
Total Liabilities	60,000
Stockholders' equity:	
Common stock, at par value	10,000
Additional paid-in-capital	190,000
Retained earnings, beginning	$958,800
Net income for the year	582,200
Retained earnings, end of year	1,541,000
Total Stockholders' Equity	1,741,000
Total Liabilities and Stockholders' Equity	$1,801,000

SUMMARY

We have followed a manufacturing company through the budgeting process. We started with a sales budget and from there we prepared a production budget, a purchases budget, a direct labor budget, a budget for manufacturing overhead and a budgeted for selling and administrative expenses. This process took us through all of the items that will affect net income due the year. We then prepared a cash flow budget which took into account the cash aspects of the items previously prepared and it also considered our plans for capital investments during the year. The cash budget is the most important as companies that get in trouble usually are in trouble because of cash flow.

Following completion of the budgets pertaining to the individual areas that affect the income statement and the cash budget, we prepared the budgeted income statement. We waited to prepare the budgeted income statement because if the cash flow budget had not turned out well we would have needed to rethink our budgets in all of the previous areas. Once the income statement budget was complete we prepared a budgeted balance sheet. The budgeted balance sheet is always the last step as information from the cash budget and from the budgeted income statement flow forward to be included in the budgeted balance sheet.

KEY TERMS

- Master budget
- Production budget
- Manufacturing overhead budget
- Budgeted income statement
- zero-base budgeting
- purchases budget
- cash budget
- budgeted balance sheet
- sales budget
- direct labor budget

EXERCISES AND PROBLEMS

9-1. Tom's Tools sells eyeglass repair tools for $1.50 each. The marketing department prepared the sales forecast in units for the first quarter. It is shown below:

January	120,000
February	125,000
March	150,000
Total	395,000

Prepare the sales budget in dollars for each month and for the quarter.

9-2. Bikes R Us produces and sells top of the line racing bicycles. At the end of July, the company had 90 bikes in inventory. The company's inventory policy is to maintain an inventory level of 10% of the next month's sales budget. The company's sales budget for the next 3 months follows:

August	1,000 bikes
September	1,200 bikes
October	1,100 bikes

What is the production budget for September?

9-3. Dave's Donuts makes specialty donuts that are sold by the dozen. Each dozen requires ¾ of a pound of flour. The company began the year with 15,000 pounds of flour in inventory, but would like have only 12,000 pounds on hand at the end of the year. Dave's expects to sell 160,000 dozen during the year.

How much flour (in pounds) will need to be purchased during the year to meet production needs and to end the year with the desired level of inventory?

9-4. Re-Hydrate Inc. sells water bottles to outdoor activity participants. The selling price of the bottles is $1.75 each. The company has prepared the following sales forecast, in units, for the first half of the year:

January	140,000
February	130,000
March	125,000
April	160,000
May	170,000
June	150,000

Historically the cash collections of sales has been as follows: 50 percent of sales collected in the month of sale; 35 percent collected in the month following the month of sale and 14 percent collected in the 2nd month following the month of sale. 1% is never collected.

Prepare a cash receipts budget for the months of April, May and June.

9-5. Hot Stuff Fireworks sells all types of fireworks. The following information was taken from the budgeted income statement for the month of May. The labor costs and rent will be paid in May, while the advertising expenses and inventory purchases will be paid June. Half of the selling expense is paid in May and the other half in June.

Labor expenses	$10,500
Advertising expense	2,500
Rent	4,000
Inventory purchases	4,500
Selling expenses	8,000

Prepare the cash disbursements budget for May, assuming there are no other expenses and that no expenses from April are to be paid in May.

9-6. Timeless Creations makes a product that is a very popular Mother's day gift. This means that their peak sales are in May each year. The company's sales budget for the second quarter is shown below (all sales are sold on account):

	April	May	June
Budgeted sales	$200,000	$600,000	$200,000

Typically, the company has collected 20% of sales in the month of sale, 65% in the month following the month of sale and 15% in the 2nd month following the month of sale. February sales were $220,000 and March sales were $190,000.

Prepare a cash collections schedule for each month of the second quarter (April, May and June).

9-7. Back at You, Ltd., has the following sales budget for the boomerang it produces:

January	40,000 units
February	60,000 units
March	75,000 units
April	70,000 units

The company is preparing its production budget for the first quarter. They feel that inventory at the end of any month should be equal to 10% of the next month's sales in units. The inventory at the end of December was 4,000 units.

Prepare a production budget for each month of the quarter (January, February, and March) and in total for the quarter.

9-8. Smell Me, Inc., makes a very popular perfume. In its perfume it uses 4 grams of a secret ingredient per bottle. The secret ingredient costs $250 per kilogram. The company has prepared the following production budget (in bottles):

2013

First quarter	65,000
Second quarter	80,000
Third quarter	100,000
Fourth quarter	150,000

2014

First quarter	75,000

Because of the popularity of the perfume and the nature of the secret ingredient the company requires its end of quarter inventory of the secret ingredient to be 25% of the next quarter's usage. There will be 65,000 grams of the secret ingredient in inventory to start 2013.

Prepare a direct material budget for 2013 by quarter and in total. Once the direct materials budget is complete for the year calculate the purchases budget in dollars for the year.

9-9. The production department of Night Owl, Inc. has prepared the forecast of units to be produced by quarter as shown below:

First quarter	7,500
Second quarter	8,000
Third quarter	9,000
Fourth quarter	7,500

Each unit requires .5 direct labor hours and direct laborers are paid $15.00 per hour.

Prepare the company's direct labor budget for the upcoming year. Assume that the direct labor work force is adjusted each quarter to match the number of hours required for producing the forecasted units.

9-10. Amy Smith and Sam Johnson are preparing a business plan for submission to venture capitalists to obtain funding for their business. The plan calls for them to spend $350,000 on equipment in the first quarter of 2013. Salaries and other operating expenses will be paid as incurred and will total $30,000 per month beginning in January 2013 and will continue at that level through 2015. The company will not have any revenue until January 2014 and will average cash collections of $25,000 per month for all of 2014. Beginning in January 2015 cash collections are expected to be $90,000 per month and will continue at that level.

Assume that the company needs funding to cover all its cash needs until the cash receipts begin to exceed the cash disbursements. How much should Amy and Sam request in venture capital funding?

9-11. Cast Me, Inc. is a wholesaler of fishing equipment. They have budgeted sales as indicated for the months below:

	June	July	August
Credit Sales	$1,750,000	$1,850,000	$1,950,000
Cash Sales	250,000	350,000	350,000

All products are marked to sell at cost plus 30%. At the beginning of each month the company wants to have inventories of 35% of that month's projected cost of goods sold.

1. Compute the company's budgeted costs of goods sold for June.
2. Compute the company's budgeted purchases for July.

9-12. The local lumber yard has prepared the following data:

- Accounts receivable, May 31 – $120,000
- Monthly forecasted sales: June, $400,000: July, $450,000: August, $500,000; and September, $500,000.

Sales consist of 75% cash and 25% credit. All credit sales are collected in the month following the month of sale.

Prepare a cash collections budget schedule for July, August and September.

9-13. See Better Lighting plans inventory levels, at cost, at the end of each month as follows: May, $250,000; June, $200,000; July, $225,000; and August, $250,000.

Sales are expected to be: June, $450,000; July, $350,000; and August, $400,000. Cost of goods sold is 60% of sales.

Purchases in April were $250,000 and in May they were $200,000. Payments on each month's purchases are made according to the following schedule: in the month of purchase, 10%; in the month following purchase, 70%: and in the next month, the remaining 29%.

Prepare a monthly schedule for purchases and purchase disbursements for June, July and August.

9-14. Happy Hats Company manufactures and distributes a wide range of hats. The company was started four years ago and has grown dramatically. The business is considering an expansion and needs to prepare cash budgeting information for presentation to the bank in order to secure a loan. The information that is applicable to the cash budget is as follows:

The company began the month, of April, with $15,000 in the bank. The budgeted sales for March through June are as follows:

	March	April	May	June
Cash sales	$15,000	$16,000	$16.500	$17,500
Credit sales	30,000	30,000	40,000	45,000

In reviewing the history of the company's credit sales it has been determined that the company typically collects 60% of credit sales in the month of sale and the remaining 40% in the month following the month of sale. Inventory is purchased equal to 60% of the month's budgeted sales each month. The company's selling and administrative costs are 30% of the month's budgeted sales, with 60% of that being depreciation. The company purchased additional equipment in April for $25,000. The owner does not receive a salary, but does take dividends as profits permit. The owner took $10,000 in dividends in April. The owner wants to maintain a minimum bank balance of $15,000 and would like to obtain a line of credit that would be sufficient to cover any cash shortfall in a given month. If there is cash in excess of the minimum desired bank balance at the end of a month it would be paid back to the bank if there were any amounts outstanding on the line of credit. For purposes of this example ignore interest payments.

1. Prepare a cash receipts budget for April, May and June.
2. Prepare a cash disbursements budget for April, May and June.
3. Prepare a summary cash budget for April, May and June.

9-15. The production department of Zoo Corporation submitted the following forecast of units to be produced by quarter for the next budget year:

First quarter.. 5,000

Second quarter.. 9,000

Third quarter.. 7,500

Fourth quarter.. 6,500

The beginning raw material inventory will be 6,000 grams and beginning accounts payable will be $ 2,500.

Each unit requires six grams of raw material that cost $1.50 per gram. The company's desired inventory level at the end of each quarter is to have raw materials equal to 25% of the next quarter's production needs. The desired inventory level for the end of the fourth quarter is 7,000 grams. The payment schedule for raw material purchases is 70% in the quarter purchased and 30% in the next quarter. Each unit requires 0.10 direct labor hours and direct laborers are paid $15.00 per hour.

1. Prepare the company's direct materials budget for the upcoming year, by quarter, and a schedule of expected cash disbursements for purchases for the same period.
2. Prepare the company's direct labor budget for the upcoming year.
   Assume that the direct labor work force is adjusted each quarter to match the number of hours required for production for the quarter.

CHAPTER 10 – VARIANCE ANALYSIS – A BASIS FOR PERFORMANCE EVALUATION

LEARNING OBJECTIVES

1. Identify and calculate variable manufacturing variances in total.
2. Determine the portion of variable manufacturing variances that are related to material. Break down the material variance into price and usage variances.
3. Determine the portion of variable manufacturing variances that are related to labor. Break down the labor variance into rate and efficiency variances.

INTRODUCTION

As was discussed in an earlier chapter one of the uses for a budget is to help the business control its activities. The budget process starts with the sales budget and goes through all other aspects of the financial plan from there. A significant part of the budgeting process (for a manufacturing firm) is spent planning the variable manufacturing expenses. The variable manufacturing expenses are direct materials, direct labor and variable overhead. The variable costs represent the majority of the costs in a manufacturing process and therefore they are the largest focus of the budgeting process. The second reason for having a budget, after planning, is for control. *Control* involves monitoring and evaluating the effectiveness of the resources used in the business. Budgets are used for control by measuring actual results against the budgeted results. By comparing the plan to the actual results on a timely basis, management can see areas that are not proceeding in the manner planned. Once areas that are not going according to plan are identified then management can look deeper into the causes.

Budgets are generally put together using dollars. The dollar amounts in the budget are based on one level of activity (sales), this is called a static budget. Some businesses put together *flexible budgets*, which will use multiple sales levels to predict the costs for an associated sales level. This is time consuming and costly and therefore normally only used by very large organizations. *Flexible budgets* can be used in a shortened method by organizations of all sizes by preparing the budgets not only in a volume of dollars, but also by identifying expenses as a percentage of sales dollars. By stating expenses as a percentage of sales dollars both in the plan (budget) and with the actual results we can evaluate variable costs regardless of the sales volume. Fixed costs are not subject to changes in volume and therefore should be compared on a dollar to dollar basis rather than based on percentages.

Once the costs have been compared to the plan by using percentages for variable costs and actual dollars for fixed costs management will want to investigate any costs that vary significantly form the plan. Management is only concerned with significant variances, not with every minor difference. This is called *management by exception* as management concerns itself only with items that vary by a predetermined percentage or amount. Management should look at all significant variances both favorable and unfavorable. *Favorable variances* means that the company is doing better than expected in an area of cost, and *unfavorable variances* means they are doing worse than plan.

As the company is putting together the budget and spending time on planning their variable costs they are establishing standard costs for production. *Standard costs* plan how much raw materials should be used per unit and at what expected price, how many direct labor hours production should take and per unit and at what hourly labor rate and finally what the variable manufacturing costs other than material and labor should be per unit. These standard costs will be the basis for evaluating actual results against the plan for the variable manufacturing costs. Most companies set their standards based upon a *practical standard*, a standard that should be attained under normal, efficient operating conditions. There are some people that feel that standards should be set using an *ideal standard*, a standard that can be attained when near perfect conditions are present The thinking behind people wanting to use ideal standards is that the business should always be moving towards near perfection. The biggest problem with using an ideal standard is that management knows that the near perfect conditions don't exist so they may not continue to analyze variances and then an opportunity for improvement could be lost.

For our purposes we are going to assume that all standards are practical standards and should be used to analyze and improve operations. The use of standards can also apply to merchandising and service organizations as well. A merchandising concern can set standards for their cost of goods sold as a percentage of sales and the labor used in the store as a percentage of sales. These standards can be compared to actual results and provide the basis for management to look for ways to improve the operation. In a service organization standards can be set for how long it should take personnel to complete a given service task and then compared to the actual amount of time the service took to complete. It would very difficult for an agricultural production company to set standards and use them for control since so many factors are beyond the control of management.

There are advantages to and criticisms of standard costing.

Advantages of standard costing include: (1) it provides an effective benchmark and overall framework for comparing and evaluating the cost of operations; (2) it facilitates management by exception; (3) it is useful in setting long range cost-plus pricing: (4) it lowers the costs of record keeping by using predetermined values when recording cost transactions; and (5) it provides a more accurate measurement of inventory.

The criticisms of standard costing include: (1) the process is out of touch with today's manufacturing environment; (2) it is too focused on labor at a time when labor is becoming a smaller portion of manufacturing costs due to increased use of machinery; (3) does not give enough focus to quality control as it is too focused on cost control; (4) it is too expensive to install and maintain, especially in industries where there are short product life cycles; and (5) creates cost variances that are untimely and therefore does not contribute to continuous improvement.

In spite of the criticisms standard costing is still the most widely used costing system in U.S. manufacturing. This is because most of the criticisms come from rapidly changing industries, which is a small portion of the total number of manufacturing firms in the U.S.

We will now look at the analysis of variable manufacturing costs.

VARIABLE MANUFACTURING COSTS

Businesses will use the budget (possibly the flexible budget) to determine if there are variances that need further investigation. Most companies with start an analysis that is similar to the one in Exhibit 10-1 below:

Exhibit 10-1 - Variance Report

	Actual	Budget	Variances	
Units	7,000	9,000	2,000	U
Sales	$224,000	$288,000	$64,000	U
Variable Costs				
Variable manufacturing costs	$160,270	$198,000	$37,730	F
Shipping costs (selling)	5,200	5,400	200	F
Administrative Costs	1,800	1,800	$0	
Total variable costs	$167,270	$205,200	$37,930	F
Contribution margin	$56,730	$82,800	$26,070	U
Fixed Expenses				
Fixed manufacturing costs	$36,600	$36,000	$600	U
Fixed S, G & A costs	33,600	34,000	400	F
Total fixed costs	$70,200	$70,000	$200	U
Operating income (loss)	($13,470)	$12,800	$26,270	U

This gives us a very quick picture using a static budget but we know that with sales being below budget by $62,000 that our profit will also be below our budgeted level. While this shows some problems we don't know if those problems are all due to the sales volume or are there items that need to be investigated further. To determine if additional investigation is warranted we will need to compare the actual sales level to a budget for that level of sales which can be obtained by calculating the ratio of costs in the static budget and applying them to the actual sales level. First, we will calculate the cost ratios for the static budget as follows in Exhibit 10-2.

Exhibit 10-2 Cost Ratios (Unit Costs) for the Static Budget

	Static Budget Infomation	Unit Costs
Sales	9,000 Units	
Sales	$288,000	$ 32.00
Variable Costs		
Variable manufacturing costs	$198,000	$ 22.00
Shipping costs (selling)	5,400	0.60
Administrative Costs	1,800	0.20
Total variable costs	$205,200	$ 22.80
Contribution margin	$82,800	$ 9.20
Fixed Expenses		
Fixed manufacturing costs	$36,000	
Fixed S, G & A costs	34,000	
Total fixed costs	$70,000	
Operating income (loss)	$12,800	

It should be noted that we did not calculate unit costs for the fixed expenses as both the budgeted sales level and the actual sales level are in the relevant range and therefore the fixed costs would be budgeted for the same amount at either sales level.

We will now apply the budgeted unit costs to the actual level of activity to determine the flexible budget for the actual sales level as shown in Exhibit 10-3 below:

Exhibit 10-3 - Flexible Budget for Actual Sales Level

	Unit Costs	Flexible Budget
Sales		7000 Units
Sales	$ 32.00	$ 224,000
Variable Costs		
Variable manufacturing costs	$ 22.00	154,000
Shipping costs (selling)	0.60	4,200
Administrative Costs	0.20	1,400
Total variable costs	$ 21.80	$ 159,600
Contribution margin	$ 9.20	$ 64,400
Fixed Expenses		
Fixed manufacturing costs		$36,000
Fixed S, G & A costs		34,000
Total fixed costs		$70,000
Operating income (loss)		$ (5,600)

We now have our flexible budget for the actual level of activity. We can now compare that to our actual results to see if there are any areas that need further review. This is shown in Exhibit 10-4 below:

Exhibit 10-4 - Comparison of Actual Results to Flexible Budget

	Actual	Flexible Budget	Variance	
Units	7,000	7,000		
Sales	$224,000	$ 224,000	$0	
Variable Costs				
Variable manufacturing costs	$160,270	154,000	$6,270	U
Shipping costs (selling)	5,200	4,200	$1,000	U
Administrative Costs	1,800	1,400	$400	U
Total variable costs	$167,270	$ 159,600	$7,670	U
Contribution margin	$56,730	$ 64,400	$7,670	U
Fixed Expenses				
Fixed manufacturing costs	$36,600	$36,000	$600	U
Fixed S, G & A costs	33,600	34,000	$400	F
Total fixed costs	$70,200	$70,000	$200	U
Operating income (loss)	($13,470)	$ (5,600)	($7,870)	U

Now we have a variance report that shows us if we need to investigate anything further. Based upon the numbers above management may wish to investigate the variable costs further. This would be done by breaking down the costs within each variable section and determining the cause for each area. Normally, management would probably not look at the variable selling and administrative costs when the variance in dollars is small but in this case they probably would look at the causes for those variances because the percentage is high.

Now we will try and isolate the causes of the variances further to see which areas need additional investigation. To show us where we may wish to investigate further we will breakdown the components of variable manufacturing costs and obtain a preliminary explanation for the variances. This is shown in Exhibit 10-5.

Exhibit 10-5 – Preliminary Review of Variance by Component

	Actual Costs	Flexible Budget	Variance	Explanation
Units	7,000	7,000		
Variable costs				
Direct Material	$ 75,980	$75,000	$980 U	Lower prices, higher usage
Direct Labor	63,500	58,000	5,500 U	Higher wage rate and usage
Indirect Labor	16,090	16,800	710 F	Decreased set up time
Supplies	4,700	4,200	500 U	Higher prices
Variable Manufacturing Costs	$160,270	$154,000	$6,270 U	
Shipping	5,200	4,200	1,000 U	Air freight
Adminstartion	1,800	1,400	400 U	Long distance calls
Total Variable Costs	$167,270	$159,600	$7,670 U	

Now we will look more in depth at some of the variances. Before we can analyze the variances further we need to know the standards and the actual results for this product. The standards are shown below:

	Standard Quantity per Unit	Standard Price per Unit
Direct material	5 pounds	$2/pound
Direct labor	½ hour	$16/hour

The actual information is as follows:

Direct material: the company purchased and used 36,400 pounds of material at an actual unit price of $1.95.

Direct labor: the company used 3,750 hours of labor at an actual hourly rate of $16.40.

We will start by looking at the direct material variance. The preliminary explanation cites both lower prices and higher usage; a manager should be interested in the impact of each part of the variance on the overall operation. To find out the impact of each part on the total we will compute both the material price variance and the material quantity variance. The *price variance* indicates whether we paid more or less than standard for the material used and the *quantity variance (commonly called usage variance)* indicates whether we used more or less than the standard quantity. These are both calculated based on the actual number of units. The formulas for calculating these variances are shown below.

Price variance = (actual price - standard price) X actual quantity used

Quantity variance = (actual quantity used - standard quantity for actual output)

X standard price

The calculations of the direct materials variances are as follows:

Price variance = (actual price - standard price) X actual quantity used

= ($1.95–$2.00) per pound X 36,400 pounds

= (-.05) per pound X 36,400 pounds

= $1,820 favorable

Quantity variance = (actual quantity - standard quantity) X standard price

= (36,400 - (7000 X 5) pounds) X $2.00 per pound

= (36,400 - 35,000) pounds X $2.00 per pound

= (1,400) pounds X $2.00 per pound

= $ 2,800 unfavorable

We can then combine these to arrive at the previously calculated total direct material variance. The calculation would be: direct materials variance = $1,820 favorable + $2,800 unfavorable, this then equals $980 favorable.

Now it is time to calculate the direct labor variances: first we will calculate the *price (commonly called rate)* variance first and then we will calculate the *quantity (commonly called efficiency)* variance. The formulas for calculating the variances are the same as we used in calculating the direct materials variances except that we use the actual and standard prices and units for labor.

Labor price (rate) variance = (actual price - standard price) X actual quantity

= ($16.40–$16.00) per hour X 3,750 hours

= ($.40) per hour X 3,750 hours

= $1,500 unfavorable

Labor quantity (efficiency) variance = (actual quantity - standard quantity) X standard rate

= (3,750 - (7,000 X ½)) hours X $16.hour

= (3,750 – 3,500) hours X $16/hour

= (250) hours X $16/hour

= $ 4,000 unfavorable

We then combine these amounts to arrive at the previously calculated total direct labor variance. The calculation is: direct labor variance = $1,500 unfavorable + $4,000 unfavorable = $5,500 unfavorable.

The management would now analyze this data to see where they can possibly make improvements. The analysis could be like this. The first item to be noticed is that the material price is less than expected; therefore the question should be asked if the material is of lesser quality than the material in the standard. If the answer is yes, this could be the reason why more material was used than in the standard. This would not pose a problem overall for the material as there is a slightly favorable variance.

The next area to look at is the labor price (rate) variance and we would ask why the rate is above the standard rate. The answer could be that we have a different mix of very experienced people to relatively inexperienced personnel. This could be influenced by several factors and probably would not be a concern.

Then we move on to the labor quantity (efficiency) variance. We should be very concerned about this variance, especially if we have a mix that has more experienced personnel than planned. With more experienced personnel the labor quantity variance would normally be favorable but it is unfavorable. Upon further investigation we find out the lower grade material that has been purchased is harder to process and therefore takes more labor. At this point we could come to the conclusion that the lower grade material is not worth using because the total direct material variance that is favorable by $980 is more than offset by the $4,000 unfavorable labor quantity variance caused by the lower grade material.

The analysis of variances is crucial for businesses of all sizes, however it can be costly and time consuming. The time and cost considerations make it unlikely that small businesses will be able to use an analysis this extensive.

Most businesses that use variance analyses like we have just gone through spend a great deal of time on cost control. In our example, the bigger issue is the sales volume variance. In this example, we sold 2,000 units less than were budgeted. When we multiply this times the unit contribution margin of $9.20 as shown in Exhibit 10-3 we find that this variance accounts for $18,400 of the decrease in profit versus the plan. This represents a sales quantity variance. A business could also have a sales price variance. To calculate a sales price variance we would take the actual selling price per unit and deduct the budgeted selling price per unit from it. We would then multiply the difference times the actual quantity sold. We would need to discuss this sales shortfall with the sales department to see if we can find the cause(s). This is where the most time should be spent in this situation.

We have focused our discussion on calculating variances for a manufacturing firm because manufacturing lends itself to an easier analysis than other types of businesses. This same type of analysis can be performed for any type of business. For example, a cattle ranch could evaluate any variances in what they have to pay for feed (corn or hay) versus what they expected to pay when the budget was prepared. The ranch could also analyze any variance in cost of ranch hands (direct labor) if they use outside labor. Another analysis that could be looked at is the actual cost of transporting the cattle to market for sale versus the planned cost in the budget. These costs could be evaluated both in total and by unit price differences.

Some businesses also do variance analysis on the variable and fixed manufacturing overhead costs. This very time consuming and it is not likely to be worth the effort for most small businesses. In our example, most small businesses would accept the preliminary explanation of higher prices on supplies and would not delve deeper into the explanation. Since our focus is on small business we will not go into any further discussion regarding variable and fixed manufacturing overhead variances.

Quite frequently large companies use performance reports to see how they are doing. These performance reports can provide a significant amount of information to management. In Exhibits 10-6 to 10-9, a sample of a comprehensive performance report is presented.

Exhibit 10-6 -Performance Report Based on Sales

SALES & STANDARD GROSS MARGIN BY PRODUCT LINE
ANY COMPANY

October			Year-to Date		
Budget	Actual		Prior Yr	Budget	Actual
		Residential			
		Residential Sump			
686	792	SALES	9670	7522	9596
102	186	GROSS MARGIN @ STD	1185	1129	1506
14.9%	23.5%	SGM %	12.3%	15.0%	15.7%
		Residential Effluent			
485	444	SALES	3489	3890	3587
187	183	GROSS MARGIN @ STD	1289	1500	1392
38.6%	41.2%	SGM %	36.9%	38.6%	38.8%
		Residential Ejector			
654	946	SALES	7220	7007	7766
271	406	GROSS MARGIN @ STD	2788	2907	3289
41.4%	42.9%	SGM %	38.6%	41.5%	42.4%
		Residential Grinders			
16	29	SALES	0	161	208
6	10	GROSS MARGIN @ STD	0	62	65
37.5%	34.5%	SGM %		38.5%	31.3%
		Residential Non-Clogs			
40	33	SALES	0	416	372
16	13	GROSS MARGIN @ STD	0	165	144
40.0%	39.4%	SGM %		39.7%	38.7%
		Total Residential Pumps			
1881	2244	SALES	20379	18996	21529
582	798	GROSS MARGIN @ STD	5262	5763	6396
30.9%	35.6%	SGM %	25.8%	30.3%	29.7%
		Residential Accessories			
51	105	SALES	795	620	987
21	38	GROSS MARGIN @ STD	301	254	374
41.2%	36.2%	SGM %	37.9%	41.0%	37.9%
		Residential Parts			
13	10	SALES	158	131	135
10	8	GROSS MARGIN @ STD	117	103	99
76.9%	80.0%	SGM %	74.1%	78.6%	73.3%

Exhibit 10-7 - Performance Report - Manufacturing Variances in Inventory

(FAVORABLE) UNFAVORABLE MANUFACTURING VARIANCES IN INVENTORY

October			Year-to-Date		
Budget	Actual		Prior Year	Budget	Actual
		Material Variance			
		Purchase Price Variance			-
		PPV - Ongoing		-	-
(129)	(79)	PPV - MRC	52	(932)	(831)
(129)	(79)	Total PPV	52	(932)	(831)
		Rebates			
		Purchase Discounts			
12	19	Surcharges	166	128	184
6	9	Pallet & Container Costs	75	58	82
		Other Material	-		
(111)	(51)	Total Material Variance	293	(746)	(565)
		Material Acquisition			
40	69	Material Acquisition Incurred	n/a	426	721
(40)	(87)	Material Acquisition Absorbed		(426)	(833)
-	(18)	Net Material Acquisition	-	-	(112)
		Direct Labor			
280	267	Direct Labor Incurred	2,666	2,846	3,535
(274)	(285)	Direct Labor Absorbed	(2,272)	(2,788)	(3,189)
6	(18)	Labor Variance	394	58	346
		Overhead Variance			
343	346	Variable Overhead	3,533	3,460	3,050
470	500	Fixed Overhead	5,281	4,764	4,987
(788)	(662)	Absorbtion	(7,598)	(7,954)	(6,954)
25	184	Total Overhead Variance	1,216	270	1,083
(80)	97	**Total Variances Incurred**	1,903	(418)	752

Exhibit 10-8 – Performance Report – Overhead by Department

OVERHEAD EXPENSES BY DEPARTMENT
ANY COMPANY

(AMOUNTS IN THOUSANDS U.S. DOLLARS)

October Budget	October Actual			Year to Date 1996	Year to Date Budget	Year to Date Actual
			Direct Departments			
7	5	112100	Vsumps/Boosters	67	72	58
40	41	112200	Fabrication	384	436	373
167	175	112300	Machine Shop	1730	1678	1648
61	52	112500	Engineered Assembly	567	590	498
63	65	112600	Residential Assembly	713	618	698
5	8	112700	Electrical	72	68	59
343	346		Total Variable Spending	3533	3462	3334
			Indirect Departments			
80	50	121010	Unit Operations	0	765	705
99	60	121020	Local Operations Management	1471	900	903
54	42	121030	Manufacturing Engineering	572	577	625
21	32	121040	Quality	302	227	346
16	19	121050	Tool Support	139	166	168
62	77	121060	Maintenance	642	681	698
29	20	121100	Industrial Engineering	314	309	243
11	4	330000	Test Lab	54	116	36
98	196	611000	Building Occupancy - 80%	1057	1021	2039
			Allocation from Material Acq Depts			0
470	500		Total Fixed Spending	4551	4762	5763
813	846		Total Manufacturing Overhead	8084	8224	9097
			Material Acquisition Departments			
40	31	231000	Purchase	383	373	369
0	35	232000	Receiving	339	53	386
0	3	233000	Incoming Inspection	8	0	35
			Allocation from Fixed Overhead	0	0	-
40	69		Total Material Acquisition	730	426	790
853	915		Total Overhead	8814	8650	9887

Exhibit 10-9 - Performance Report - Overhead Expense by Category

OVERHEAD EXPENSES BY CATEGORY
ANY COMPANY

(AMOUNTS IN THOUSANDS U.S. DOLLARS)

October				YEAR TO DATE	
Budget	Actual	Cost Category	1996	Budget	Actual
426	362	Indirect Labor	3008	4556	3551
37	112	Fringe	857	398	1059
51	16	Other employee Related Expenses	412	328	238
84	62	Production Costs	762	712	576
6	8	Facilities	40	61	60
26	43	Supplies & Equipment	108	278	319
0	0	Depreciation	0	0	0
7	5	Services	145	75	89
0	0	Taxes	0	0	0
0	0	Telecommunications	0	0	1
(26)	0	Misc Operating Expenses	7	(286)	1
104	42	Shared Services		919	704
715	650	Subtotal	5339	7041	6598
98	196	Building Occupancy - 80%	1057	1021	1439
40	69	Material Acquisition Costs	730	588	721
853	915	Total Overhead	7126	8650	8758

In Exhibits 10-6 through 10-9 the column labeled 1996 represents the previous years' actual through the month of October to provide a year to year comparison.

SUMMARY

This chapter has covered the basics in variance analysis and standard costing and how they can be used for performance evaluation. We looked at a traditional static budget and how that can be adapted by using actual sales volume to a flexible budget. Then it was discussed how that flexible budget can be compared to actual results to identify areas that have variances that should be investigated further. After determining the variances for the variable manufacturing costs it was decided to further analyze the direct materials and direct labor variances.

Based on the example given the direct materials variances for price and quantity were calculated. Then the direct labor variance for rate and efficiency were calculated. Finally, the sales variance was calculated. A discussion of what management should see or ask about each of these variances followed the calculation of the variances. We did not do any analysis of variable manufacturing overhead variances since that would be beyond what small business would normally do.

KEY TERMS

- Control
- Flexible budgets
- Management by exception
- Favorable variance
- Unfavorable variance
- Standard costs
- Practical standard
- Ideal standard
- Price variance
- Quantity variance
- Usage variance
- Rate variance
- Efficiency variance

EXERCISES AND PROBLEMS

10-1. Slam Dunk Enterprises made 45,000 basketballs this year. The company had total variable manufacturing costs of $360,000 and total fixed manufacturing cost of $90,000. Assume the company will experience no price change for its direct materials and no rate changes for its direct labor for next year. Also assume no changes in the company's production methods.

Compute the production costs for producing 54,000 basketballs for next year.

10-2. The city is in the midst of preparing its budget for next year. As part of the budget process the city is attempting to plan for the cost of having a police car on the streets. The city is interested in the cost running the vehicle but is not concerned with cost of the officers that will be in each car. The city is not sure how many miles each car should be budgeted for and how many cars should be in the budget. The cost to operate vehicle includes variable costs of $.25 per mile and $5,000 depreciation per car. If the cars average 30,000 miles per car the city will need 15 vehicles on the street, if the cars average 40,000 per car the city will need 12 cars on the street and if the cars average 50,000 miles per car the city will need 9 cars which is the fewest cars the city can have and provide adequate police coverage.

1. Calculate the total budgeted vehicle expense per car for each level of operation (30,000, 40,000, or 50,000 miles).
2. Calculate the total vehicle costs for the department at each operating level.

10-3. Polson Steel provides a variety of steel products to its customers. The expenses related to material handling are driven by the amount of material handled. The company's budget called for the material handling department to move 840,000 pounds of material at a cost of $.30 per pound. Due to a shortage of customer orders, the department only moved 672,000 pounds of materials during the year. The department had expenses of $215,000 for the year.

Compare actual material handling costs to budgeted material handling costs for both the static budget and the flexible budget based on activity level.

10-4. Western Montana Specialty Aluminum uses a special aluminum alloy in the production of its products. Western purchased and used 400,000 pounds of the special alloy during the year at a total alloy cost of $540,000. The standard cost for Western calls for the use of 50 pounds of alloy per unit of production at a price of $1.40 per pound. During the year Western produced 7,500 units of their specialty product.

Compute the direct materials price variance and the direct materials quantity variance for the year.

10-5. Western Montana Specialty Aluminum budgeted their direct labor based on the following information: It takes 8 man-hours to produce one unit of the final product. The average labor rate was budgeted at $15.00 per hour and average worker works 2,000 hours per year. The budget called for the production of 8,250 units. During the year the company produced 8,000 units with 29 production workers at an average rate of $15.50 per hour.

Compute the direct labor price (rate) variance and the direct labor quantity (efficiency) variance.

10-6. Bigfoot Enterprises has accumulated the following information:

Standard direct labor rate	$14.25
Actual direct labor rate	$13.00
Standard direct labor hours	12,000
Direct labor quantity (efficiency) variance – unfavorable	$10,800
Standard unit price of materials	$ 4.50
Actual quantity purchased and used	1,900
Standard quantity allowed for actual production	1750
Materials purchase price variance (favorable)	$ 380

1. Compute the actual hours worked, round to the nearest hour
2. Compute the actual purchase per unit of materials, round to the nearest penny

10-7 Below is information related to a small manufacturing company:

	Direct Materials	Direct Labor
Costs incurred (actual units x actual price)	$166,000	$82,000
Actual inputs x expected prices	$180,000	$77,500
Standard inputs allowed for actual outputs achieved expected prices	$185,000	$75,000

Compute the price, quantity and flexible budget variances for direct materials and direct labor. Label the variances as favorable or unfavorable.

10-8. A local CPA firm has budgeted $80,000 per month in fixed charges for the tax department. It budget showed the following variable expenses per tax return: supplies $4; labor costs $50; and computer time $10. The firm expects to prepare 1500 tax returns per month per month at an average charge of $140. During the current month the firm actually prepared 1,650 tax returns at an average charge of $ 135 each. Actual supplies expense was $7,000, labor costs were $85,000, and computer time charges were $16,250. The actual fixed expenses were the budgeted amount.

Prepare a flexible budget for the CPA firm for the current month.

10-9.Using the information from 10-8 compute the direct labor variance for the month. Label it as favorable or unfavorable.

10-10. Local Hardware Store had planned on a cost of sales of 56% of sales during its budgeting process. Using the trial balance for Local Hardware Store in Appendix A, calculate the flexible budget for the cost of sales based on the actual sales volume and then calculate the flexible budget variance. The variance should be labeled as favorable or unfavorable.

10-11. Double Bar Ranch and Cattle Company budgeted their cost of goods sold at 2% of net sales and their ranch labor at 8.25% of net sales.

1. Using the trial balance in Appendix A calculate the flexible budget amount for cost of goods sold and ranch labor.
2. Calculate the flexible budget variance for both cost of goods sold and ranch labor and label each as favorable or unfavorable.

10-12. ABC Hospital Corporation planned on their lab technicians' wages being 48% of the lab revenue. They further planned that pharmacy cost of sales would be equal to 48% of pharmacy revenue.

1. Using the ABC Hospital Corporation trial balance in Appendix A, calculate the flexible budget for the lab technicians' wages and the pharmacy cost of goods sold.
2. Calculate the flexible budget variances for the lab technicians' wages and the pharmacy cost of goods sold. Label each as favorable or unfavorable.

10-13. The Lower Montana Arts Council recently held a dinner and costume ball for fund-raising purposes. The original (static) budget and the actual results are shown below:

	Budget	Actual
Number of guests	90	100
Revenue	$ 2,700	$ 3,000
Food costs at $18 each	1,620	1,825
Beverages–$5 per person	450	475
Room rental–$75	75	75
Music - 2 hours at $80/hour	160	150
Profit	$ 395	$ 475

Food, beverages and music costs are considered to be variable costs.

1. Calculate the flexible budget for the revenue and each of the variable costs.
2. Using Exhibit 10-5 as a guideline prepare a schedule showing each actual cost, each flexible budget cost and the flexible budget variance.

10-14. The emergency room at a major urban hospital showed the following data for the month of September:

	Budget	Actual
Number of patients	4,400	4,600
Nurse -hours	3,300	3,680
Nursing costs	$66,000	$75,440
Supplies	$33,000	$36,064

The hospital has set the following rates during its budgeting process: nurse hours per patient 0.75, nursing costs $20 per hour and supplies cost $10 per nursing hour.

1. Calculate the flexible budget for the variable costs.
2. Calculate all price and quantity variances for the variable costs based on the flexible budget.

10-15. XYZ Manufacturing, Inc. set the following standards during its annual budgeting process: sales price per unit $1,325; direct material 66 pounds per unit at a cost of $4.50 per pound; direct labor at 8 hours per unit with a cost of $16.25 per hour. The actual sales value for the year was 7,000 units which matches the budgeted quantity. The production department used 55,000 direct labor hours for production during the year. The actual cost of material was $4.25 per pound.

1. Prepare a flexible budget based on the data shown in the XYZ Manufacturing, Inc. trial balance in Appendix A and the applicable data above.
2. Calculate all applicable quantity and price variances based on the flexible budget and label them as favorable or unfavorable.
3. Based upon the variances that are calculated in item 2, prepare a list of questions that you feel management should obtain answers for.

CHAPTER 11 – FINANCIAL STATEMENT ANALYSIS

LEARNING OBJECTIVES

1. Understand the calculation of the liquidity ratios and what they mean.
2. Understand the calculation of asset management ratios,
3. Understand the calculation of debt management ratios.
4. Understand the calculation of profitability ratios.
5. Understand the market value ratios.

INTRODUCTION

One of the most common pieces of corporate information, that is available for public companies, is the annual report which contains the financial statements of the company. This information is readily available for publicly traded companies. All of the financial statements of publicly traded companies have to be reported annually to the Securities and Exchange Commission (SEC). This is done through the filing of form 10-K with the SEC. In the 10-K, which is the company's annual formal report to the SEC, the financial statements are included as item 8 or a reference telling the users where to find the financial statements is included in item 8. The filings the company makes with the SEC are public information and can be reviewed through the SEC's website or can be requested from the company. If a person wishes to review the filings of a company they can access those filings through the following website: www.sec.gov/edgar.shtml.

For anyone interested in seeing how a particular company is doing this is a very good place to find public information. Once the available public information has been obtained it is then advisable to further analyze the information if you are interested in investing in the company. One common way of doing additional analysis is through examining the relationships between some of the amounts reflected in the financial statements. This is done through ratio analysis of the financial statements. After ratio analysis has been done the results can be compared to other companies both in the same industry and in other industries. On an annual basis ratio averages for industries are published and can usually be found at local libraries or at university libraries.

In this chapter we are going to cover ratio analysis and what each ratio tells an individual about the company. We will do this by breaking the ratios into categories so that similar ratios are discussed at the same time. The categories we are going to discuss are: liquidity ratios, asset management ratios, debt management ratios, profitability ratios and market value ratios. In the case of the market value ratios the ratios are only appropriate for use on publicly traded companies. To begin the analysis we will need a set of financial statements to use. Below you will find a balance sheet, a statement of income and a statement of cash flows for a company. The statement of changes in stockholders' equity is not included as it does not contain any information necessary to ratio analysis.

Exhibit 11-1 – Balance Sheet

My Manufacturing Company
Balance Sheet
December 31, 20X1

	20X1
ASSETS	
Current Assets	
Cash and cash equivalents	$793,189
Accounts receivable, net	3,734,824
Inventories	5,375,132
Prepaid expenses	722,818
Total current assets	$10,625,963
Property, plant & equipment, net	5,882,036
Intangible assets	2,246,950
Total Assets	$18,754,949
LIABILITIES & STOCKHOLDERS' EQUITY	
Current liabilities	
Current portion of long-term debt	$977,454
Current portion of capital lease obligations	70,728
Account payable	2,705,753
Accrued expenses	1,606,872
Total current liabilities	$5,360,807
Long-term debt	2,530,737
Capital lease obligation (long-term)	1,388,024
Other long-term liabilities	448,642
Stockholder's equity	
Common stock, $1 par value	13,100
Additional paid-in-capital	636,900
Retained earnings	8,362,512
Other comprehensive income	14,227
	9,026,739
Total liabilities and stockholders' equity	$18,754,949

Exhibit 11-2 - Statement of Income

My Manufacturing Company
Statement of Income
Year ended December 31, 20X1

	20X1
Net Sales	$36,477,460
Cost of goods sold	26,036,564
Gross margin	10,440,896
S, G & A expenses	6,590,110
Operating income	3,850,786
Interest expense	629,602
Income before income taxes	3,221,184
Provision for income taxes	647,587
Net income	$2,573,597

Exhibit 11-3 – Statement of Cash Flows

My Manufacturing Company
Statement of Cash Flows
Year ended December 31, 20X1

	20X1
Cash flows from operating activities	
Net income	$2,573,597
Adjustments to net income to reconcile to cash from operating activities	
Depreciation and amortization	1,410,267
Pension expense	108,779
Changes to assets and liabilities	
Accounts receivable	(421,906)
Inventories	114,458
Prepaid expenses	(107,648)
Accounts payable	(238,087)
Accrued expenses	(140,193)
Net cash from operating activities	3,299,267
Cash flows from investing activities	
Additions to plant and equipment	(1,391,508)
Net cash from investing activities	(1,391,508)
Cash flows from financing activities	
Payments on capital lease obligation	(59,466)
Proceeds from issuance of long-term debt	7,700,635
Payments of long-term debt	(7,624,793)
Cash dividends paid	(2,226,316)
Net cash from financing activities	(2,209,940)
Net change in cash and cash equivalents	(302,181)
Cash and cash equivalents at beginning of year	1,095,370
Cash and cash equivalents at end of year	$ 793,189

LIQUIDITY RATIOS

Now that we have a set of financial statements we can begin our ratio analysis. The starting point in ratio analysis is the liquidity ratios. These ratios deal with current assets, which are cash and those items that will turn cash in the normal operating cycle (usually considered a year).and current liabilities, which are those bills that will come due and need to be paid in the next operating cycle. These ratios are designed to measure the company's ability to pay its bills as they come due. The liquidity ratios are of particular interest to the company's creditors.

The first liquidity ratio is the current ratio. This is simply the current assets from the balance sheet divided by the current liabilities from the balance sheet. This is expressed as the number of times the current assets would be able to pay the current liabilities. In our example the calculation would be:

$$\text{Current ratio} = \frac{\text{Current assets (10,625,963)}}{\text{Current liabilities (5,360,807)}} = 1.98 \text{ Times}$$

This means that, in the normal course of the next operating cycle, the company will have sufficient cash pay its bills as they come due. Generally anything above 1.25 times for a manufacturing firm is considered to be a good position. For most industries anything above 1.2 is considered good.

The next ratio is the quick (acid-test) ratio. This measures the assets that will quickly turn to cash in the normal operating cycle and how many times they would cover the current liabilities. The assets that will quickly turn to cash are all current assets except inventories. In this ratio we exclude the value of the inventories from the calculation. The calculation is as follows:

$$\text{Quick ratio} = \frac{\text{Current assets - inventories (10,625,968 - 5,375,132)}}{\text{Current liabilities (5,360,807)}} = 0.98 \text{ times}$$

Anything over 0.8 times is considered good for a manufacturing firm and in general all firms are considered in good shape if the ratio is above 0.75 times.

Creditors are interested in these ratios since they show the company's ability to pay its bills as they come due. In the second ratio the inventories are not considered because in the event of a catastrophe the inventories may not be able to be turned to cash.

These are the only two ratios in the liquidity ratio category. We will now move on to the asset management ratios.

ASSET MANAGEMENT RATIOS

The asset management ratios are designed to measure the effectiveness of the business in using its assets to create sales. These are measured in terms of the number of times that the asset being measured is used during the year (turnover). It should be noted here that in many parts of the world the term turnover is used in business to mean sales so it can be easy to confuse the meaning between here and Europe for example.

The first asset management ratio we are going to calculate is inventory turnover. This is calculated by dividing the cost of goods sold (sometimes called cost of sales or cost of revenue) by the inventory. The cost of goods sold comes from the income statement and the inventory comes from the balance sheet. In our example the calculation is as follows:

$$\text{Inventory turnover} = \frac{\text{Cost of goods sold (26,036,564)}}{\text{Inventory (5,375,132)}} = 4.84 \text{ turns}$$

In a manufacturing setting companies are looking for inventory turns of between 4 and 8 times so this would be an acceptable level of inventory turnover. In merchandising companies would generally like to be between 8 and 12 turns. This ratio generally cannot be calculated for service companies and agricultural production companies as they don't have inventory. If a service or agricultural production company has inventory it is generally small and therefore would make this calculation meaningless.

The next asset management ratio to be calculated is the days' sales outstanding (DSO). This gives us a measurement on how fast we are collecting our accounts receivable (sometimes called trade receivables). It is calculated by dividing the accounts receivable balance by the average daily credit sales. If a company does not show credit sales in its financial statements then it would be appropriate to use the net sales (net revenue) amount from the income statement and divide that by 360 to get the average daily sales. The accounts receivable figure will come from the balance sheet. In our example the calculation would be:

$$\text{Days' sales outstanding} = \frac{\text{Accounts receivable (3,734,824)}}{\text{(Net sales/360)} = \text{(36,477,460/360)}} = 36.9 \text{ days}$$

If we were to assume that the company sells on normal credit terms of net, 30 days. Then this would telling us that on average the company collects its account receivable within one week of when they are due. This would be considered good. Generally, merchandising firms do not have significant amounts in accounts receivable as the majority of their sales are for cash or on a major credit card, therefore this measurement would have very little meaning for a merchandising company. There could be an exception if the merchandising company has its own credit card and has a large portion of its sales charged to the credit card it issues. For agricultural production companies this would have very little meaning as generally they sell production once a year and receive their cash almost immediately. They then have to manage cash for the next year but don't have to worry about collecting accounts receivable. In the case of service companies the use of this measure varies by the type of service. Some types of services receive payment immediately and other types can have very long collection periods. As examples: a CPA firm normally will have the client pay for the preparation of their tax return at the time the tax return is picked up and therefore there is no extended time in accounts receivable; however, a hospital that provides services to a patient that does not have insurance may be collecting on the bill for a year or sometimes even more.

The next asset management ratio to be calculated is the fixed assets turnover ratio. This measures how many times a year the fixed assets are creating sales. The ratio is calculated by taking the annual sales (net sales, net revenue) from the income statement and dividing it by the net fixed assets (plant and equipment) on the balance sheet. In our example the calculation is as follows:

$$\text{Fixed assets turnover} = \frac{\text{Net sales } (36{,}477{,}460)}{\text{Fixed Assets } (5{,}882{,}036)} = 6.2 \text{ times}$$

This ratio would be considered very good as it means that, in essence, the use of the fixed assets in the business is creating sales equal to the investment in fixed assets in just under 2 months. This measurement is very useful in evaluating any type of business. It would generally be significantly lower for an agricultural production company than for any other type of business due to the investment in the land used for production. Generally the highest level would be shown for service companies, but it would matter on the type of service.

The final asset management ratio we are going to calculate is the total assets turnover. This is calculated by dividing net sales by the total assets shown on the balance sheet. Based on the financial statements we are using the calculation would be as follows:

$$\text{Total assets turnover} = \frac{\text{Net sales } (36{,}477{,}460)}{\text{Total Assets } (18{,}754{,}949)} = 1.95 \text{ times}$$

Manufacturing firms generally look for at least 2 times in this ratio so this company is very close but just a little bit low. This ratio is useful in evaluating businesses in any industry but must be used in comparison with the industry average for the appropriate industry.

We have finished the calculations of the asset management ratios. We will next look at the debt management ratios.

DEBT MANAGEMENT RATIOS

Not all companies use debt as part of their financing, but for that do use debt it has important implications as listed below:

1. If the firm uses debt it can obtain additional financing without the current stockholders needing to invest more in the business or without the current stockholders having their ownership interest reduced (diluted) by bringing in any additional stockholders.
2. Creditors, those lending money to the firm, will look to the portion of the financing of the firm provided by the stockholders (owners) as a margin of safety. If the percentage of funds provided by the owners is relatively small it means that the majority of the risk associated with the company is falling on the creditors.
3. If the firm earns more through the use of borrowed funds than it pays in interest, then the owners' capital is increased (leveraged).

If a company borrows funds for investment in the business it affects the owners expected rate of return because: (1) the interest paid is tax deductible, while dividends paid are not tax deductible; and (2) if the company is healthy it invests the funds at a greater rate of return than the interest it pays. Because of these two aspects of borrowing the successful operation of the company will create a magnified return to the owners. In this case the *financial leverage* is positive for the firm and the owners.

Because of the impact of financial leverage both the owners and the creditors will pay close attention to the debt management ratios. The first ratio to be covered is the debt ratio. This ratio shows what portion, of the total assets, is financed by debt. It is calculated by dividing total liabilities by total assets. Both of these amounts come from the balance sheet. Based on the financial statements we are using the calculation will be as follows:

$$\text{Debt ratio} = \frac{\text{Total liabilities } (5{,}360{,}807+2{,}530{,}737+1{,}388{,}024+448{,}642)}{\text{Total assets } (18{,}754{,}949)} = 51.9\%$$

For a small to medium sized, privately held (not publicly traded) company the creditors generally like this ratio to be around 50% or lower. In this case the company is slightly above 50% of its financing being from borrowing but this would probably not be of concern to the creditors based upon what we saw in the liquidity and asset management ratios. Those ratios showed effective use of the assets and a good position for paying the bills as they come due. With the effective use of assets it means that the company will probably be experiencing a reasonable level of profitability which will increase the owners' share of the financing.

The next debt management ratio to be discussed is the times interest earned ratio. This is a measurement that measures how many times the earnings before interest and taxes (EBIT), covers the payment of the interest on borrowing. This ratio is of particular interest to those lenders who are collecting interest on the borrowed funds as they want to be confident in the receipt of the interest they are due. The earnings before interest and taxes can be calculated for companies by going to the income statement and finding the earnings before income taxes and adding back the amount of the interest expense (interest charges). In the case of the financial statements above it is equal to operating income (earnings from operations) but this not always the case. The calculation is EBIT divided by interest expense (interest charges). In our example, the calculation is:

$$\text{Times interest earned} = \frac{\text{EBIT } (3{,}850{,}786)}{\text{Interest expense } (629{,}602)} = 6.1 \text{ times}$$

This is a very good ratio. Most banks and other lenders are looking for 3 to 5 times to feel comfortable with the coverage.

The final debt management ratio we are going to discuss is the fixed charge coverage ratio. This is calculated by adding EBIT and any lease payments together and then dividing the result by the sum of the interest expense plus the lease payments plus the value of any bond sinking fund payments required divided by 1-the company's tax rate.

The general calculation would be below:

$$\text{Fixed charge coverage} = \frac{\text{EBIT} + \text{Lease payments}}{\text{Interest expense} + \text{lease payments} + \{\text{sinking fund payments}) \,/\, (1 - \text{tax rate})}$$

Most companies do not have bond sinking fund payments so the most common calculation is EBIT + lease payments / interest expense + lease payments. It should be noted that companies that have bank loans may have a different calculation for the bank loan as frequently banks will want a specific calculation that will be specified in the loan agreement. The EBIT and interest expense amounts come from the income statement and the amount of lease payments and bond sinking funds payments, if any, come from the cash flows from financing activities section of the statement of cash flows. For our company, the calculation is as follows (the company does not have any bond sinking fund payments):

$$\text{Fixed charge coverage} = \frac{\text{EBIT} + \text{Lease payments}}{\text{interest expense} + \text{lease payments}} = \frac{(3{,}850{,}786 + 59{,}466)}{(629{,}602 + 59{,}466)} = 5.67 \text{ times}$$

This is also very good as banks would normally be looking for between 2 and 3 times. If a company does not have any lease payments or bond sinking fund contributions then this calculation is the same as the times interest earned calculation and does not carry any special meaning at that point.

We have now completed our coverage of debt management ratios. We will next cover profitability ratios.

PROFITABILITY RATIOS

Profitability ratios are expressed as percentages and are used to determine what rates of return on various bases are being earned. These are items that would be of the greatest interest of potential investors. Potential investors will be looking for rates of returns that will cover their cost of capital and also cover the rate of inflation. For our purposes we are going to calculate 3 profitability ratios. The first ratio is the net profit margin and it is calculated by dividing net income by net sales. Both amounts used in this calculation come from the income statement. With the data we have been using the calculation is as follows:

$$\text{Net profit margin} = \frac{\text{Net income (2,573,597)}}{\text{Net sales (36,477,460)}} = 7.06\%$$

This is a relatively low net profit margin as most investors would be looking for a minimum of 10-12% for a manufacturing firm. Investors probably would be looking for differing margin rates for merchandising firms, service firms and agricultural production firms than they look for with manufacturing firms.

The next profitability ratio to be calculated is the Return on Assets (ROA). This is calculated by dividing net income by total assets. This is a measurement that shows management and ownership the return that firm in earning on the total investment in the firm. The net income comes from the income statement and the total assets come from the balance sheet. The calculation for our example is as follows:

$$\text{Return on Assets} = \frac{\text{Net income (2,573,597)}}{\text{Total Assets (18,754,949)}} = 13.72\%$$

Again this ratio is less than investors would normally expect from a manufacturing firm. Investors would typically be looking for a minimum return on assets of 16-20%. Also the return on assets goals would be different for other types of firms (nonmanufacturing).

The final profitability ratio we will examine is the Return on Equity (ROE). This shows the stockholders the percentage return they are getting on their investment in the company. This is the calculation that current ownership would the most interest in. it is calculated by dividing net income by common stockholders' equity. The net income comes from the income statement and the stockholders' equity comes from the balance sheet. In our example the calculation is as follows:

$$\text{Return on Equity} = \frac{\text{Net income (2,573,597)}}{\text{Stockholders' equity (9,026,739)}} = 28.51\%$$

This is very good as most investors look for a minimum return on equity of 20-25% for manufacturing firms. This concludes our calculations of profitability ratios. We will move on to calculating the market value ratios.

MARKET VALUE RATIOS

These ratios are used for publicly traded companies only, as the market value is only easily obtainable for companies whose stock is traded on a stock exchange. We will illustrate these ratios by assuming the market price per share of our example company is $900. If this were a publicly traded company the market price per share could be obtained online from a number of locations or the previous trading day's last trade could be found in the Wall Street Journal.

As our example company is a privately held company the number of shares is very small and thus all of the values calculated here will be larger than would be normal for a publicly traded company. The number of shares outstanding would be shown on the balance sheet of a publicly traded company. In our example it is not shown but the number can be calculated by dividing the value of common stock by the par value per share, this is therefore $13,100/$1 per share which gives us 13,100 shares of stock in the company.

We will use the number of shares to calculate earnings per share. This is calculated by taking the net income from the income statement and dividing it by the number of shares. For our example the calculation would be $2,573,597/13,100 which would give us earnings per share of $196.46. For a public traded company the earnings per share would be shown on the bottom of the income statement and for the calculations to follow the basic earnings per share would be used.

The calculation of book value per share is stockholders' equity (from the balance sheet) divided by the number of shares. Using our example company this would be $9,026,739/13,100 which equals $689.06. Now we are ready to do the market value calculations.

The first calculation is the price earnings ratio which compares the stock price to the earnings per share. Our calculation is as follows:

$$\text{Price earnings ratio} = \frac{\text{Market price per share (\$900.00)}}{\text{Earnings per share (\$196.46)}} = 4.58 \text{ times}$$

This represents how many years' worth of earnings it would take for the company to earn an amount equivalent to the share price. For top public companies that are mature and have reasonable growth prospects the normal trading range for the stock would between 12 and 18 times earnings. For companies with unusually high growth potential the stock would trade at a higher multiple of earnings. The multiple can also be affected by the industry the company is in.

The second measurement of market value is the market to book ratio. This is calculated by dividing the share price by the book value per share. Using our example company the calculation is as follows:

$$\text{Market/Book} = \frac{\text{Market price per share (\$900.00)}}{\text{Book value per share (\$689.06)}} = 1.31 \text{ times}$$

This ratio is not as widely used as the other ratios that we have calculated. How this ratio is viewed is very dependent upon the individual investor Because this is so individualized there is no set range of what investors would expect However, as a general rule higher is better.

Below is a recap of the ratios as they were calculated above:

Liquidity Ratios

Current ratio....................1.98 times

Quick (acid test) ratio.................... .98 times

Asset Management Ratios

Inventory turnover.................... 4.84 times

Days' sales outstanding (DSO) .... 36.9 days

Fixed assets turnover.................... 6.2 times

Total assets turnover....................1.95 times

Debt Management Ratios

Debt ratio 51.9%

Times interest earned.................... 6.1 times

Fixed charge coverage ....5.67 times

Profitability Ratios

Net profit margin 7.06%

Return on assets (ROA) 13.72%

Return on equity (ROE) 28.51%

Market Value Ratios

Price/earnings ratio .... 4.58 times

Market/book .... 1.31 times

SUMMARY

This chapter has covered the basics of financial statement analysis. It has taken us through the calculations of the most commonly calculated ratios and what they ratios tell us. It has also provided some explanation as to how the ratios are used by potential investors or potential creditors.

In some places we mentioned industry averages. The industry averages can be found based on the company's Standard Industrial Classification (SIC) or North American Industrial Classification System (NAICS) code. There are books published each year that track industry averages. The Risk Management Association publishes industry averages for small and medium sized companies based on data collected from companies that have bank loans. Leo Troy, PhD, publishes an annual book based on data from U.S. federal income tax returns that are filed, this publication tracks businesses of all sizes.

KEY TERMS

- Liquidity ratios
- Current ratio
- Quick Ratio
- Asset management ratios
- Profitability ratios
- Inventory turnover
- Days' sales outstanding
- Fixed assets turnover
- Total assets turnover
- Debt management ratios
- Debt ratio
- Times interest earned
- Return on assets
- Return on equity
- Market Value ratios
- Price/earnings ratio
- Market/book
- Fixed charge coverage
- Net profit margin

EXERCISES AND PROBLEMS

11-1. Edelweiss Corporation has $1,425,000 in current assets and $ 550,000 in current liabilities. Its' current inventory level is $250,000 but management feels that level is too low. To increase its' inventory level the company will issue notes payable with a maturity of nine months from the date of issue. The company wants to increase its inventory level to $400,000 dollars.

Calculate the current ratio and the quick ratio for the company as they stand today and as they will stand after the issuance of the notes and the investment of the proceeds in inventory.

11-2. Assume that you are provided with the following information regarding Zero Gravity Corporation.

Total Assets Turnover	3.0x
Return on Assets (ROA)	7.5%
Return on Equity (ROE)	10.0%

Calculate the company's net profit margin.

11-3.The following information relates to a company in the music industry. (amounts in millions)

	Year 1	Year 2
Sales	$250	$325
Total Assets	$ 85	$120
Net profit margin	8%	10%

Compute the total assets turnover and ROA for the company for each year.

11-4.The following financial information was gathered from the accounting records of Sunset Corporation:

Total Assets	$3,500,000
Long term debt (10% interest rate)	$ 600,000
Total stockholders' equity	$2,100,000
Net Income	$ 315,000
Interest expense	$ 60,000

The net income above is after tax and the corporation's tax rate is 30%.

1. Compute the ROA
2. Compute the ROE
3. Compute the times interest earned ratio.

11-5. Albacore Corporation has published its' financial statements. A review of the statements shows the following information.

Inventory	$575,000
Sales	$5,750,000
Cost of goods sold	40% of sales
Accounts receivable	$495,140
Plant & equipment	$805,000
Total Assets	$2,875,000
Total Liabilities	$1,150,000

1. Calculate inventory turnover.
2. Calculate days' sales outstanding
3. Calculate fixed assets turnover
4. Calculate total assets turnover
5. Calculate the debt ratio.

11-6. Brighton, Inc. has taken the following information from their financial statements and has asked you to compute certain ratios for them:

Total current assets	$750,000
Total fixed assets	$550,000
Total assets	$ 2,505,000
Total liabilities	$ 1,202,400
Net income	$280,000
Income taxes	$120,000
Interest expense	$ 50,000

In addition you have looked at the statement of cash flows and found that the company made long term lease payments of $ 50,000 during the year. The information requested by the company is:

1. Compute the company's ROA
2. Compute the company's ROE
3. Compute the debt ratio
4. Compute the times interest earned
5. Compute the company's fixed charge coverage (assume no sinking fund payments)

11-7. Nightmare, Inc. a Halloween decoration manufacturer is concerned about the financial position of the company but they are unsure how to determine if they have reason for concern. You have been hired to provide them with information regarding their financial situation. You have taken the following information from their financial records:

Current assets	$275,000
Current liabilities	$200,000
Inventory	$110,000
Total assets	$575,000
Total liabilities	$250,000
Net sales	$900,000
Net income	$180,000
Interest expense	$ 5,000

1. Calculate the liquidity ratios
2. Calculate the profitability ratios
3. Prepare a summary report of your findings and determine if the owners should be concerned about their financial situation. State the reasons why you feel they should or should not be concerned.

11-8. Midnight Auto Parts has been experiencing some cash flow difficulties. They have pulled together the following information for your review:

Accounts receivable $135,000

Inventory $400,000

Total current assets $600,000

Total current liabilities $550,000

Upon review you find the following additional information: (1) the DSO is 45 days but management feels they can get it down to 30 days with a little more effort; (2) the inventory can be reduced by 20% without affecting sales volume; and (3) all of the funds from the accounts receivable and inventory reductions will be used to pay current liabilities.

1. Calculate the liquidity ratios as they are today.
2. Calculate the liquidity ratios if all of the changes are made.
3. Will the changes put the company in a better liquidity position?

11-9.The management of Paytheon Corporation is not sure if they are meeting the owners' expectations. The owners have told them that they require a net profit margin of 10%, a return on assets of 8% and a return on equity of 18%. The management is unsure how to calculate these amounts but have provided the following information:

Net income $255,000

Net sales $2,600,000

Current assets $600,000

Total assets $3,000,000

Total liabilities $1,600,000

Interest expense (7% Onterest) $112,000

1. Is the company meeting the goals of the owners?
2. If not where are the shortcomings and could the information be presented to the owners in a way that would look good for management?

11-10. Pantomime, Inc. has had some good results recently and as a result their stock price has risen significantly. The following information is available:

Net income	$12,000,000
Shares outstanding	8,000,000
Stockholders' equity	$64,000,000
Share price	$27 per share

1. Calculate the market value ratios for Pantomime, Inc.

11-11. Beta Alpha has the following current assets and current liabilities at the beginning of the year:

Cash	$75,000
Accounts receivable	$175,000
Inventory	$225,000
Prepaid expenses	$25,000
Accounts payable	$175,000
Notes payable	$40,000
Accrued expenses	$20,000

During the year the company had the following transactions:

a. Issued additional common stock for $75,000

b. Sold inventory costing $40,000 for $75,000 on account

c. Paid accounts payable $45,000

d. Purchased inventory for $45,000

e. Paid off the notes payable, $40,000

f. Purchased equipment for cash, $20,000

g. Collected cash on accounts receivable, $75,000

1. Calculate the current ratio and the quick ratio at the beginning of the year
2. Show how each transaction would affect current assets and current liabilities, an increase or a decrease
3. Calculate the ending balance for each of the current assets and current liabilities
4. Calculate the ending current ratio and quick ratio.

11-12.Using the trial balance in Appendix A for ABC Hospital Corporation, calculate all ratios that the trial balance provides information for. Assume all sales to be credit sales.

11-13. Using the trial balance for Local Hardware Company in Appendix A, calculate all ratios that there is sufficient information for. Assume that 80% of sales are cash sales.

11-14.Using the trial balance for Double Bar Ranch in Appendix A, calculate all ratios that there is sufficient information for. Assume all sales are credit sales.

11-15.Using the trial balance for XYZ Manufacturing in Appendix A, calculated all ratios there is sufficient data for. Assume that all sales are credit sales and that there are 10,500 shares of stock outstanding. The company is privately held so there is no market price for the stock, but you should calculate the earnings per share and the book value per share for the company.

CHAPTER 12 – CASH FLOW PLANNING

LEARNING OBJECTIVES

1. Identify methods for predicting cash receipts
2. Identify methods for predicting cash disbursements
3. Develop a monthly cash plan for a business

INTRODUCTION

The most important issue faced by businesses of all sizes is the planning and management of cash flow. This is even more critical for small businesses. Businesses that fail generally fail because they run out of cash. Running out of cash can be caused by the business have continuing losses that are not caused by non-cash expenses such as depreciation or because of their cash planning and management. The areas that need to be addressed in cash planning are cash receipts and cash disbursements. As a general rule, businesses have the most difficulty in predicting and planning for cash receipts if the business makes the majority of their sales on credit. It is much easier for businesses to predict their cash receipts if the majority of their sales are cash or on national credit cards (not company credit cards). Cash disbursements are easier to plan for as many of the cash expenditures are routine, such as rent, utilities, wages and payroll taxes and most other expenditures. The difficulty in planning cash expenditures can come in the areas of unexpected major repairs or inventory purchases for businesses where inventory is a significant portion of their expenditures.

CASH RECEIPTS

If the business primarily sells their product or service for cash or on national credit cards such as Visa or Discover, predicting cash receipts becomes a fairly easy task. The business can plan their cash receipts based on their sales volume less the amounts they are charged by the credit card companies for the use of credit cards at their business. At this point the only major variable will be the level of sales. The company can predict the sales level by looking at their sales by month for the last three years and if there are no major changes in their business or competition they can use the average sales by month to predict their sales for the next year. The company would then use the percentage of cash or credit card sales to predict their cash receipts by month. If the company is a small merchandising company they would probably have 100% of their sales in cash or by credit card. They could predict their sales volume and then discount their credit card sales by the fees they are charged to predict their cash receipts. If the company is charged 4% by the credit card companies then they would plan their cash receipts to be 96% (100% -4%) of their planned sales. If half of their sales are for cash and the half on credit card then they would apply the credit card charges only to the credit card sales. In this case they would plan on the following cash receipts based on sales: (50% + (50%–(50% x 4%) which would equal a plan of 98% of sales becoming cash receipts. This same type of cash receipts planning would be used for restaurants, hotels and motels, health spas and most personal services as these businesses traditionally make all sales either for cash or on credit cards.

The companies that have the hardest time predicting their cash receipts are those companies that have cash sales of 5% or less and the rest of their sales are on credit that they manage. These companies first have to predict their sales the same as the companies that sell for cash but then they have to predict when their customers will pay for the sales on credit. Predicting the cash receipts for these types of companies involves developing company specific models for when collecting of credit sales can be planned. In the chapter on budgeting we assumed collection patterns, but in reality each business has to develop those patterns for their business. Collection patterns cannot be assumed to be consistent from company to company. Each company has aspects of its business that make its collection pattern unique. Each company will have to predict their sales, what percentage of their sales will be on credit, and when the credit sales will be collected. In developing the models the longer the base period that can be used the better but the base period should be at least three years and should be updated at least annually to reflect the most recent information.

The company should have information on sales, accounts receivable balances and collections in the following month for each month of the base period. With this information we can prepare the cash receipts plan. The starting point will be planning the sales amount. We will start with the information in Exhibit 12-1 below:

Exhibit 12-1 – Sales History

Oct-08	820,828
Nov-08	621,716
Dec-08	537,981
Jan-09	505,945
Feb-09	667,062
Mar-09	634,207
Apr-09	794,928
May-09	669,239
Jun-09	765,858
Jul-09	547,586
Aug-09	557,618
Sep-09	1,060,946
Oct-09	1,213,153
Nov-09	381,929
Dec-09	191,446
Jan-10	677,197
Feb-10	661,240
Mar-10	1,538,162
Apr-10	893,838
May-10	729,690
Jun-10	842,401
Jul-10	799,327
Aug-10	478,903
Sep-10	708,344
Oct-10	999,832
Nov-10	894,198
Dec-10	313,063
Jan-11	600,474
Feb-11	651,653
Mar-11	1,042,652
Apr-11	771,959
May-11	700,859
Jun-11	815,035
Jul-11	645,582
Aug-11	459,535
Sep-11	925,866

Based on this history information we can then plan our sales for the next year. If the company has had no major changes in their business or in their competition they can base their sales plan by month on an average of the last three years. The sales plan would be as shown in Exhibit 12-2.

Exhibit 12-2 - Sales Plan

January	594,539
February	659,985
March	1,071,674
April	820,242
May	699,929
June	807,765
July	664,165
August	498,685
September	898,385
October	1,011,271
November	632,614
December	347,497

The next information we would need to consider is the history of the beginning of the month accounts receivable (A/R) balance and the collections in the month. This will allow us to develop a pattern on collections to use in planning our cash receipts in the future. The information needed can usually be found in the company's computerized accounting system. The system should be able to provide the company with information regarding the end of the month accounts receivable balances, the end of the month balances become the beginning of the month balances for the following month. It may be more difficult to obtain the cash collections information from the computerized accounting system. If the system does not have a report that shows the receipts on accounts receivable during the month there are other ways to obtain the information. One way to obtain the information is to look at the bank statements for the months where information is needed and take the amount of total deposits. The next way would be to take the beginning accounts receivable balance, add the month's sales to that amount and subtract the ending accounts receivable balance from it; this will give the collections during the month. The information, once obtained would look like the information in Exhibit 12-3.

Exhibit 12-3 - Accounts Receivable and Cash Collections

	Opening A/R Balance	Cash Collected
Oct-08	1485690	776062
Nov-08	1530456	765326
Dec-08	1386846	953533
Jan-09	971294	578909
Feb-09	898330	488964
Mar-09	1076428	278797
Apr-09	1431838	644931
May-09	1581835	864902
Jun-09	1386172	1037361
Jul-09	1114669	725015
Aug-09	937240	750726
Sep-09	744132	749804
Oct-09	1055274	720547
Nov-09	1547880	577984
Dec-09	1351825	560450
Jan-10	982821	631488
Feb-10	1028530	735536
Mar-10	954234	992655
Apr-10	1499740	884677
May-10	1508902	777357
Jun-10	1461234	967968
Jul-10	1335667	834043
Aug-10	1300951	760480
Sep-10	1019374	867744
Oct-10	859974	724523
Nov-10	1135283	730956
Dec-10	1298525	715789
Jan-11	895799	548408
Feb-11	947865	574217
Mar-11	1025301	615283
Apr-11	1452670	713406
May-11	1511223	796414
Jun-11	1415668	985035
Jul-11	1245668	790999
Aug-11	1100251	734087
Sep-11	825699	720835

From this information we can build a history schedule that shows the collection percentage which we will use to predict cash collections by month. This is shown in Exhibit 12-4 below:

Exhibit 12-4 - Cash Collection Percentages

	Opening A/R Balance	Cash Collected	% Collected
Oct-08	1485690	776062	52.24%
Nov-08	1530456	765326	50.01%
Dec-08	1386846	953533	68.76%
Jan-09	971294	578909	59.60%
Feb-09	898330	488964	54.43%
Mar-09	1076428	278797	25.90%
Apr-09	1431838	644931	45.04%
May-09	1581835	864902	54.68%
Jun-09	1386172	1037361	74.84%
Jul-09	1114669	725015	65.04%
Aug-09	937240	750726	80.10%
Sep-09	744132	749804	100.76%
Oct-09	1055274	720547	68.28%
Nov-09	1547880	577984	37.34%
Dec-09	1351825	560450	41.46%
Jan-10	982821	631488	64.25%
Feb-10	1028530	735536	71.51%
Mar-10	954234	992655	104.03%
Apr-10	1499740	884677	58.99%
May-10	1508902	777357	51.52%
Jun-10	1461234	967968	66.24%
Jul-10	1335667	834043	62.44%
Aug-10	1300951	760480	58.46%
Sep-10	1019374	867744	85.13%
Oct-10	859974	724523	84.25%
Nov-10	1135283	730956	64.39%
Dec-10	1298525	715789	55.12%
Jan-11	895799	548408	61.22%
Feb-11	947865	574217	60.58%
Mar-11	1025301	615283	60.01%
Apr-11	1452670	713406	49.11%
May-11	1511223	796414	52.70%
Jun-11	1415668	985035	69.58%
Jul-11	1245668	790999	63.50%
Aug-11	1100251	734087	66.72%
Sep-11	825699	720835	87.30%

The information would be used to get an average collections percentage, by month, to be applied to the beginning accounts receivable balance, by month, for the next year. We would average the three years' percentages and then we would want to adjust the average for anything unusual. As an example the information above shows the following collection percentages for March: 25.90%; 104.03%; and 60.01%. This gives us an average of 63.31%. In considering what percentage to use for March for planning purposes we are faced with a decision because there is a wide variation in the percentages. We investigate what happened in March for each of the years and we find the following; the company's customers were badly affected by the economic conditions in early 2009 and thus paid slower than normal; the company received a large down payment from a new customer in 2010; and 2011 was a normal year. Based on this additional information the 2011 percentage should be used in the plan. The planned percentages are shown in Exhibit 12-5

Exhibit 12-5 - Planned Collection Percentages

January	61.69%
February	62.17%
March	60.01%
April	51.05%
May	52.97%
June	70.22%
July	63.66%
August	68.43%
September	91.06%
October	68.26%
November	50.58%
December	55.11%

The company has now determined what percentages to use in planning their cash collections. The next step is to estimate the beginning accounts receivable balances to apply the percentages to. All of the information, needed to estimate the balances, is available except the beginning accounts receivable balance for January, for our purpose we will say that the beginning balance is $922,654. The monthly balances can be estimated by taking the beginning balance each month and adding the sales to it and then subtracting the collections from it. The tricky part becomes estimating the collections part and the balance part at the same time. This can be done by setting up a spreadsheet where the known information is entered and the formulas for calculating everything else are in the appropriate cells. The end result will look like Exhibit 12-6.

Exhibit 12-6 - Cash Collections and Beginning Balance Plan

	Beginning A/R Balance	Cash Collections Percentage	Cash Collections	Sales	Ending Balance
January	922,654	61.69%	569,199	594,539	947,994
February	947,994	62.17%	589,411	659,985	1,018,568
March	1,018,568	60.01%	611,242	1,071,674	1,478,999
April	1,478,999	51.05%	754,984	820,242	1,544,257
May	1,544,257	52.97%	817,916	699,929	1,426,270
June	1,426,270	70.22%	1,001,529	807,765	1,232,505
July	1,232,505	63.66%	784,642	664,165	1,112,029
August	1,112,029	68.43%	760,907	498,685	849,807
September	849,807	91.06%	773,855	898,385	974,337
October	974,337	68.26%	665,036	1,011,271	1,320,572
November	1,320,572	50.58%	667,911	632,614	1,285,275
December	1,285,275	55.11%	708,348	347,497	924,425

In the use of the spreadsheet the cash collections are arrived at by multiplying the beginning balance by the collections percentage. The beginning balance and the sales amount are added together and the cash collections subtracted to arrive at the ending balance. The ending balance becomes the beginning balance for the next month. After going through these steps we have arrived at a cash collections plan for the next year..

The example we have been using shows significant fluctuations based on the time of year in both the beginning balance and the collections percentage. A business with this kind of seasonal cash collections will have to be aware of the need to save some cash from the season to help with expenditures during the slow time of year. During the slow time of year the company may need to plan the cash flow on a shorter time frame possibly weekly. The procedures outlined above won't necessarily serve this planning need. The company has some options for short term planning depending upon the capabilities of their computerized accounting system.

If the system has good capabilities it may be possible to trace the average days to pay by customer. If this can be done the company could potentially develop a report that can be run on demand that takes the average days to pay by customer and matches that against open invoices by each customer and then projects the weekly collections for the next 4 to 6 weeks based upon open invoices.

If the system lacks the capabilities described above then the process will need to be more manual in nature. In this case the accountant may need to prepare a schedule showing weekly collections for the slow period for at least the last two years and then by week project the percentage of the beginning

accounts receivable balance that was collected. The information as to weekly collections may need to be taken from the deposits made to the bank which can be obtained from the bank statements or from the deposit slip copies in the deposit book. If the company uses a lockbox for their customers' payments a weekly lockbox report may be available that could be used to develop the history that will be needed for making the projections going forward.

Now that the company has completed their cash collections plan, either long term or short term, it now needs to put together the cash expenditures plan for the same period.

CASH EXPENDITURES

The cash expenditures plan is generally easier than the cash collections plan. Several parts of the cash expenditures plan don't change significantly from year to year. If the business doesn't change significantly from year to year then the cost of wages, salaries and payroll taxes will only change by the amounts of any planned annual wage and salary increases, so it easy to use the current payroll reports and add the percentage change to the amounts. Utilities expenses normally will only change by the percentage increase that the utility company adds to the previous year's amount, there will be some small changes from year to year based on differences in weather but these differences generally aren't significant. Utilities should be planned for based on the bills received by month plus an increase for the amount of rate increase from the utility company. Most business supplies won't change dramatically from year to year either. The main area for concern for most businesses is in the cost of the inventory they use to make and sell to their products to their customers or the products that they buy and resell to their customers. This is of special concern for businesses that use commodities in their business as commodity prices can fluctuate wildly. In this case the company has to make their best estimate based upon the best information available when they put the cash plan together and then adapt quickly to changes in prices.

In our example the company has determined that payroll costs are equal to 10% of sales, utilities are equal to 2% of sales and other expenses (excluding materials) are equal to 8% of sales. Materials are equal to 60% of sales. All expenses are paid in the month of the sales except for the materials which are paid in the month following the month of sales. Based on this information the cash expenditures for operations are shown in Exhibit 12-7.

Exhibit 12-7 - Cash Expenditures for Operations

	Sales	Materials	Labor	Utilities	Other	Total
January	594,539	367,270	59,454	11,891	47,563	486,178
February	659,985	356,723	65,998	13,200	52,799	488,720
March	1,071,674	395,991	107,167	21,433	85,734	610,326
April	820,242	643,004	82,024	16,405	65,619	807,052
May	699,929	492,145	69,993	13,999	55,994	632,131
June	807,765	419,958	80,776	16,155	64,621	581,511
July	664,165	484,659	66,416	13,283	53,133	617,492
August	498,685	398,499	49,869	9,974	39,895	498,236
September	898,385	299,211	89,839	17,968	71,871	478,888
October	1,011,271	539,031	101,127	20,225	80,902	741,285
November	632,614	606,763	63,261	12,652	50,609	733,285
December	347,497	379,569	34,750	6,950	27,800	449,068

The company now has to look at the final items, not included above, that will affect cash, and these are income taxes and equipment purchases. The company has an income tax rate of 30%. This would be applicable to the excess of cash collections over cash expenditures from operations. The total cash collections are $8,704,980 and the total cash expenditures for operations are $7,124,172 which leaves an excess of $1,580,808. This would mean that income taxes would be $474,242 ($1,580,808 x 30%). The company will have to plan for making payments for the taxes (the payments will be due in March, June, September and December). Each payment will be 25% of the total. The company plans to make equipment purchases that total $ 250,000 during the year with half in May and half in September.

With the company having identified all of the components they can now put the cash plan, by month, together. This is shown is exhibit 12-8 below.

CASH PLAN

Exhibit 12-8 – Cash Plan

	Cash Collections	Cash Expenditures	Income Tax	Equipment	Net Cash Flow
January	569,199	486,178			83,021
February	589,411	488,720			100,691
March	611,242	610,326	118,561		-117,644
April	754,984	807,052			-52,069
May	817,916	632,131		125,000	60,786
June	1,001,529	581,511	118,561		301,457
July	784,642	617,492			167,150
August	760,907	498,236			262,671
September	773,855	478,888	118,561	125,000	51,406
October	665,036	741,285			-76,249
November	667,911	733,285			-65,375
December	708,348	449,068	118,561		140,719

The cash plan above shows positive cash flow for most months but shows negative cash flow for four months. Management will have to ensure that they have sufficient cash from the positive months to allow them to get through the negative months. This situation would be normal for many businesses and requires the effective management of cash to ensure sufficient funds to operate year round. This situation could be worse for a business that is highly seasonal.

SUMMARY

This chapter has covered the basics of cash flow planning by looking at ways to predict cash receipts and a brief look at predicting cash disbursements. At the end the company ended up with a cash flow plan by month which shows the months they will have positive cash flow and the months where there will be negative cash flow. The management of the company will need to plan on holding cash from the positive months to ensure that they will have cash for the negative months. Management will also need to make adjustments to account for any differences in sales or expenditures from the plan.

KEY TERMS

- cash collections
- cash disbursements

QUESTIONS

1. What information does a company need to collect to attempt to predict cash receipts if their sales are on credit rather than for cash or on national credit cards?
2. Which part of putting together a cash plan is usually the most difficult?
3. Which cash disbursement is likely to be the most difficult to plan?
4. What cash disbursements do some businesses have other than operating disbursements?
5. What does the business need to do if the cash plan shows negative cash flow in some months?

EXERCISES AND PROBLEMS

12-1. Assume that the sales plan from Exhibit 12-2 and the collection percentages from Exhibit 12-5 relate to XYZ Manufacturing. Using the trial balance in Appendix A to determine the percentages for expenditures put together a cash plan for XYZ Manufacturing. Assume that the company will make expenditures for equipment of $50,000 each in April and August. Use only cash expenses and ignore income taxes.

12-2.

	Opening A/R Balance	Cash Collected
Oct-08	482,585	303,443
Nov-08	437,249	303,971
Dec-08	243,726	206,364
Jan-09	263,766	158,258
Feb-09	418,738	240,610
Mar-09	816,180	675,359
Apr-09	831,628	463,498
May-09	833,484	423,200
Jun-09	1,028,839	933,814
Jul-09	711,387	673,087
Aug-09	379,234	374,491
Sep-09	267,067	237,017
Oct-09	243,841	227,941
Nov-09	243,841	160,527
Dec-09	234,852	171,718
Jan-10	207,719	127,848
Feb-10	210,937	458,545
Mar-10	298,276	716,569
Apr-10	568,032	586,896
May-10	638,343	340,133
Jun-10	654,358	969,337
Jul-10	1,029,775	782,679
Aug-10	838,120	451,833
Sep-10	462,316	285,128
Oct-10	337,147	185,954
Nov-10	311,107	244,033
Dec-10	338,862	243,797

Based on the information above calculate the collection percentages by month that should be used for predicting cash collections for the next year.

12-3. Based on the information shown in 12-2 above and assuming no significant changes plan the sales for the company for the next year. Assume the ending accounts receivable balance for December is $214,222.

12-4. Based on the information in 12-2 above and the information calculated in 12-2 and 12-3 prepare a cash collection plan for the business.

12-5. Assume that the company buys and resells products. Using the calculations in 12-2 through 12-4 above and using the following information prepare a cash plan for the business:

a. Materials cost is 70% of sales and is paid for in the following month.

b. Materials costs to be paid for in January are $162,750.

c. Labor costs are 10% of sales and are paid for in the month of the sales.

d. Other costs are 5% of sales and are paid for in the month of the sales.

e. The company's tax rate is 25% and it makes equal payments in March, June, September and December.

CHAPTER 13 – IMPACT OF TAXES ON SMALL BUSINESS

LEARNING OBJECTIVES

1. The student will understand the payroll taxes paid by small businesses.
2. The student will understand workers' compensation.
3. The student will become familiar with the total tax impact on small business (excluding income taxes).

INTRODUCTION

All businesses pay taxes on the wages and salaries they pay their employees. These taxes are paid at both the state and federal level. In addition companies pay for workers' compensation insurance which is in essence another tax since it is legally mandated in all states. These taxes are a burden on business and especially a burden on small business as they represent a higher portion of expenses for the small business. We will discuss the federal payroll taxes, then the state level payroll taxes and finally workers' compensation.

PAYROLL TAXES

There are payroll taxes paid to the federal, by business, on every employee. The most commonly known payroll tax is Social Security. Social Security is a shared tax in that one half of the tax is withheld from the employee's pay and the other half is paid by the employer. The social security tax rate is 12.4% of wages paid, which means that 6.2% is withheld from the employee and 6.2% is paid by the employer. The total tax of 12.4% means that for every $100 in wages and salaries paid there are taxes of $12.40. Social Security taxes are limited, this means that once an employee's wages exceed an amount specified by law the tax is no longer required to be paid. This amount of the limit changes each year as it is indexed to inflation, in 2012 the limit was $110,100 of wages and for 2013 it is $113,700 of wages. This limit means that Social Security taxes have a maximum of $7,049.40 for each the employee and the employer in 2013. If an employee works for more than one employer the limit applies separately to each employer. If the employee has more than the limit withheld during the year because of working for more than one employer the employee can get the excess refunded on their individual income tax return, however the employers cannot get any of the amounts they paid refunded.

The next federal payroll tax is the Medicare tax. This also is a shared tax between the employee and the employer. The tax rate is 2.9% of wages paid or 1.45% each to the employee and the employer. The total tax rate of 2.9% means that for every $100 of wages paid there are taxes paid of $2.90. Unlike the Social Security tax there is no limit on the amount of wages subject to the tax. All wages paid are subject to withholding and to the employer's matching amount.

The employer has a legal responsibility to track the amounts withheld and the amounts they have to pay to match the withholding and must file a tax return each quarter of the year reporting the amount owed to the federal government and showing the amounts of payments made during the quarter. The deadline for making payment depends upon the amount of taxes due to the federal government. The total taxes due to the federal government also will include any federal income tax withheld from the employees' pay. The quarterly tax return that must be filed to report these taxes is the federal Form 941. A copy of the form is included in Appendix C.

The final federal payroll tax is federal unemployment. Unlike the Social Security tax and the Medicare tax this is not a shared tax as it is paid 100% by the employer. The basic tax rate is 5.4% of wages paid but it is limited to the first $ 7,000 paid to each employee. In addition if the employer is covered by state unemployment there is a credit of 4.8% which means the next amount is .6% as shown on the top of federal Form 940. If the amount owed exceeds $500 in any quarter the employer must pay the amount via electronic transfer at the end of the quarter. Form 940 is only filed at the end of each year and shows the total amount of wages, the amount of wages in excess of $7,000 per employee, the amount of taxable wages and the amount of tax owed for the year. There is a section for showing any payments made during the year and then a place to show any amount still owing. A copy of Form 940 is included in Appendix C.

The purpose of federal unemployment is assist any state whose state unemployment funds run out. The state can then borrow from the funds at the federal level so they can continue to provide unemployment benefits. These loans have to be repaid from the state to the federal government. When a state has borrowed from the federal government it can affect any employer in the state. The first of these effects comes from the federal government as employers, in any state that owes the federal government money for unemployment, will not get the full 4.8% credit for state unemployment. The problem for employers is that they do not know the amount of the credit they will be allowed until the end of the year and they can end up with a large tax bill that is unexpected. As an example of this, the

State of Michigan was particularly hard hit with unemployment during the economic downturn and had to borrow a significant amount of money from the federal unemployment funds. An employer in Michigan was still losing some of the credit in 2011. For one particular employer with 70 employees the unexpected bill at the end of the year was $2,720.00. When you compare this with what the employer originally paid during the year, the taxes almost doubled. The taxes paid during the year were: 70 employees x $7,000 X .006 = $2,940.00. For a small business an expected tax like this can be a serious issue.

This concludes the discussion of federal payroll taxes. We will now move on to state payroll taxes.

Most states impose an unemployment tax on all employers that pay employees located in the state. Like federal unemployment there is a cap on the wages subject to the tax but the cap varies state by state. For example, the cap in Michigan in 2011 was $18,000 in wages for any individual employee while in Montana it is $ 27,000 for any individual employee. This cap applies to each employer that a given employee works for during the year, therefore if the employee works the first half of the year for one employer and exceeds the cap and then goes to work for another employer the wages paid by the new employer start working towards the cap again. If the employee reached the cap at both employers the state will collect double the money for that employee for that year. States that have unemployment taxes have a base rate for new employers that is based on the experience of other employers in the same line of business within the state, the starting rate is usually near the average of the rates for the other employers in the same line of business. The rate is then modified as the company conducts business based on the amount of unemployment claims filed by employees that worked for the individual business. If the experience of the individual business is better than average then their rate will go down and if their experience is worse their rate will go up. The adjustment of rates is normally based on a moving 3 year average of claims. Even if a business has no claims ever they will still have to pay state unemployment tax as there is a minimum rate of tax based on the line of business. Usually the minimum rate of tax is between 3% and 5% of the base taxable wages per employee. If a state owes funds to the federal government they will generally increase the rates for companies in the state to pay the funds back. In the case of Michigan, the state added a surcharge of over 10% to begin to pay the federal government back. As an example a company's rate of 10.3% before the surcharge became 11.4% once the surcharge was added.

Claims are filed by employees when they no longer work for the employer through no fault of the employee. This means that generally if an employee quits or is fired for a valid reason the employee cannot collect unemployment against that employer's account. However, they may be able to collect unemployment against a previous employer's account if the previous employer laid them off.

Generally, the period that the state will look back is 3 years and for an employer to have the claim charged against their account and normally the employee must have worked for the employer for a minimum of 6 months.

As a rule rates are higher for industries that have a higher claim rate than other industries. This would normally affect those businesses that are seasonal in nature more than those businesses that are year round.

Employers are required to file unemployment tax reports for the state on a quarterly basis in most states. The form will usually include a listing of each employee, the employee's social security number and the wages paid by employee for the quarter. There will also be a place to identify the total amount of wages in excess of the taxable limit during the quarter. The net amount will be taxed at the individual company's tax rate. A copy of the unemployment tax report for Montana is shown in Appendix C. This form is very similar to the forms for other states.

Businesses need to manage their payroll taxes by being judicial with hiring and layoffs. Let's look at an example of how this might work. A company feels it needs an additional employee for the busy season. This employee would work for six months and then be laid off. Since the employee would have worked for the employer for six months and would have lost the job through no fault of their own, they would be eligible to collect unemployment benefits. Since this is a six month, full time position the employee will be assumed to work 1040 hours (26 weeks x 40 hours). Before adding this employee the employer had 30 employees, all of whom exceeded the unemployment base of $25,000. The employer's unemployment tax rate is currently 8%. The new employee's wage rate will be $15.00. The average hourly wage for the other employees in the same position is $16.00 per hour. The other option the company has is for the current workers to work overtime at time and one half or $24.00 ($16.00 x 1 1/2) per hour to cover the 1040 hours of additional work needed.

We will discuss the relevant costs involved in this decision. The relevant costs for this decision are: the difference in wage rate between the new worker and overtime of $9.00 per hour ($24–$15); the amount of federal and state unemployment taxes that would be paid to cover the new worker; and the impact of a change in state unemployment tax rate due to the layoff of the seasonal worker, in this case the rate will go to 8.25%.

The analysis of this decision is as follows:

Additional wages paid by using overtime (1040 x $ 9)		$ 9,360
Savings in federal unemployment ($7,000 x .006)	$ 42	
Savings in state unemployment (1040 x $15 x .08)	1,248	
Savings in future unemployment costs ((\$25,000 x 30) x (8.25%–8%) x 3 years)	5,625	
		(6,915)
Net savings by using new worker		$2,445

In this case it would be better for the company to use the new worker for the seasonal workload increase. If the impact on the unemployment tax rate had been to raise it to 8.5% then it would be better for the company to use overtime as the amount of future unemployment costs would have doubled to $11,250 and the total relevant cost savings related to the use of a new worker would have been $12,540 which would have exceeded the cost of the overtime.

We did not consider the cost of Social Security or Medicare taxes in the calculation as they do not differ between the alternatives.

WORKERS' COMPENSATION

Workers' compensation is insurance that covers a business' employees for injuries incurred while performing the necessary functions of their jobs. The insurance will pay for the cost of medical treatment and if the worker is unable to work it will also pay for a portion of lost wages. Although it is insurance it is also a tax as it is mandated by state law in all states. Depending upon the state the employer may have one or more options in how to cover their employees. They may be required to use a state pool, they may be able to be self-insured by filing appropriate paperwork with the state or they may be able to use private insurance through an insurance company, these options will be based on the law in the state(s) in which they conduct business. If the business has employees located in more than one state they will come under different rules and different rates in each state.

The rates charged may be expressed as an hourly rate, a rate per $100 of payroll or as a percentage of pay. The rates are different for different job classifications. To give an example of this we will discuss a hypothetical business that has office employees, salespersons, and warehouse workers. In this case the workers' compensation rates are based on each $100 of payroll. The rates are as follows: office workers, $.29; salespersons, $.61; and warehouse workers, $8.96. The difference in rates is based on the rate of claims due to injuries in each of the job classifications. The warehouse rate is the highest because it is not unusual for warehouse workers to have back or arm strains from lifting items in the warehouse where office workers very seldom have claims.

The management of workers' compensation claims is very important for small businesses are these rates are also based upon the experience of the individual company. As with state unemployment rates there are minimum rates for each classification. A small company can be devastated by one claim based on how it can affect their rates. In most states the rates that a company pays are based on their claims history for the preceding 3 years. This means that a significant claim will continue to affect the company for 3 years after the claim is closed and all amounts are paid.

Let's examine the case of a small company with 10 employees, 2 of which are warehouse employees. The company pays $180,000 per year in office wages (6 employees), $80,000 per year in warehouse wages and $100,000 per year in salespersons wages (2 employees). Their rates are $.25 per $100 paid for office employees; $.50 per $100 paid for salespersons and $5.00 per $100 paid for warehouse personnel. This means that their total workers' compensation costs would be: (($.25 x $180,000 / $100) + ($.50 x $100,000 /$100) + ($5.00 x $80,000 /$100)) = $4,950. If there were to be an accident where one of the warehouse workers was injured and the total cost of the claim was $10,000 their workers' compensation rate for warehouse workers would increase to approximately $9.16 per $100 paid. This means that the new annual cost of workers' compensation would be: (($.25 x $180,000 / $100) + ($.50 x $100,000 /$100) + ($9.16 x $80,000 /$100)) = $ 8,278 or an increase of 67%. This new rate would remain in effect until three years after the final expenses were paid on the claim.

Based on the example above it is easy to see why it is important for businesses to maintain a safe workplace and conduct safety training regularly in order to avoid injuries.

Unlike unemployment compensation there is no minimum time an employee has to work for an employer before they are covered by workers' compensation. This makes the management of workers' compensation an important function for small business managers and owners.

Let's take the an example where we hire an employee expecting to keep them for 6 months which means they would be eligible for unemployment. However, the business volume falls off after four months so we need to lay the person off earlier than planned. The employee now will not be eligible for unemployment. If we tell the person ahead of time that they are going to be laid off at a certain date, the individual could sustain an injury, before being laid off, that allows them to continue to be paid partial wages through workers' compensation when they would not have be able receive unemployment benefits. We are going to assume that the worker is a warehouse worker and that his wage rate was $12 per hour. His injury is a back strain and his medical bills total $ 1,000 and he is able to

continue to collect 2/3 of his pay for six weeks due to the injury. The amount of workers' compensation he is able to collect is: $1,920 ($12 x 2/3 x 240 hours), this makes the total cost of the injury $3,940. Using the same company as we did before this would raise the warehouse to approximately $6.64 per $100 paid. This would increase the company's workers compensation costs by approximately $1,312 per year for the next 3 years.

In this case, if the injury is questionable, the company is incurring additional costs for 3 years because they gave the employee advanced warning of the lay off. If the management wants to manage their workers' compensation costs they should not tell the employee until the end of the last day of his employment unless required to give advance notice by law.

The total payroll tax burden on small business is a key cost in running the operation. We are going to use the example of the small business with 10 employees used above to illustrate the total cost of payroll related taxes for the company. The company pays total wages of $360,000 ($180,000 + $80,000 + $100,000). On these wages the business would have the following taxes:

Social Security taxes ($360,000 x 6.2%)	$ 22,320
Medicare taxes ($360,000 x 1.45%)	5,220
Federal unemployment taxes (10 x $7,000 x .6%)	420
State unemployment (10 x $25,000 x 5%)	12,500
Workers' compensation (calculated above)	4,950
Total	$ 45,410

This means that in this case, where we have assumed the minimums, the total payroll tax burden is 12.61% ($45,410 / $360,000). This represents a significant amount of money for a small business. If we were to assume some of the cases presented throughout the chapter the analysis would look like this.

Social Security taxes ($360,000 x 6.2%)	$ 22,320
Medicare taxes ($360,000 x 1.45%)	5,220
Federal unemployment taxes (10 x $7,000 x .6%)	420
Federal unemployment additional ($ 2,720 / $2,940 x $420) 388	
State unemployment (10 x $25,000 x 11.4%)	28,500
Workers' compensation (calculated above)	8,278
Total	$ 65,126

This now represents 18.09% of payroll. If the company is in a state that owes the federal government funds for borrowing unemployment and also has not managed their unemployment and workers' compensation well the payroll tax burden can strangle the company.

SUMMARY

In this chapter we have discussed payroll taxes imposed upon a business by both the federal and state governments. We have also discussed how to weigh the impacts of payroll taxes in a decision involving short term hiring versus using overtime. We then discussed workers' compensation and again explored a scenario where the cost of workers' compensation could be impacted for the future and a possible way to eliminate the negative impact. We then brought the total costs of these payroll related taxes together to show the burden they place on small business.

KEY TERMS

- Social Security Tax
- Medicare Tax
- Federal unemployment tax
- State unemployment tax
- Workers' compensation

EXERCISES AND PROBLEMS

13-1. Based on the trial balance for ABC Hospital Corporation, in Appendix A, calculate the total payroll tax burden for the company in both dollars and as a percentage of payroll.

13-2. Based on the trial balance for Double Bar Ranch and Cattle Company, in Appendix A, calculate the total payroll tax burden for the company in both dollars and as a percentage of payroll.

13-3. Based on the trial balance for Local Hardware Company, in Appendix A, calculate the total payroll tax burden for the company in both dollars and as a percentage of payroll.

13-4. Based on the trial balance for XYZ Manufacturing, Inc., in Appendix A, calculate the total payroll tax burden for the company in both dollars and as a percentage of payroll. This should be calculated for the production area, the selling and administrative area and the company as a whole. Be sure to include workers' compensation.

CHAPTER 14 – OVERVIEW OF FEDERAL INCOME TAXES

LEARNING OBJECTIVES

1. The student will understand what tax forms are used for a sole proprietorship.
2. The student will understand what main tax forms are used for a partnership.
3. The student will understand what tax forms are used for a corporation.
4. The student will understand what tax forms are used for special entities.

INTRODUCTION

This chapter is presented so that business owners or managers that have the responsibility for reviewing and/or signing tax returns will be able to tell if the information is being entered on the proper form. Any small business will need to file the tax forms appropriate for it based upon its legal structure. The legal structure can be a sole proprietorship, a partnership, a corporation or a special entity such as an S Corporation or an L.L.C. Each of these business types has specific forms that need to be filed for its federal income tax. Also, the type of business, as well as the legal structure, may make a difference in the form(s) required. All businesses that have depreciable assets will include form 4562 in their tax filing. This form relates to all business types and legal structures. In this chapter we are going to briefly cover the forms required based on the business type and legal structure. We will only be discussing businesses entered into for profit. Not for profit businesses have special forms and those will not be discussed.

SOLE PROPRIETORSHIP

A sole proprietorship is a business that is owned by one individual and has not adopted any legal structure that would require specific legal documentation. This type of business could be very small or could be quite large depending upon the business. The business could also be in any industry or could be as simple as a family farm. In filing income taxes related to a sole proprietorship all forms that are required for the specific business are filed with the individual's personal income tax return and are schedules that are attached to the form 1040 filed by the individual. Depending upon the business transactions during the year the forms and schedules that will be attached to the form 1040 can be relatively simple or quite involved.

For purposes of our discussion we are going to assume a small business without any transactions that would add more forms or that would make the tax filing more complex. We will deal with a simple small business that has some depreciable assets and discuss the tax forms and schedules required for that. If the business is not farming or a ranch then the individual will need to have a Schedule C for form 1040 prepared to reflect the business activities during the year, a sample of Schedule C is included in Appendix C. In the case of a business with depreciable assets there will also need to be a form 4562 added to the return to report the information on the depreciable assets. The depreciation from form 4562 is carried over to the Schedule C and reflected on the appropriate line. If the business sells products it will be required to fill out the cost of goods section that is on page 2 of the Schedule C. This calculation for taxes may vary slightly from the calculations that have been shown in earlier chapters of this book. Generally the Schedule C is prepared on the cash basis of accounting as the taxpayer prepares his/her entire form 1040 on the cash basis of accounting.

Once the Schedule C is completed then the net profit is carried to both the front page of form 1040 and to the Schedule SE for form 1040. Schedule SE is used to calculate the self-employment taxes owed by the owner. The self-employment taxes represent the combined Social Security and Medicare taxes that would have been paid by both the individual and the business had the owner worked for someone else. As was discussed in the last chapter the base combined rate for Social Security is 12.4% subject to the earnings limit and the base combined rate for Medicare is 2.9% and there is no limit on the earnings subject to the tax. This combined tax rate is 15.3% given the two base rates. There is a Schedule SE included in Appendix C. This form shows the combined rate for the taxes at 13.3% because for 2012 there was a temporary reduction in the Social Security tax.

If the business is a farm or ranch then the taxpayer will need to Schedule F for form 1040 prepared instead of Schedule C. Schedule F has been adapted to reflect those features that are unique to farming when the farm is a sole proprietorship. The income section is different than Schedule C and there is no section for calculating the cost of goods sold. Normally the Schedule F would be prepared using the cash basis of accounting but if the owner wishes to use the accrual basis of accounting then the section on page 2, of Schedule F, would need to be completed. A Schedule F is included in Appendix C. Once the Schedule F is completed then, like the Schedule C, the net income will need to be brought over to page 1 of form 1040 and to the Schedule SE.

The Schedule F is designed only to be used when a proprietor has a producing farm where he or she is actively involved. If the farm owner is not actively involved in the operation of the farm but instead rents the farm to another party that does the production then a Schedule F would not be appropriate. The taxpayer would then use a form 4835 which would be attached to their form 1040. A form 4835 is included in Appendix C. The net income from form 4835 is brought for to a schedule E (included in Appendix C) and combined with other items before going to page 1 of form 1040. If the farm is rented and therefore reported on form 4835 the net income is not subject to self-employment tax and therefore no Schedule SE is required.

Now we will move on for a brief discussion of tax forms for partnerships.

PARTNERSHIP

A partnership is a business organization that has two or more owners who have agreed to do business as a partnership. Normally, there is a partnership agreement that spells out certain areas of agreement such as: the amount that each partner is going to invest in the partnership; how the profits will be divided and how the management of the partnership will be run. There does not have to be a formal written partnership agreement for a partnership to exist.

A partnership has a special tax return just for its use, the form 1065 (included in Appendix C). This form is used to report the income from partnership activities. The form 1065 is relatively straight forward for the reporting of income on a tax basis, however, there can be differences between accounting income for financial statement purposes and income for income tax purposes. If this occurs then the reconciliation of accounting income to tax income makes the form become more complex. If the business sells products then there will need to be a calculation for cost of goods sold on form 1125-A (included in Appendix C) which is brought forward to page 1 of the form 1065. Like the calculation on schedule C this may vary somewhat from the calculations we have shown in earlier chapters of this book. The partnership will also need form 4562 if they have depreciable assets.

The partnership does not pay federal income tax but rather the net income of the partnership flows through to the individual partners, based on their individual shares, for reporting on their personal income tax. The flow through amount of income is reported on Schedule E before it comes through to page 1 of form 1040. There may also be other items from the partnership that will need to be reported on form 1040 these items will be shown on a Schedule K-1 that the individual partners will receive based on the information on form 1065.

Normally the income that flows through from the partnership is subject to self-employment income and therefore would need to be reported on Schedule SE. This means that the individual partner will have the responsibility to pay this tax in addition to the income tax on the profits of the partnership.

We will now move on to a discussion of taxes for corporations.

CORPORATION

A corporation is a legal entity that is separate from it owners and it requires that there be formal articles of incorporation be prepared and filed with the Secretary of State for the state where the business is incorporated.

A corporation has a tax form that is separate from any forms required by the owners. The corporation files and pays its taxes separately from the owners. The corporation tax form is form 1120 (included in Appendix C). This form is filed separately and signed by an officer, the officer may or may not be an owner. Like the other business forms we have discussed the corporation will have to include form 4562 if it has depreciable assets. Like the partnership the corporation will have to attach form 1125-A to show the calculation of cost of goods sold if the business sells products.

Since the corporation is a separate legal entity and has its own taxes nothing from the corporate tax return flows through to the owners tax returns. A corporation that is completely separate from its owners for tax purposes is referred to as a C corporation.

We will now move on to a discussion of special entities.

SPECIAL ENTITIES

In terms of federal income tax, a special entity is any type of organization (excluding not for profit organizations) that is not one of the organization types previously described. These special entities have special rules and may have their own tax return forms. The first type of special entity we will discuss is a limited liability corporation (LLC). This is basically a partnership that has been legally organized under the laws of the state it was organized in, to take advantages of some items that make the corporation form of business more desirable while retaining some of the aspects of the partnership form of business. A LLC is most often taxed as a partnership and thus files form 1065. It has all of the other same requirements regarding taxes as a partnership. For the description of these items refer to the discussion of partnerships above.

The other special entity we are going to discuss is an S corporation. An S corporation is a corporation that has elected to be taxed differently from a C corporation. The difference is that the corporation's profits flow through to the individuals owners and are reported on the owners' tax returns. An S corporation uses form 1120S (included in Appendix C) for filing of its tax return. This form has parts that are similar to both a form 1065 (partnerships) and a form 1120 (corporations). The flow through of income is reported on Schedule E of the form 1040. Like a partnership there may be other tax items that affect the owners and these will be reported on a Schedule K-1. In this case the corporation pays no separate income tax. There are limitations regarding what corporations can elect to be taxed this way. The most common limitations are that there cannot be any owners that are not U.S. citizens and there is a limitation on the total number of stockholders (owners).

Both of these special entities would use form 4562 if they have depreciable assets and would use form 1125-A to calculate the cost of goods sold if the business sells products.

SUMMARY

In this chapter we have given a brief overview of federal income taxes for businesses based on the legal structure of the business. There has been a brief discussion of sole proprietorships, partnerships, corporations and special entities (LLC and S corporations). This has included a brief overview of which tax forms are appropriate for each entity.

KEY TERMS

- Sole proprietorship
- Partnership
- Corporation
- Limited Liability Corporation
- S Corporation

EXERCISES AND PROBLEMS

14-1 Assume that Local Hardware Store shown on the trial balance in Appendix A is a sole proprietorship. Prepare a Schedule C based upon the trial balance and the following information: the cost of labor includes the amounts shown for salaries and wages, payroll taxes and benefits; the amount shown as cost of sales in the trial balance is the amount of purchases; and the beginning inventory was $145,750. Ignore any header information and form 4562.

14-2 Assume that Double Bar Ranch and Cattle Company shown in the trial balance in Appendix A is a sole proprietorship. Prepare a Schedule F based on the trial balance and the following information: ranch labor, payroll taxes and benefits equal the cost of labor; the cost of goods sold on the trial balance represents the cost of products with no adjustment needed for changes in inventory; and the cost of feed and water is part of the cost of goods sold for the tax return. Ignore any header information and form 4562.

14-3 Assume that XYZ Manufacturing, Inc. shown in the trial balance in Appendix A is an LLC that is taxed as a partnership. Prepare the first page of form 1065 and form 1125-A. Assume the following information: the cost of labor should include direct labor, indirect labor and supervisory salaries as well as the payroll taxes, benefits and workers' compensation related to them; the purchases should be equal to the amount shown as material cost of goods sold; all of the other costs shown between the spaces, except depreciation should be treated as other costs for form 1125-A; and the beginning inventory, net of the reserve for inventory shrink was $1,215,776. Ignore any header information and form 4562.

14-4 Assume that ABC Hospital Corporation shown in the trial balance in Appendix A is a C corporation. Prepare the first page of form 1120 (through line 28) and form 1125-A for the corporation. The following information is needed to prepare the return: beginning inventory was $4,250; the purchases are equal to the amounts shown on the trial balance for patient supplies, surgical supplies, laboratory supplies, emergency room supplies and pharmacy cost of sales; the cost of labor is equal to the lab technician wages, the pharmacy salaries and payroll taxes equal to 10% of the combined wages for these two areas. Ignore any header information and form 4562.

INDEX

T

U

V

W

Z

APPENDIX A

ILLUSTRATIVE TRIAL BALANCES

ABC Hospital Corporation
Trial Balance
December 31, 20xx

Cash	372,425
Accounts receivable	783,558
Allowance for bad debts	(80,525)
Inventory	3,575
Property, plant and equipment	1,145,165
Accumulated depreciation	(408,988)
Other assets	89,030
Accounts payable	(476,581)
Accrued expenses	(63,224)
Long term debt	(258,725)
Common stock	(500,000)
Retained earnings	(488,252)
Inpatient revenue	(3,053,910)
Outpatient revenue	(469,832)
Surgical revenue	(652,177)
Laboratory revenue	(313,442)
Pharmacy revenue	(208,962)
Patient supplies	442,817
Surgical supplies	114,130
Emergency room supplies	70,475
Laboratory supplies	31,344
Pharmacy cost of sales	104,481

Physicians salaries	657,707
Nursing salaries & wages	1,221,457
Lab technicians wages	141,049
Pharmacy salaries	73,137
Housekeeping wages	124,782
Payroll taxes	221,817
Maintenance wages	162,357
Payroll taxes - maintenance	16,235
Benefits	99,816
Benefits - maintenance	7,306
Depreciation	163,595
Electricity	202,616
Natural gas	72,851
Other utilities	55,224
Administrative salaries	252,341
Administrative payroll taxes	25,234
Administrative benefits	12,617
Advertising	75,422
Office supplies	45,789
Postage	24,782
Interest	122,331
Income taxes	39,153

Double Bar Ranch and Cattle Company
Trial Balance
December 31, 20xx

Cash	275,000
Account receivable	560,000
Allowance for bad debts	(5,000)
Inventory	1,350,000
Other current assets	156,000
Land	250,000
Buildings	850,000
Equipment & vehicles	1,650,000
Accumulated depreciation	(611,000)
Other non-current assets	425,000
Accounts payable	(196,000)
Short-term notes payable	(1,078,000)
Income taxes payable	(37,500)
Other current liabilities	(294,000)
Long term debt	(1,150,000)
Common stock	(500,000)
Retained earnings	(1,382,000)
Net sales	(5,390,000)
Cost of goods sold	100,000
Ranch labor	450,000
Payroll taxes on ranch labor	45,000
Benefits for ranch labor	150,000

Cost of feed/grazing fees	2,000,000
Cost of water	350,000
Veterinary fees	250,000
Repairs	350,000
Transportation expense	550,000
Utilities	300,000
Depreciation expense	200,000
Miscellaneous expenses	100,000
Interest expense	245,000
Income taxes	37,500

XYZ Manufacturing, Inc.

Trial Balance

December 31, 20xx

Cash	99,742
Accounts receivable	1,111,022
Allowance for doubtful accounts	(47,768)
Finished goods inventory	545,122
Work in process inventory	286,818
Raw materials inventory	437,789
Reserve for inventory shrink/obs	(115,842)
Land	300,000
Building	700,000
Machinery/equipment	4,083,353
Accumulated depreciation	(659,339)
Accumulated amortization of intangibles	(256,228)
Intangibles	1,165,865
Accounts payable	(371,113)
Accrued expenses	(322,146)
Long term revolving loan	(855,006)
Common stock	(1,695,000)
Paid in capital	(611,396)
Retained earnings	(3,614,244)
Sales	(9,135,000)
Sales returns	21,504

Cash deduction allowance	45,906
Freight out	25,908
MANUAFACTURING EXPENSES	
Material - cost of goods sold	2,034,509
Freight-in	195,110
Direct labor	902,644
Indirect labor- manufacturing	296,425
Group insurance	193,970
Workers compensation	250,824
Payroll taxes - production workers	156,386
Manufacturing supplies	328,634
Perishable/portable tools	121,788
Machine repair and maintenance	150,669
Electricity	235,559
Natural gas	108,310
Water	4,645
Obsolete inventory and shrink	75,016
Scrap from work in process	240,669
Hourly vacation expense	80,961
Hourly holiday expense	22,348
Supervisory salaries	143,285
Other production salaries	100,839

Group insurance	18,375
Payroll taxes production salaries	29,823
Travel & lodging	366
Meals & entertainment	33
Office supplies	275
Environmental	1,554
Rental items expense	5,629
Waste disposal - trash	2,537
Security services	10,209
Janitorial service	13,521
Janitorial supplies	321
Packaging/shipping supplies	5,672
Depreciation	557,414
Property tax	94,988
General insurance	245,788

SELLING AND ADMINISTRATIVE EXPENSES

Salaries	1,128,791
Group insurance	139,062
Payroll taxes - salaries	129,399
Travel & entertainment	54,212
Dues & subscriptions	3,931
Engineering testing	80,891
Office supplies	40,838

Postage	13,036
Payroll service	9,944
Legal - general	100,009
Annual audit	50,693
Hardware lease	36,651
Hardware maintenance	9,895
Software maintenance	18,121
Software license agreements	15,687
Commissions	5,878
Advertising	53,704
Depreciation	2,484
Amortization of intangibles	192,560
Other taxes	32,794
Telephone	10,374
Interest expense	102,000

APPENDIX B

PRESENT VALUE TABLES

Present Value of $1 Due in *n* Periods

Factor = $\frac{1}{(1+r)^n}$

Periods	1%	2%	3%	4%	5%	6%	7%	8%	9%	10%	12%	14%	15%	16%	18%	20%	24%
1	0.9901	0.9804	0.9709	0.9615	0.9524	0.9434	0.9346	0.9259	0.9174	0.9091	0.8929	0.8772	0.8696	0.8621	0.8475	0.8333	0.8065
2	0.9803	0.9612	0.9426	0.9426	0.9070	0.8900	0.8734	0.8573	0.8417	0.8264	0.7972	0.7695	0.7561	0.7432	0.7182	0.6944	0.6504
3	0.9706	0.9423	0.9151	0.8890	0.8638	0.8396	0.8163	0.7938	0.7722	0.7513	0.7118	0.6750	0.6575	0.6407	0.6086	0.5787	0.5245
4	0.9610	0.9238	0.8885	0.8548	0.8227	0.7921	0.7629	0.7350	0.7084	0.6830	0.6355	0.5921	0.5718	0.5523	0.5158	0.4823	0.4230
5	0.9515	0.9057	0.8626	0.8219	0.7835	0.7473	0.7130	0.6806	0.6499	0.6209	0.5674	0.5194	0.4972	0.4761	0.43731	0.4019	0.3411
6	0.9420	0.8880	0.8375	0.7903	0.7462	0.7050	0.6663	0.6302	0.5963	0.5645	0.5066	0.4556	0.4323	0.4104	0.3704	0.3349	0.2751
7	0.9327	0.8706	0.8131	0.7599	0.7107	0.6651	0.6227	0.5835	0.5470	0.5132	0.4523	0.3996	0.3759	0.3538	0.3139	0.2791	0.2218
8	0.9235	0.8535	0.7894	0.7307	0.6768	0.6274	0.5820	0.5403	0.5019	0.4665	0.4039	0.3506	0.3269	0.3050	0.2660	0.2326	0.1789
9	0.9143	0.8368	0.7664	0.7026	0.6446	0.5919	0.5439	0.5002	0.4604	0.4241	0.3606	0.3075	0.2843	0.2630	0.2255	0.1938	0.1443
10	0.9053	0.8203	0.7441	0.6756	0.6139	0.5584	0.5083	0.4632	0.4224	0.3855	0.3220	0.2697	0.2472	0.2267	0.1911	0.1615	0.1164
11	0.8963	0.8043	0.7224	0.6496	0.5847	0.5268	0.4751	0.4289	0.3875	0.3505	0.2875	0.2366	0.2149	0.1954	0.1619	0.1346	0.0938
12	0.8874	0.7885	0.7014	0.6246	0.5568	0.4970	0.4440	0.3971	0.3555	0.3186	0.2567	0.2076	0.1869	0.1685	0.1372	0.1122	0.0757
13	0.8787	0.7730	0.6810	0.6006	0.5303	0.4688	0.4150	0.3677	0.3262	0.2897	0.2292	0.1821	0.1625	0.1452	0.1163	0.0935	0.0610
14	0.8700	0.7579	0.6611	0.5775	0.5051	0.4423	0.3878	0.3405	0.2992	0.2633	0.2046	0.1597	0.1413	0.1252	0.0985	0.0779	0.0492
15	0.8613	0.7430	0.6419	0.5553	0.4810	0.4173	0.3624	0.3152	0.2745	0.2394	0.1827	0.1401	0.1229	0.1079	0.0835	0.0649	0.0397
16	0.8528	0.7284	0.6232	0.5339	0.4581	0.3936	0.3387	0.2919	0.2519	0.2176	0.1631	0.1229	0.1069	0.0930	0.0708	0.0541	0.0320
17	0.8444	0.7142	0.6050	0.5134	0.4363	0.3714	0.3166	0.2703	0.2311	0.1978	0.1456	0.1078	0.0929	0.0802	0.0600	0.0451	0.0258
18	0.8360	0.7002	0.5874	0.4936	0.4155	0.3503	0.2959	0.2502	0.2120	0.1799	0.1300	0.0946	0.0808	0.0691	0.0508	0.0376	0.0208
19	0.8277	0.6864	0.5703	0.4746	0.3957	0.3305	0.2765	0.2317	0.1945	0.1635	0.1161	0.0829	0.0703	0.0596	0.0431	0.0313	0.0168
20	0.8195	0.6730	0.5537	0.4564	0.3769	0.3118	0.2584	0.2145	0.1784	0.1486	0.1037	0.0728	0.0611	0.0514	0.0365	0.0261	0.0135
21	0.8114	0.6598	0.5375	0.4388	0.3589	0.2942	0.2415	0.1987	0.1637	0.1351	0.0926	0.0638	0.0531	0.0443	0.0309	0.0217	0.0109
22	0.8034	0.6468	0.5219	0.4220	0.3418	0.2775	0.2257	0.1839	0.1502	0.1228	0.0826	0.0560	0.0462	0.0382	0.0262	0.0181	0.0088
23	0.7954	0.6342	0.5067	0.4057	0.3256	0.2618	0.2109	0.1703	0.1378	0.1117	0.0738	0.0491	0.0402	0.0329	0.0222	0.0151	0.0071
24	0.7876	0.6217	0.4919	0.3901	0.3101	0.2470	0.1971	0.1577	0.1264	0.1015	0.0659	0.0431	0.0349	0.0284	0.0188	0.0126	0.0057
25	0.7798	0.6095	0.4776	0.3751	0.2953	0.2330	0.1842	0.1460	0.1160	0.0923	0.0588	0.0378	0.0304	0.0245	0.0160	0.0105	0.0046
26	0.7720	0.5976	0.4637	0.3607	0.2812	0.2198	0.1722	0.1352	0.1064	0.0839	0.0525	0.0331	0.0264	0.0211	0.0135	0.0087	0.0037
27	0.7644	0.5859	0.4502	0.3468	0.2678	0.2074	0.1609	0.1252	0.0976	0.0763	0.0469	0.0291	0.0230	0.0182	0.0115	0.0073	0.0030
28	0.7568	0.5744	0.4371	0.3335	0.2551	0.1956	0.1504	0.1159	0.0895	0.0693	0.0419	0.0255	0.0200	0.0157	0.0097	0.0061	0.0024
29	0.7493	0.5631	0.4243	0.3207	0.2429	0.1846	0.1406	0.1073	0.0822	0.0630	0.0374	0.0224	0.0174	0.0135	0.0082	0.0051	0.0020
30	0.7419	0.5521	0.4120	0.3083	0.2314	0.1741	0.1314	0.0994	0.0754	0.0573	0.0334	0.0196	0.0151	0.0116	0.0070	0.0042	0.0016

Present Value of an Annuity of $1 per Period

$$\text{Factor} = \frac{1 - \frac{1}{(1+r)^n}}{r}$$

Periods	1%	2%	3%	4%	5%	6%	7%	8%	9%	10%	12%	14%	15%	16%	18%	20%	24%
								r									
1	0.9901	0.9804	0.9709	0.9615	0.9524	0.9434	0.9346	0.9259	0.9174	0.9091	0.8929	0.8772	0.8696	0.8621	0.8475	0.8333	0.8065
2	1.9704	1.9416	1.9135	1.8861	1.8594	1.8334	1.8080	1.7833	1.7591	1.7355	1.6901	1.6467	1.6257	1.6052	1.5656	1.5278	1.4568
3	2.9410	2.8839	2.8286	2.7751	2.7232	2.6730	2.6243	2.5771	2.5313	2.4869	2.4018	2.3216	2.2832	2.2459	2.1743	2.1065	1.9813
4	3.9020	3.8077	3.7171	3.6299	3.5460	3.4651	3.3872	3.3121	3.2397	3.1699	3.0373	2.9137	2.8550	2.7982	2.6901	2.5887	2.4043
5	4.8534	4.7135	4.5797	4.4518	4.3295	4.2124	4.1002	3.9927	3.8897	3.7908	3.6048	3.4331	3.3522	3.2743	3.1272	2.9906	2.7454
6	5.7955	5.6014	5.4172	5.2421	5.0757	4.9173	4.7665	4.6229	4.4859	4.3553	4.1114	3.8887	3.7845	3.6847	3.4976	3.3255	3.0205
7	6.7282	6.4720	6.2303	6.0021	5.7864	5.5824	5.3893	5.2064	5.0330	4.8684	4.5638	4.2883	4.1604	4.0386	3.8115	3.6046	3.2423
8	7.6517	7.3255	7.0197	6.7327	6.4632	6.2098	5.9713	5.7466	5.5348	5.3349	4.9676	4.6389	4.4873	4.3436	4.0776	3.8372	3.4212
9	8.5660	8.1622	7.7861	7.4353	7.1078	6.8017	6.5152	6.2469	5.9952	5.7590	5.3282	4.9464	4.7716	4.6065	4.3030	4.0310	3.5655
10	9.4713	8.9826	8.5302	8.1109	7.7217	7.3601	7.0236	6.7101	6.4177	6.1446	5.6502	5.2161	5.0188	4.8332	4.4941	4.1925	3.6819
11	10.3676	9.7868	9.2526	8.7605	8.3064	7.8869	7.4987	7.1390	6.8052	6.4951	5.9377	5.4527	5.2337	5.0286	4.6560	4.3271	3.7757
12	11.2551	10.5753	9.9540	9.3851	8.8633	8.3838	7.9427	7.5361	7.1607	6.8137	6.1944	5.6603	5.4206	5.1971	4.7932	4.4392	3.8514
13	12.1337	11.3484	10.6350	9.9856	9.3936	8.8527	8.3577	7.9038	7.4869	7.1034	6.4235	5.8424	5.5831	5.3423	4.9095	4.5327	3.9124
14	13.0037	12.1062	11.2961	10.5631	9.8986	9.2950	8.7455	8.2442	7.7862	7.3667	6.6283	6.0021	5.7245	5.4675	5.0081	4.6106	3.9616
15	13.8651	12.8493	11.9379	11.1184	10.3797	9.7122	9.1079	8.5595	8.0607	7.6061	6.8109	6.1422	5.8474	5.5755	5.0916	4.6755	4.0013
16	14.7179	13.5777	12.5611	11.6523	10.8378	10.1059	9.4466	8.8514	8.3126	7.8237	6.9740	6.2651	5.9542	5.6685	5.1624	4.7296	4.0333
17	15.5623	14.2919	13.1661	12.1657	11.2741	10.4773	9.7632	9.1216	8.5436	8.0216	7.1196	6.3729	6.0472	5.7487	5.2223	4.7746	4.0591
18	16.3983	14.9920	13.7535	12.6593	11.6896	10.8276	10.0591	9.3719	8.7556	8.2014	7.2497	6.4674	6.1280	5.8178	5.2732	4.8122	4.0799
19	17.2260	15.6785	14.3238	13.1339	12.0853	11.1581	10.3356	9.6036	8.9501	8.3649	7.3658	6.5504	6.1982	5.8775	5.3162	4.8435	4.0967
20	18.0456	16.3514	14.8775	13.5903	12.4622	11.4699	10.5940	9.8181	9.1285	8.5136	7.4694	6.6231	6.2593	5.9288	5.3527	4.8696	4.1103
21	18.8570	17.0112	15.4150	14.0292	12.8212	11.7641	10.8355	10.0168	9.2922	8.6487	7.5620	6.6870	6.3125	5.9731	5.3837	4.8913	4.1212
22	19.6604	17.6580	15.9369	14.4511	13.1630	12.0416	11.0612	10.2007	9.4424	8.7715	7.6446	6.7429	6.3587	6.0113	5.4099	4.9094	4.1300
23	20.4558	18.2922	16.4436	14.8568	13.4886	12.3034	11.2722	10.3711	9.5802	8.8832	7.7184	6.7921	6.3988	6.0422	5.4321	4.9245	4.1371
24	21.2434	18.9139	16.9355	15.2470	13.7986	12.5504	11.4693	10.5288	9.7066	8.9847	7.7843	6.8351	6.4338	6.0726	5.4509	4.9371	4.1428
25	22.0232	19.5235	17.4131	15.6221	14.0939	12.7834	11.6536	10.6748	9.8226	9.0770	7.8431	6.8729	6.4641	6.0971	5.4669	4.9476	4.1474
26	22.7952	20.1210	17.8768	15.9828	14.3752	13.0332	11.8258	10.8100	9.9290	9.1609	7.8957	6.9061	6.4906	6.1182	5.4804	4.9563	4.1511
27	23.5596	20.7069	18.3270	16.3296	14.6430	13.2105	11.9867	10.9352	10.0266	9.2372	7.9426	6.9352	6.5135	6.1364	5.4919	4.9636	4.1542
28	24.3164	21.2813	18.7641	16.6631	14.8981	13.4062	12.1371	11.0511	10.1161	9.3066	7.9844	6.9607	6.5335	6.1520	5.5016	4.9697	4.1566
29	25.0658	21.8444	19.1885	16.9837	15.1411	13.5907	12.2777	11.1584	10.1983	9.3696	8.0218	6.9830	6.5509	6.1656	5.5098	4.9747	4.1585
30	25.8077	22.3965	19.6004	17.2920	15.3725	13.7648	12.4090	11.2578	10.2737	9.4269	8.0552	7.0027	6.5660	6.1772	5.5168	4.9789	4.1601

APPENDIX C

TAX FORMS

SCHEDULE C (Form 1040)

Department of the Treasury
Internal Revenue Service (99)

Profit or Loss From Business
(Sole Proprietorship)

▶ For information on Schedule C and its instructions, go to *www.irs.gov/schedulec*.

▶ Attach to Form 1040, 1040NR, or 1041; partnerships generally must file Form 1065.

OMB No. 1545-0074

2012

Attachment Sequence No. **09**

Name of proprietor	Social security number (SSN)
A Principal business or profession, including product or service (see instructions)	B Enter code from instructions ▶
C Business name. If no separate business name, leave blank.	D Employer ID number (EIN), (see instr.)

E Business address (including suite or room no.) ▶
City, town or post office, state, and ZIP code

F Accounting method: (1) ☐ Cash (2) ☐ Accrual (3) ☐ Other (specify) ▶

G Did you "materially participate" in the operation of this business during 2012? If "No," see instructions for limit on losses . ☐ Yes ☐ No

H If you started or acquired this business during 2012, check here . . . ▶ ☐

I Did you make any payments in 2012 that would require you to file Form(s) 1099? (see instructions) . . . ☐ Yes ☐ No

J If "Yes," did you or will you file required Forms 1099? . . . ☐ Yes ☐ No

Part I Income

1	Gross receipts or sales. See instructions for line 1 and check the box if this income was reported to you on Form W-2 and the "Statutory employee" box on that form was checked . . . ▶ ☐	1	
2	Returns and allowances (see instructions) . . .	2	
3	Subtract line 2 from line 1 . . .	3	
4	Cost of goods sold (from line 42) . . .	4	
5	**Gross profit.** Subtract line 4 from line 3 . . .	5	
6	Other income, including federal and state gasoline or fuel tax credit or refund (see instructions) . . .	6	
7	**Gross income.** Add lines 5 and 6 . . . ▶	7	

Part II Expenses

Enter expenses for business use of your home only on line 30.

8	Advertising . . .	8		18	Office expense (see instructions)	18	
9	Car and truck expenses (see instructions) . . .	9		19	Pension and profit-sharing plans .	19	
10	Commissions and fees .	10		20	Rent or lease (see instructions):		
11	Contract labor (see instructions)	11		a	Vehicles, machinery, and equipment	20a	
12	Depletion . . .	12		b	Other business property . . .	20b	
13	Depreciation and section 179 expense deduction (not included in Part III) (see instructions) . . .	13		21	Repairs and maintenance . . .	21	
				22	Supplies (not included in Part III) .	22	
				23	Taxes and licenses . . .	23	
14	Employee benefit programs (other than on line 19) . .	14		24	Travel, meals, and entertainment:		
15	Insurance (other than health)	15		a	Travel . . .	24a	
16	Interest:			b	Deductible meals and entertainment (see instructions) .	24b	
a	Mortgage (paid to banks, etc.)	16a		25	Utilities . . .	25	
b	Other . . .	16b		26	Wages (less employment credits) .	26	
17	Legal and professional services	17		27a	Other expenses (from line 48) . .	27a	
				b	**Reserved for future use** . . .	27b	

28	**Total expenses** before expenses for business use of home. Add lines 8 through 27a . . . ▶	28	
29	Tentative profit or (loss). Subtract line 28 from line 7 . . .	29	
30	Expenses for business use of your home. Attach **Form 8829.** Do **not** report such expenses elsewhere . .	30	
31	**Net profit or (loss).** Subtract line 30 from line 29. • If a profit, enter on both **Form 1040, line 12** (or **Form 1040NR, line 13**) and on **Schedule SE, line 2.** (If you checked the box on line 1, see instructions). Estates and trusts, enter on **Form 1041, line 3.** • If a loss, you **must** go to line 32.	31	

32 If you have a loss, check the box that describes your investment in this activity (see instructions).

- If you checked 32a, enter the loss on both **Form 1040, line 12,** (or **Form 1040NR, line 13**) and on **Schedule SE, line 2.** (If you checked the box on line 1, see the line 31 instructions). Estates and trusts, enter on **Form 1041, line 3.**
- If you checked 32b, you **must** attach **Form 6198.** Your loss may be limited.

32a ☐ All investment is at risk.
32b ☐ Some investment is not at risk.

Part III Cost of Goods Sold (see instructions)

33 Method(s) used to value closing inventory: a ☐ Cost b ☐ Lower of cost or market c ☐ Other (attach explanation)

34 Was there any change in determining quantities, costs, or valuations between opening and closing inventory? If "Yes," attach explanation . . . ☐ Yes ☐ No

35	Inventory at beginning of year. If different from last year's closing inventory, attach explanation . . .	35		
36	Purchases less cost of items withdrawn for personal use . . .	36		
37	Cost of labor. Do not include any amounts paid to yourself . . .	37		
38	Materials and supplies . . .	38		
39	Other costs . . .	39		
40	Add lines 35 through 39 . . .	40		
41	Inventory at end of year . . .	41		
42	**Cost of goods sold.** Subtract line 41 from line 40. Enter the result here and on line 4 . . .	42		

Part IV Information on Your Vehicle. Complete this part **only** if you are claiming car or truck expenses on line 9 and are not required to file Form 4562 for this business. See the instructions for line 13 to find out if you must file Form 4562.

43 When did you place your vehicle in service for business purposes? (month, day, year) ► / /

44 Of the total number of miles you drove your vehicle during 2012, enter the number of miles you used your vehicle for:

a Business ______ b Commuting (see instructions) ______ c Other ______

45 Was your vehicle available for personal use during off-duty hours? . . . ☐ Yes ☐ No

46 Do you (or your spouse) have another vehicle available for personal use?. . . ☐ Yes ☐ No

47a Do you have evidence to support your deduction? . . . ☐ Yes ☐ No

b If "Yes," is the evidence written? . . . ☐ Yes ☐ No

Part V Other Expenses. List below business expenses not included on lines 8–26 or line 30.

48 Total other expenses. Enter here and on line 27a . . .	48		

SCHEDULE F (Form 1040)

Department of the Treasury Internal Revenue Service (99)

Profit or Loss From Farming

▶ Attach to Form 1040, Form 1040NR, Form 1041, Form 1065, or Form 1065-B.

▶ Information about Schedule F and its separate instructions is at *www.irs.gov/form1040*.

OMB No. 1545-0074

2012

Attachment Sequence No. 14

Name of proprietor | Social security number (SSN)

A Principal crop or activity | B Enter code from Part IV ▶ | C Accounting method: ☐ Cash ☐ Accrual | D Employer ID number (EIN), (see instr)

E Did you "materially participate" in the operation of this business during 2012? If "No," see instructions for limit on passive losses ☐ Yes ☐ No

F Did you make any payments in 2012 that would require you to file Form(s) 1099 (see instructions) ☐ Yes ☐ No

G If "Yes," did you or will you file required Forms 1099? ☐ Yes ☐ No

Part I **Farm Income—Cash Method.** Complete Parts I and II (Accrual method. Complete Parts II and III, and Part I, line 9.)

1a	Sales of livestock and other resale items (see instructions)	1a		
b	Cost or other basis of livestock or other items reported on line 1a	1b		
c	Subtract line 1b from line 1a		1c	
2	Sales of livestock, produce, grains, and other products you raised		2	
3a	Cooperative distributions (Form(s) 1099-PATR)	3a	3b Taxable amount 3b	
4a	Agricultural program payments (see instructions)	4a	4b Taxable amount 4b	
5a	Commodity Credit Corporation (CCC) loans reported under election		5a	
b	CCC loans forfeited	5b	5c Taxable amount 5c	
6	Crop insurance proceeds and federal crop disaster payments (see instructions)			
a	Amount received in 2012	6a	6b Taxable amount 6b	
c	If election to defer to 2013 is attached, check here ▶ ☐		6d Amount deferred from 2011 6d	
7	Custom hire (machine work) income		7	
8	Other income (see instructions)		8	
9	**Gross income.** Add amounts in the right column (lines 1c, 2, 3b, 4b, 5a, 5c, 6b, 6d, 7, and 8). If you use the accrual method, enter the amount from Part III, line 50 (see instructions) ▶		9	

Part II **Farm Expenses—Cash and Accrual Method.** Do not include personal or living expenses (see instructions).

10	Car and truck expenses (see instructions). Also attach **Form 4562**	10		23	Pension and profit-sharing plans	23	
				24	Rent or lease (see instructions):		
11	Chemicals	11		a	Vehicles, machinery, equipment	24a	
12	Conservation expenses (see instructions)	12		b	Other (land, animals, etc.)	24b	
13	Custom hire (machine work)	13		25	Repairs and maintenance	25	
14	Depreciation and section 179 expense (see instructions)	14		26	Seeds and plants	26	
				27	Storage and warehousing	27	
15	Employee benefit programs other than on line 23	15		28	Supplies	28	
				29	Taxes	29	
16	Feed	16		30	Utilities	30	
17	Fertilizers and lime	17		31	Veterinary, breeding, and medicine	31	
18	Freight and trucking	18		32	Other expenses (specify):		
19	Gasoline, fuel, and oil	19		a		32a	
20	Insurance (other than health)	20		b		32b	
21	Interest:			c		32c	
a	Mortgage (paid to banks, etc.)	21a		d		32d	
b	Other	21b		e		32e	
22	Labor hired (less employment credits)	22		f		32f	

33	**Total expenses.** Add lines 10 through 32f. If line 32f is negative, see instructions ▶	33	
34	**Net farm profit or (loss).** Subtract line 33 from line 9	34	

If a profit, stop here and see instructions for where to report. If a loss, complete lines 35 and 36.

35 Did you receive an applicable subsidy in 2012? (see instructions) ☐ Yes ☐ No

36 Check the box that describes your investment in this activity and see instructions for where to report your loss.

a ☐ All investment is at risk. b ☐ Some investment is not at risk.

Part III Farm Income—Accrual Method (see instructions).

37	Sales of livestock, produce, grains, and other products (see instructions)				37	
38a	Cooperative distributions (Form(s) 1099-PATR)	38a		38b Taxable amount	38b	
39a	Agricultural program payments	39a		39b Taxable amount	39b	
40	Commodity Credit Corporation (CCC) loans:					
a	CCC loans reported under election				40a	
b	CCC loans forfeited	40b		40c Taxable amount	40c	
41	Crop insurance proceeds				41	
42	Custom hire (machine work) income				42	
43	Other income (see instructions)				43	
44	Add amounts in the right column for lines 37 through 43 (lines 37, 38b, 39b, 40a, 40c, 41, 42, and 43)				44	
45	Inventory of livestock, produce, grains, and other products at beginning of the year. Do not include sales reported on Form 4797	45				
46	Cost of livestock, produce, grains, and other products purchased during the year	46				
47	Add lines 45 and 46	47				
48	Inventory of livestock, produce, grains, and other products at end of year	48				
49	Cost of livestock, produce, grains, and other products sold. Subtract line 48 from line 47*				49	
50	**Gross income.** Subtract line 49 from line 44. Enter the result here and on Part I, line 9 ▶				50	

*If you use the unit-livestock-price method or the farm-price method of valuing inventory and the amount on line 48 is larger than the amount on line 47, subtract line 47 from line 48. Enter the result on line 49. Add lines 44 and 49. Enter the total on line 50 and on Part I, line 9.

Part IV Principal Agricultural Activity Codes

CAUTION

Do not file Schedule F (Form 1040) to report the following.

- *Income from providing agricultural services such as soil preparation, veterinary, farm labor, horticultural, or management for a fee or on a contract basis. Instead file Schedule C (Form 1040) or Schedule C-EZ (Form 1040).*
- *Income from breeding, raising, or caring for dogs, cats, or other pet animals. Instead file Schedule C (Form 1040) or Schedule C-EZ (Form 1040).*
- *Sales of livestock held for draft, breeding, sport, or dairy purposes. Instead file Form 4797.*

These codes for the Principal Agricultural Activity classify farms by their primary activity to facilitate the administration of the Internal Revenue Code. These six-digit codes are based on the North American Industry Classification System (NAICS).

Select the code that best identifies your primary farming activity and enter the six-digit number on line B.

Crop Production

111100 Oilseed and grain farming
111210 Vegetable and melon farming
111300 Fruit and tree nut farming
111400 Greenhouse, nursery, and floriculture production
111900 Other crop farming

Animal Production

112111 Beef cattle ranching and farming
112112 Cattle feedlots
112120 Dairy cattle and milk production
112210 Hog and pig farming
112300 Poultry and egg production
112400 Sheep and goat farming
112510 Aquaculture
112900 Other animal production

Forestry and Logging

113000 Forestry and logging (including forest nurseries and timber tracts)

SCHEDULE SE (Form 1040)

Department of the Treasury
Internal Revenue Service (99)

Self-Employment Tax

▶ Information about Schedule SE and its separate instructions is at *www.irs.gov/form1040.*

▶ Attach to Form 1040 or Form 1040NR.

OMB No. 1545-0074

2012

Attachment Sequence No. **17**

Name of person with **self-employment** income (as shown on Form 1040)	Social security number of person with **self-employment** income ▶	

Before you begin: To determine if you must file Schedule SE, see the instructions.

May I Use Short Schedule SE or Must I Use Long Schedule SE?

Note. Use this flowchart **only if** you must file Schedule SE. If unsure, see *Who Must File Schedule SE* in the instructions.

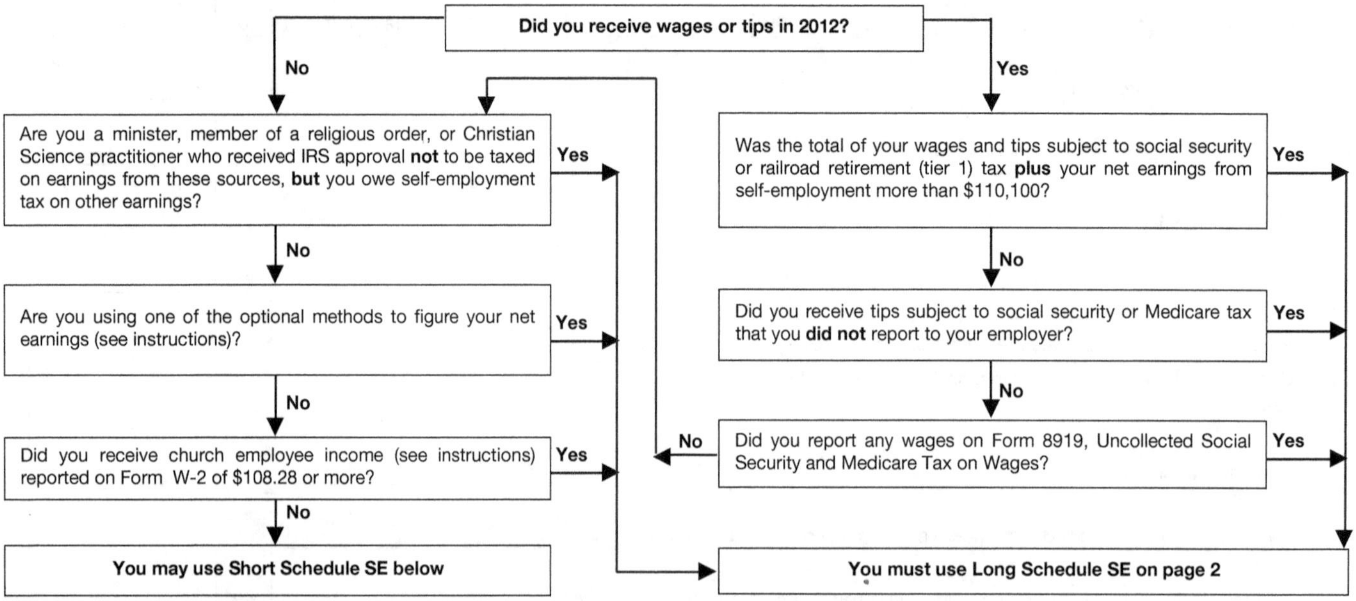

Section A—Short Schedule SE. Caution. Read above to see if you can use Short Schedule SE.

1a	Net farm profit or (loss) from Schedule F, line 34, and farm partnerships, Schedule K-1 (Form 1065), box 14, code A	**1a**	
b	If you received social security retirement or disability benefits, enter the amount of Conservation Reserve Program payments included on Schedule F, line 4b, or listed on Schedule K-1 (Form 1065), box 20, code Y	**1b**	( )
2	Net profit or (loss) from Schedule C, line 31; Schedule C-EZ, line 3; Schedule K-1 (Form 1065), box 14, code A (other than farming); and Schedule K-1 (Form 1065-B), box 9, code J1. Ministers and members of religious orders, see instructions for types of income to report on this line. See instructions for other income to report	**2**	
3	Combine lines 1a, 1b, and 2	**3**	
4	Multiply line 3 by 92.35% (.9235). If less than $400, you do not owe self-employment tax; **do not** file this schedule unless you have an amount on line 1b . . . . ▶	**4**	
	Note. If line 4 is less than $400 due to Conservation Reserve Program payments on line 1b, see instructions.		
5	**Self-employment tax.** If the amount on line 4 is: • $110,100 or less, multiply line 4 by 13.3% (.133). Enter the result here and on **Form 1040, line 56,** or **Form 1040NR, line 54** • More than $110,100, multiply line 4 by 2.9% (.029). Then, add $11,450.40 to the result. Enter the total here and on **Form 1040, line 56,** or **Form 1040NR, line 54**	**5**	
6	**Deduction for employer-equivalent portion of self-employment tax.** If the amount on line 5 is: • $14,643.30 or less, multiply line 5 by 57.51% (.5751) • More than $14,643.30, multiply line 5 by 50% (.50) and add $1,100 to the result. Enter the result here and on **Form 1040, line 27,** or **Form 1040NR, line 27** **6**		

Part III Farm Income—Accrual Method (see instructions).

37	Sales of livestock, produce, grains, and other products (see instructions)			37	
38a	Cooperative distributions (Form(s) 1099-PATR)	38a	38b Taxable amount	38b	
39a	Agricultural program payments	39a	39b Taxable amount	39b	
40	Commodity Credit Corporation (CCC) loans:				
a	CCC loans reported under election			40a	
b	CCC loans forfeited	40b	40c Taxable amount	40c	
41	Crop insurance proceeds			41	
42	Custom hire (machine work) income			42	
43	Other income (see instructions)			43	
44	Add amounts in the right column for lines 37 through 43 (lines 37, 38b, 39b, 40a, 40c, 41, 42, and 43)			44	
45	Inventory of livestock, produce, grains, and other products at beginning of the year. Do not include sales reported on Form 4797	45			
46	Cost of livestock, produce, grains, and other products purchased during the year	46			
47	Add lines 45 and 46	47			
48	Inventory of livestock, produce, grains, and other products at end of year	48			
49	Cost of livestock, produce, grains, and other products sold. Subtract line 48 from line 47*			49	
50	**Gross income.** Subtract line 49 from line 44. Enter the result here and on Part I, line 9 ▶			50	

*If you use the unit-livestock-price method or the farm-price method of valuing inventory and the amount on line 48 is larger than the amount on line 47, subtract line 47 from line 48. Enter the result on line 49. Add lines 44 and 49. Enter the total on line 50 and on Part I, line 9.

Part IV Principal Agricultural Activity Codes

CAUTION *Do not file Schedule F (Form 1040) to report the following.*

- *Income from providing agricultural services such as soil preparation, veterinary, farm labor, horticultural, or management for a fee or on a contract basis. Instead file Schedule C (Form 1040) or Schedule C-EZ (Form 1040).*
- *Income from breeding, raising, or caring for dogs, cats, or other pet animals. Instead file Schedule C (Form 1040) or Schedule C-EZ (Form 1040).*
- *Sales of livestock held for draft, breeding, sport, or dairy purposes. Instead file Form 4797.*

These codes for the Principal Agricultural Activity classify farms by their primary activity to facilitate the administration of the Internal Revenue Code. These six-digit codes are based on the North American Industry Classification System (NAICS).

Select the code that best identifies your primary farming activity and enter the six-digit number on line B.

Crop Production

111100 Oilseed and grain farming
111210 Vegetable and melon farming
111300 Fruit and tree nut farming
111400 Greenhouse, nursery, and floriculture production
111900 Other crop farming

Animal Production

112111 Beef cattle ranching and farming
112112 Cattle feedlots
112120 Dairy cattle and milk production
112210 Hog and pig farming
112300 Poultry and egg production
112400 Sheep and goat farming
112510 Aquaculture
112900 Other animal production

Forestry and Logging

113000 Forestry and logging (including forest nurseries and timber tracts)

SCHEDULE SE (Form 1040)

Department of the Treasury Internal Revenue Service (99)

Self-Employment Tax

► Information about Schedule SE and its separate instructions is at *www.irs.gov/form1040.*

► Attach to Form 1040 or Form 1040NR.

OMB No. 1545-0074

2012

Attachment Sequence No. **17**

Name of person with **self-employment** income (as shown on Form 1040)	Social security number of person with **self-employment** income ►	

Before you begin: To determine if you must file Schedule SE, see the instructions.

May I Use Short Schedule SE or Must I Use Long Schedule SE?

Note. Use this flowchart **only if** you must file Schedule SE. If unsure, see *Who Must File Schedule SE* in the instructions.

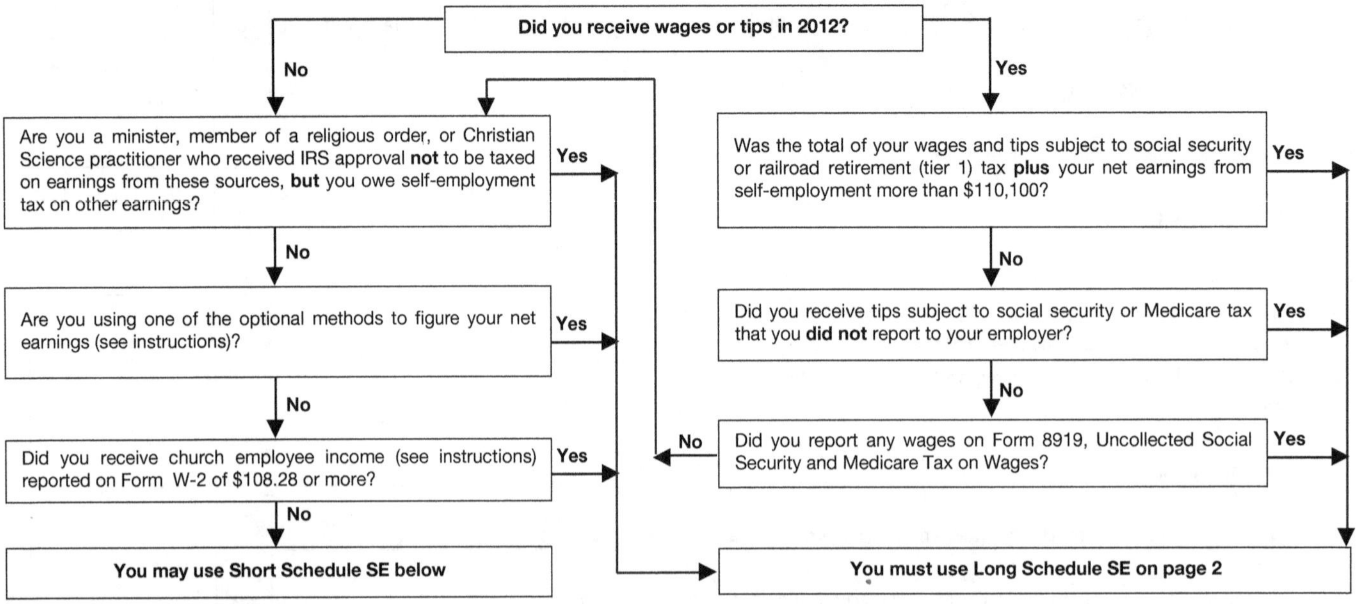

Section A—Short Schedule SE. Caution. Read above to see if you can use Short Schedule SE.

1a	Net farm profit or (loss) from Schedule F, line 34, and farm partnerships, Schedule K-1 (Form 1065), box 14, code A	**1a**	
b	If you received social security retirement or disability benefits, enter the amount of Conservation Reserve Program payments included on Schedule F, line 4b, or listed on Schedule K-1 (Form 1065), box 20, code Y	**1b**	( )
2	Net profit or (loss) from Schedule C, line 31; Schedule C-EZ, line 3; Schedule K-1 (Form 1065), box 14, code A (other than farming); and Schedule K-1 (Form 1065-B), box 9, code J1. Ministers and members of religious orders, see instructions for types of income to report on this line. See instructions for other income to report	**2**	
3	Combine lines 1a, 1b, and 2	**3**	
4	Multiply line 3 by 92.35% (.9235). If less than $400, you do not owe self-employment tax; **do not** file this schedule unless you have an amount on line 1b . . . . . ►	**4**	
	Note. If line 4 is less than $400 due to Conservation Reserve Program payments on line 1b, see instructions.		
5	**Self-employment tax.** If the amount on line 4 is: • $110,100 or less, multiply line 4 by 13.3% (.133). Enter the result here and on **Form 1040, line 56,** or **Form 1040NR, line 54** • More than $110,100, multiply line 4 by 2.9% (.029). Then, add $11,450.40 to the result. Enter the total here and on **Form 1040, line 56,** or **Form 1040NR, line 54**	**5**	
6	**Deduction for employer-equivalent portion of self-employment tax.** If the amount on line 5 is: • $14,643.30 or less, multiply line 5 by 57.51% (.5751) • More than $14,643.30, multiply line 5 by 50% (.50) and add $1,100 to the result. Enter the result here and on **Form 1040, line 27,** or **Form 1040NR, line 27** **6**		

Name of person with **self-employment** income (as shown on Form 1040)	Social security number of person with **self-employment** income ▶	

Section B—Long Schedule SE

Part I Self-Employment Tax

Note. If your only income subject to self-employment tax is **church employee income,** see instructions. Also see instructions for the definition of church employee income.

A	If you are a minister, member of a religious order, or Christian Science practitioner **and** you filed Form 4361, but you had $400 or more of **other** net earnings from self-employment, check here and continue with Part I . . . . ▶ ☐			
1a	Net farm profit or (loss) from Schedule F, line 34, and farm partnerships, Schedule K-1 (Form 1065), box 14, code A. **Note.** Skip lines 1a and 1b if you use the farm optional method (see instructions)	1a		
b	If you received social security retirement or disability benefits, enter the amount of Conservation Reserve Program payments included on Schedule F, line 4b, or listed on Schedule K-1 (Form 1065), box 20, code Y	1b	(	)
2	Net profit or (loss) from Schedule C, line 31; Schedule C-EZ, line 3; Schedule K-1 (Form 1065), box 14, code A (other than farming); and Schedule K-1 (Form 1065-B), box 9, code J1. Ministers and members of religious orders, see instructions for types of income to report on this line. See instructions for other income to report. **Note.** Skip this line if you use the nonfarm optional method (see instructions)	2		
3	Combine lines 1a, 1b, and 2	3		
4a	If line 3 is more than zero, multiply line 3 by 92.35% (.9235). Otherwise, enter amount from line 3	4a		
	Note. If line 4a is less than $400 due to Conservation Reserve Program payments on line 1b, see instructions.			
b	If you elect one or both of the optional methods, enter the total of lines 15 and 17 here . .	4b		
c	Combine lines 4a and 4b. If less than $400, **stop**; you do not owe self-employment tax. **Exception.** If less than $400 and you had **church employee income,** enter -0- and continue ▶	4c		
5a	Enter your **church employee income** from Form W-2. See instructions for definition of church employee income . . . 5a			
b	Multiply line 5a by 92.35% (.9235). If less than $100, enter -0-	5b		
6	Add lines 4c and 5b	6		
7	Maximum amount of combined wages and self-employment earnings subject to social security tax or the 4.2% portion of the 5.65% railroad retirement (tier 1) tax for 2012	7	110,100	00
8a	Total social security wages and tips (total of boxes 3 and 7 on Form(s) W-2) and railroad retirement (tier 1) compensation. If $110,100 or more, skip lines 8b through 10, and go to line 11 8a			
b	Unreported tips subject to social security tax (from Form 4137, line 10) 8b			
c	Wages subject to social security tax (from Form 8919, line 10) 8c			
d	Add lines 8a, 8b, and 8c	8d		
9	Subtract line 8d from line 7. If zero or less, enter -0- here and on line 10 and go to line 11 . ▶	9		
10	Multiply the **smaller** of line 6 or line 9 by 10.4% (.104)	10		
11	Multiply line 6 by 2.9% (.029)	11		
12	**Self-employment tax.** Add lines 10 and 11. Enter here and on **Form 1040, line 56,** or **Form 1040NR, line 54**	12		
13	**Deduction for employer-equivalent portion of self-employment tax.** Add the two following amounts. • 59.6% (.596) of line 10. • One-half of line 11. Enter the result here and on **Form 1040, line 27,** or **Form 1040NR, line 27** 13			

Part II Optional Methods To Figure Net Earnings (see instructions)

Farm Optional Method. You may use this method **only** if **(a)** your gross farm income[1] was not more than $6,780, **or (b)** your net farm profits[2] were less than $4,894.

14	Maximum income for optional methods	14	4,520	00
15	Enter the **smaller** of: two-thirds (2/3) of gross farm income[1] (not less than zero) **or** $4,520. Also include this amount on line 4b above	15		

Nonfarm Optional Method. You may use this method **only** if **(a)** your net nonfarm profits[3] were less than $4,894 and also less than 72.189% of your gross nonfarm income,[4] **and (b)** you had net earnings from self-employment of at least $400 in 2 of the prior 3 years. **Caution.** You may use this method no more than five times.

16	Subtract line 15 from line 14	16		
17	Enter the **smaller** of: two-thirds (2/3) of gross nonfarm income[4] (not less than zero) **or** the amount on line 16. Also include this amount on line 4b above	17		

[1] From Sch. F, line 9, and Sch. K-1 (Form 1065), box 14, code B.

[2] From Sch. F, line 34, and Sch. K-1 (Form 1065), box 14, code A—minus the amount you would have entered on line 1b had you not used the optional method.

[3] From Sch. C, line 31; Sch. C-EZ, line 3; Sch. K-1 (Form 1065), box 14, code A; and Sch. K-1 (Form 1065-B), box 9, code J1.

[4] From Sch. C, line 7; Sch. C-EZ, line 1; Sch. K-1 (Form 1065), box 14, code C; and Sch. K-1 (Form 1065-B), box 9, code J2.

Form **4835**

Department of the Treasury
Internal Revenue Service (99)

Farm Rental Income and Expenses

(Crop and Livestock Shares (Not Cash) Received by Landowner (or Sub-Lessor))
(Income not subject to self-employment tax)
▶ Attach to Form 1040 or Form 1040NR.
▶ Information about Form 4835 and its instructions is at *www.irs.gov/form4835*.

OMB No. 1545-0074
2012
Attachment Sequence No. **37**

Name(s) shown on tax return | **Your social security number**

Employer ID number (EIN), if any

A Did you actively participate in the operation of this farm during 2012 (see instructions)? . . . . ☐ Yes ☐ No

Part I Gross Farm Rental Income—Based on Production. Include amounts converted to cash or the equivalent.

1	Income from production of livestock, produce, grains, and other crops		1	
2a	Cooperative distributions (Form(s) 1099-PATR)	2a	**2b** Taxable amount	2b	
3a	Agricultural program payments (see instructions)	3a	**3b** Taxable amount	3b	
4	Commodity Credit Corporation (CCC) loans (see instructions):			
a	CCC loans reported under election		4a	
b	CCC loans forfeited	4b	**4c** Taxable amount	4c	
5	Crop insurance proceeds and federal crop disaster payments (see instructions):			
a	Amount received in 2012	5a	**5b** Taxable amount	5b	
c	If election to defer to 2013 is attached, check here ▶ ☐		**5d** Amount deferred from 2011	5d	
6	Other income, including federal and state gasoline or fuel tax credit or refund (see instructions)		6	
7	**Gross farm rental income.** Add amounts in the right column for lines 1 through 6. Enter the total here and on Schedule E (Form 1040), line 42 . . . . ▶		7	

Part II Expenses—Farm Rental Property. Do not include personal or living expenses.

8	Car and truck expenses (see Schedule F (Form 1040) instructions). Also attach **Form 4562**	8		21	Pension and profit-sharing plans . . .	21
9	Chemicals	9		22	Rent or lease:	
10	Conservation expenses (see instructions)	10		a	Vehicles, machinery, and equipment (see instructions)	22a
11	Custom hire (machine work) .	11		b	Other (land, animals, etc.)	22b
12	Depreciation and section 179 expense deduction not claimed elsewhere	12		23	Repairs and maintenance	23
				24	Seeds and plants . .	24
				25	Storage and warehousing	25
13	Employee benefit programs other than on line 21 (see Schedule F (Form 1040) instructions). . .	13		26	Supplies	26
				27	Taxes	27
				28	Utilities	28
14	Feed	14		29	Veterinary, breeding, and medicine . . .	29
15	Fertilizers and lime	15				
16	Freight and trucking . . .	16		30	Other expenses (specify):	
17	Gasoline, fuel, and oil . . .	17				
18	Insurance (other than health).	18		a		30a
19	Interest:			b		30b
a	Mortgage (paid to banks, etc.)	19a		c		30c
b	Other	19b		d		30d
20	Labor hired (less employment credits) (see Schedule F (Form 1040) instructions)	20		e		30e
				f		30f
				g		30g

31	**Total expenses.** Add lines 8 through 30g (see instructions) . . . . ▶	31	
32	**Net farm rental income or (loss).** Subtract line 31 from line 7. If the result is income, enter it here and on Schedule E (Form 1040), line 40. If the result is a loss, you **must** go to lines 33 and 34 .	32	
33	Did you receive an applicable subsidy in 2012? (see instructions)	33 ☐ Yes ☐ No	
34	If line 32 is a loss, check the box that describes your investment in this activity (see instructions)	34a ☐ All investment is at risk. 34b ☐ Some investment is not at risk.	
c	You may have to complete **Form 8582** to determine your deductible loss, regardless of which box you checked (see instructions). If you checked box 34b, you **must** complete **Form 6198** before going to Form 8582. In either case, enter the **deductible loss** here and on Schedule E (Form 1040), line 40	34c	

Form **1065**
Department of the Treasury
Internal Revenue Service

U.S. Return of Partnership Income

For calendar year 2012, or tax year beginning ______________, 2012, ending ______________, 20 ______.
▶ Information about Form 1065 and its separate instructions is at *www.irs.gov/form1065*.

OMB No. 1545-0099

2012

	Print or type.	
A Principal business activity		Name of partnership	D Employer identification number
B Principal product or service		Number, street, and room or suite no. If a P.O. box, see the instructions.	E Date business started
C Business code number		City or town, state, and ZIP code	F Total assets (see the instructions) $

G Check applicable boxes: (1) ☐ Initial return (2) ☐ Final return (3) ☐ Name change (4) ☐ Address change (5) ☐ Amended return
(6) ☐ Technical termination - also check (1) or (2)

H Check accounting method: (1) ☐ Cash (2) ☐ Accrual (3) ☐ Other (specify) ▶ ______________

I Number of Schedules K-1. Attach one for each person who was a partner at any time during the tax year ▶ ______________

J Check if Schedules C and M-3 are attached . . . . . ☐

Caution. *Include **only** trade or business income and expenses on lines 1a through 22 below. See the instructions for more information.*

Income	1a	Gross receipts or sales	1a			
	b	Returns and allowances	1b			
	c	Balance. Subtract line 1b from line 1a			1c	
	2	Cost of goods sold (attach Form 1125-A)			2	
	3	Gross profit. Subtract line 2 from line 1c			3	
	4	Ordinary income (loss) from other partnerships, estates, and trusts (attach statement)			4	
	5	Net farm profit (loss) (attach Schedule F (Form 1040))			5	
	6	Net gain (loss) from Form 4797, Part II, line 17 (attach Form 4797)			6	
	7	Other income (loss) (attach statement)			7	
	8	**Total income (loss).** Combine lines 3 through 7			8	
Deductions (see the instructions for limitations)	9	Salaries and wages (other than to partners) (less employment credits)			9	
	10	Guaranteed payments to partners			10	
	11	Repairs and maintenance			11	
	12	Bad debts			12	
	13	Rent			13	
	14	Taxes and licenses			14	
	15	Interest			15	
	16a	Depreciation (if required, attach Form 4562)	16a			
	b	Less depreciation reported on Form 1125-A and elsewhere on return	16b		16c	
	17	Depletion **(Do not deduct oil and gas depletion.)**			17	
	18	Retirement plans, etc.			18	
	19	Employee benefit programs			19	
	20	Other deductions (attach statement)			20	
	21	**Total deductions.** Add the amounts shown in the far right column for lines 9 through 20			21	
	22	**Ordinary business income (loss).** Subtract line 21 from line 8			22	

Sign Here

Under penalties of perjury, I declare that I have examined this return, including accompanying schedules and statements, and to the best of my knowledge and belief, it is true, correct, and complete. Declaration of preparer (other than general partner or limited liability company member manager) is based on all information of which preparer has any knowledge.

▶ Signature of general partner or limited liability company member manager ▶ Date

May the IRS discuss this return with the preparer shown below (see instructions)? ☐ Yes ☐ No

Paid Preparer Use Only

Print/Type preparer's name	Preparer's signature	Date	Check ☐ if self- employed	PTIN
Firm's name ▶			Firm's EIN ▶	
Firm's address ▶			Phone no.	

Schedule B Other Information

		Yes	No
1	What type of entity is filing this return? Check the applicable box: a ☐ Domestic general partnership b ☐ Domestic limited partnership c ☐ Domestic limited liability company d ☐ Domestic limited liability partnership e ☐ Foreign partnership f ☐ Other ▶		
2	At any time during the tax year, was any partner in the partnership a disregarded entity, a partnership (including an entity treated as a partnership), a trust, an S corporation, an estate (other than an estate of a deceased partner), or a nominee or similar person?		
3	At the end of the tax year:		
a	Did any foreign or domestic corporation, partnership (including any entity treated as a partnership), trust, or tax-exempt organization, or any foreign government own, directly or indirectly, an interest of 50% or more in the profit, loss, or capital of the partnership? For rules of constructive ownership, see instructions. If "Yes," attach Schedule B-1, Information on Partners Owning 50% or More of the Partnership		
b	Did any individual or estate own, directly or indirectly, an interest of 50% or more in the profit, loss, or capital of the partnership? For rules of constructive ownership, see instructions. If "Yes," attach Schedule B-1, Information on Partners Owning 50% or More of the Partnership		
4	At the end of the tax year, did the partnership:		
a	Own directly 20% or more, or own, directly or indirectly, 50% or more of the total voting power of all classes of stock entitled to vote of any foreign or domestic corporation? For rules of constructive ownership, see instructions. If "Yes," complete (i) through (iv) below		

(i) Name of Corporation	(ii) Employer Identification Number (if any)	(iii) Country of Incorporation	(iv) Percentage Owned in Voting Stock

b	Own directly an interest of 20% or more, or own, directly or indirectly, an interest of 50% or more in the profit, loss, or capital in any foreign or domestic partnership (including an entity treated as a partnership) or in the beneficial interest of a trust? For rules of constructive ownership, see instructions. If "Yes," complete (i) through (v) below		

(i) Name of Entity	(ii) Employer Identification Number (if any)	(iii) Type of Entity	(iv) Country of Organization	(v) Maximum Percentage Owned in Profit, Loss, or Capital

		Yes	No
5	Did the partnership file Form 8893, Election of Partnership Level Tax Treatment, or an election statement under section 6231(a)(1)(B)(ii) for partnership-level tax treatment, that is in effect for this tax year? See Form 8893 for more details		
6	Does the partnership satisfy **all four** of the following conditions?		
a	The partnership's total receipts for the tax year were less than $250,000.		
b	The partnership's total assets at the end of the tax year were less than $1 million.		
c	Schedules K-1 are filed with the return and furnished to the partners on or before the due date (including extensions) for the partnership return.		
d	The partnership is not filing and is not required to file Schedule M-3 If "Yes," the partnership is not required to complete Schedules L, M-1, and M-2; Item F on page 1 of Form 1065; or Item L on Schedule K-1.		
7	Is this partnership a publicly traded partnership as defined in section 469(k)(2)?		
8	During the tax year, did the partnership have any debt that was cancelled, was forgiven, or had the terms modified so as to reduce the principal amount of the debt?		
9	Has this partnership filed, or is it required to file, Form 8918, Material Advisor Disclosure Statement, to provide information on any reportable transaction?		
10	At any time during calendar year 2012, did the partnership have an interest in or a signature or other authority over a financial account in a foreign country (such as a bank account, securities account, or other financial account)? See the instructions for exceptions and filing requirements for Form TD F 90-22.1, Report of Foreign Bank and Financial Accounts. If "Yes," enter the name of the foreign country. ▶		

Schedule B Other Information *(continued)*

		Yes	No
11	At any time during the tax year, did the partnership receive a distribution from, or was it the grantor of, or transferor to, a foreign trust? If "Yes," the partnership may have to file Form 3520, Annual Return To Report Transactions With Foreign Trusts and Receipt of Certain Foreign Gifts. See instructions		
12a	Is the partnership making, or had it previously made (and not revoked), a section 754 election? . . . . See instructions for details regarding a section 754 election.		
b	Did the partnership make for this tax year an optional basis adjustment under section 743(b) or 734(b)? If "Yes," attach a statement showing the computation and allocation of the basis adjustment. See instructions		
c	Is the partnership required to adjust the basis of partnership assets under section 743(b) or 734(b) because of a substantial built-in loss (as defined under section 743(d)) or substantial basis reduction (as defined under section 734(d))? If "Yes," attach a statement showing the computation and allocation of the basis adjustment. See instructions.		
13	Check this box if, during the current or prior tax year, the partnership distributed any property received in a like-kind exchange or contributed such property to another entity (other than disregarded entities wholly-owned by the partnership throughout the tax year) . . . . ▶ ☐		
14	At any time during the tax year, did the partnership distribute to any partner a tenancy-in-common or other undivided interest in partnership property?		
15	If the partnership is required to file Form 8858, Information Return of U.S. Persons With Respect To Foreign Disregarded Entities, enter the number of Forms 8858 attached. See instructions ▶		
16	Does the partnership have any foreign partners? If "Yes," enter the number of Forms 8805, Foreign Partner's Information Statement of Section 1446 Withholding Tax, filed for this partnership. ▶		
17	Enter the number of Forms 8865, Return of U.S. Persons With Respect to Certain Foreign Partnerships, attached to this return. ▶		
18a	Did you make any payments in 2012 that would require you to file Form(s) 1099? See instructions		
b	If "Yes," did you or will you file required Form(s) 1099?		
19	Enter the number of Form(s) 5471, Information Return of U.S. Persons With Respect To Certain Foreign Corporations, attached to this return. ▶		
20	Enter the number of partners that are foreign governments under section 892. ▶		

Designation of Tax Matters Partner (see instructions)

Enter below the general partner or member-manager designated as the tax matters partner (TMP) for the tax year of this return:

Name of designated TMP ▶		Identifying number of TMP ▶	
If the TMP is an entity, name of TMP representative ▶		Phone number of TMP ▶	
Address of designated TMP ▶			

Section	Line	Schedule K — Partners' Distributive Share Items		Line	Total amount
Income (Loss)	1	Ordinary business income (loss) (page 1, line 22)		1	
	2	Net rental real estate income (loss) (attach Form 8825)		2	
	3a	Other gross rental income (loss)	3a		
	b	Expenses from other rental activities (attach statement)	3b		
	c	Other net rental income (loss). Subtract line 3b from line 3a		3c	
	4	Guaranteed payments		4	
	5	Interest income		5	
	6	Dividends: **a** Ordinary dividends		6a	
		b Qualified dividends	6b		
	7	Royalties		7	
	8	Net short-term capital gain (loss) (attach Schedule D (Form 1065))		8	
	9a	Net long-term capital gain (loss) (attach Schedule D (Form 1065))		9a	
	b	Collectibles (28%) gain (loss)	9b		
	c	Unrecaptured section 1250 gain (attach statement)	9c		
	10	Net section 1231 gain (loss) (attach Form 4797)		10	
	11	Other income (loss) (see instructions) Type ▶		11	
Deductions	12	Section 179 deduction (attach Form 4562)		12	
	13a	Contributions		13a	
	b	Investment interest expense		13b	
	c	Section 59(e)(2) expenditures: **(1)** Type ▶ ____ **(2)** Amount ▶		13c(2)	
	d	Other deductions (see instructions) Type ▶		13d	
Self-Employment	14a	Net earnings (loss) from self-employment		14a	
	b	Gross farming or fishing income		14b	
	c	Gross nonfarm income		14c	
Credits	15a	Low-income housing credit (section 42(j)(5))		15a	
	b	Low-income housing credit (other)		15b	
	c	Qualified rehabilitation expenditures (rental real estate) (attach Form 3468)		15c	
	d	Other rental real estate credits (see instructions) Type ▶		15d	
	e	Other rental credits (see instructions) Type ▶		15e	
	f	Other credits (see instructions) Type ▶		15f	
Foreign Transactions	16a	Name of country or U.S. possession ▶			
	b	Gross income from all sources		16b	
	c	Gross income sourced at partner level		16c	
		Foreign gross income sourced at partnership level			
	d	Passive category ▶ ____ **e** General category ▶ ____ **f** Other ▶		16f	
		Deductions allocated and apportioned at partner level			
	g	Interest expense ▶ ____ **h** Other ▶		16h	
		Deductions allocated and apportioned at partnership level to foreign source income			
	i	Passive category ▶ ____ **j** General category ▶ ____ **k** Other ▶		16k	
	l	Total foreign taxes (check one): ▶ Paid ☐ Accrued ☐		16l	
	m	Reduction in taxes available for credit (attach statement)		16m	
	n	Other foreign tax information (attach statement)			
Alternative Minimum Tax (AMT) Items	17a	Post-1986 depreciation adjustment		17a	
	b	Adjusted gain or loss		17b	
	c	Depletion (other than oil and gas)		17c	
	d	Oil, gas, and geothermal properties—gross income		17d	
	e	Oil, gas, and geothermal properties—deductions		17e	
	f	Other AMT items (attach statement)		17f	
Other Information	18a	Tax-exempt interest income		18a	
	b	Other tax-exempt income		18b	
	c	Nondeductible expenses		18c	
	19a	Distributions of cash and marketable securities		19a	
	b	Distributions of other property		19b	
	20a	Investment income		20a	
	b	Investment expenses		20b	
	c	Other items and amounts (attach statement)			

Analysis of Net Income (Loss)

1	Net income (loss). Combine Schedule K, lines 1 through 11. From the result, subtract the sum of Schedule K, lines 12 through 13d, and 16l . . .				1	

2 Analysis by partner type:	(i) Corporate	(ii) Individual (active)	(iii) Individual (passive)	(iv) Partnership	(v) Exempt organization	(vi) Nominee/Other
a General partners						
b Limited partners						

Schedule L Balance Sheets per Books

Assets	Beginning of tax year (a)	(b)	End of tax year (c)	(d)
1 Cash				
2a Trade notes and accounts receivable				
b Less allowance for bad debts				
3 Inventories				
4 U.S. government obligations				
5 Tax-exempt securities				
6 Other current assets (attach statement)				
7a Loans to partners (or persons related to partners)				
b Mortgage and real estate loans				
8 Other investments (attach statement)				
9a Buildings and other depreciable assets				
b Less accumulated depreciation				
10a Depletable assets				
b Less accumulated depletion				
11 Land (net of any amortization)				
12a Intangible assets (amortizable only)				
b Less accumulated amortization				
13 Other assets (attach statement)				
14 Total assets				
Liabilities and Capital				
15 Accounts payable				
16 Mortgages, notes, bonds payable in less than 1 year				
17 Other current liabilities (attach statement)				
18 All nonrecourse loans				
19a Loans from partners (or persons related to partners)				
b Mortgages, notes, bonds payable in 1 year or more				
20 Other liabilities (attach statement)				
21 Partners' capital accounts				
22 Total liabilities and capital				

Schedule M-1 Reconciliation of Income (Loss) per Books With Income (Loss) per Return

Note. Schedule M-3 may be required instead of Schedule M-1 (see instructions).

1 Net income (loss) per books		6 Income recorded on books this year not included on Schedule K, lines 1 through 11 (itemize): a Tax-exempt interest $	
2 Income included on Schedule K, lines 1, 2, 3c, 5, 6a, 7, 8, 9a, 10, and 11, not recorded on books this year (itemize):			
3 Guaranteed payments (other than health insurance)		7 Deductions included on Schedule K, lines 1 through 13d, and 16l, not charged against book income this year (itemize): a Depreciation $	
4 Expenses recorded on books this year not included on Schedule K, lines 1 through 13d, and 16l (itemize): a Depreciation $ b Travel and entertainment $		8 Add lines 6 and 7	
		9 Income (loss) (Analysis of Net Income (Loss), line 1). Subtract line 8 from line 5	
5 Add lines 1 through 4			

Schedule M-2 Analysis of Partners' Capital Accounts

1 Balance at beginning of year		6 Distributions: a Cash	
2 Capital contributed: a Cash		b Property	
b Property		7 Other decreases (itemize):	
3 Net income (loss) per books			
4 Other increases (itemize):		8 Add lines 6 and 7	
5 Add lines 1 through 4		9 Balance at end of year. Subtract line 8 from line 5	

Form **1125-A**

(Rev. December 2012)

Department of the Treasury
Internal Revenue Service

Cost of Goods Sold

▶ Attach to Form 1120, 1120-C, 1120-F, 1120S, 1065, or 1065-B.
▶ Information about Form 1125-A and its instructions is at *www.irs.gov/form1125a.*

OMB No. 1545-2225

Name	Employer identification number

1	Inventory at beginning of year	1	
2	Purchases	2	
3	Cost of labor	3	
4	Additional section 263A costs (attach schedule)	4	
5	Other costs (attach schedule)	5	
6	**Total.** Add lines 1 through 5	6	
7	Inventory at end of year	7	
8	**Cost of goods sold.** Subtract line 7 from line 6. Enter here and on Form 1120, page 1, line 2 or the appropriate line of your tax return (see instructions)	8	

9a Check all methods used for valuing closing inventory:

(i) ☐ Cost

(ii) ☐ Lower of cost or market

(iii) ☐ Other (Specify method used and attach explanation.) ▶ ______

b Check if there was a writedown of subnormal goods ▶ ☐

c Check if the LIFO inventory method was adopted this tax year for any goods (if checked, attach Form 970) ▶ ☐

d If the LIFO inventory method was used for this tax year, enter amount of closing inventory computed under LIFO . . . **9d** ______

e If property is produced or acquired for resale, do the rules of section 263A apply to the entity (see instructions)? ☐ Yes ☐ No

f Was there any change in determining quantities, cost, or valuations between opening and closing inventory? If "Yes," attach explanation ☐ Yes ☐ No

Section references are to the Internal Revenue Code unless otherwise noted.

General Instructions

Purpose of Form

Use Form 1125-A to calculate and deduct cost of goods sold for certain entities.

Who Must File

Filers of Form 1120, 1120-C, 1120-F, 1120S, 1065, or 1065-B, must complete and attach Form 1125-A if the applicable entity reports a deduction for cost of goods sold.

Inventories

Generally, inventories are required at the beginning and end of each tax year if the production, purchase, or sale of merchandise is an income-producing factor. See Regulations section 1.471-1. If inventories are required, you generally must use an accrual method of accounting for sales and purchases of inventory items.

Exception for certain taxpayers. If you are a qualifying taxpayer or a qualifying small business taxpayer (defined below), you can adopt or change your accounting method to account for inventoriable items in the same manner as materials and supplies that are not incidental.

Under this accounting method, inventory costs for raw materials purchased for use in producing finished goods and merchandise purchased for resale are deductible in the year the finished goods or merchandise are sold (but not before the year you paid for the raw materials or merchandise, if you are also using the cash method).

If you account for inventoriable items in the same manner as materials and supplies that are not incidental, you can currently deduct expenditures for direct labor and all indirect costs that would otherwise be included in inventory costs. See the instructions for lines 2 and 7.

For additional guidance on this method of accounting, see Pub. 538, Accounting Periods and Methods. For guidance on adopting or changing to this method of accounting, see Form 3115, Application for Change in Accounting Method, and its instructions.

Qualifying taxpayer. A qualifying taxpayer is a taxpayer that, (a) for each prior tax year ending after December 16, 1998, has average annual gross receipts of $1 million or less for the 3 prior tax years and (b) its business is not a tax shelter (as defined in section 448(d)(3)). See Rev. Proc. 2001-10, 2001-2 I.R.B. 272.

Qualifying small business taxpayer. A qualifying small business taxpayer is a taxpayer that, (a) for each prior tax year ending on or after December 31, 2000, has average annual gross receipts of $10 million or less for the 3 prior tax years, (b) whose principal business activity is not an ineligible activity, and (c) whose business is not a tax shelter (as defined in section 448 (d)(3)). See Rev. Proc. 2002-28, 2002-18 I.R.B. 815.

Uniform capitalization rules. The uniform capitalization rules of section 263A generally require you to capitalize, or include in inventory, certain costs incurred in connection with the following.

- The production of real property and tangible personal property held in inventory or held for sale in the ordinary course of business.
- Real property or personal property (tangible and intangible) acquired for resale.
- The production of real property and tangible personal property by a corporation for use in its trade or business or in an activity engaged in for profit.

See the discussion on section 263A uniform capitalization rules in the instructions for your tax return before completing Form 1125-A. Also see Regulations sections 1.263A-1 through 1.263A-3. See Regulations section 1.263A-4 for rules for property produced in a farming business.

Form **1120**
Department of the Treasury
Internal Revenue Service

U.S. Corporation Income Tax Return

For calendar year 2012 or tax year beginning ______, 2012, ending ______, 20 ___

► Information about Form 1120 and its separate instructions is at *www.irs.gov/form1120*.

OMB No. 1545-0123

2012

A Check if:
1a Consolidated return (attach Form 851) ☐
b Life/nonlife consolidated return . . ☐
2 Personal holding co. (attach Sch. PH) . ☐
3 Personal service corp. (see instructions) . ☐
4 Schedule M-3 attached ☐

TYPE OR PRINT

Name

Number, street, and room or suite no. If a P.O. box, see instructions.

City or town, state, and ZIP code

B Employer identification number

C Date incorporated

D Total assets (see instructions)
$

E Check if: **(1)** ☐ Initial return **(2)** ☐ Final return **(3)** ☐ Name change **(4)** ☐ Address change

Income

1a	Gross receipts or sales	1a			
b	Returns and allowances	1b			
c	Balance. Subtract line 1b from line 1a			1c	
2	Cost of goods sold (attach Form 1125-A)			2	
3	Gross profit. Subtract line 2 from line 1c			3	
4	Dividends (Schedule C, line 19)			4	
5	Interest			5	
6	Gross rents			6	
7	Gross royalties			7	
8	Capital gain net income (attach Schedule D (Form 1120))			8	
9	Net gain or (loss) from Form 4797, Part II, line 17 (attach Form 4797)			9	
10	Other income (see instructions—attach statement)			10	
11	**Total income.** Add lines 3 through 10 ►			11	

Deductions (See instructions for limitations on deductions.)

12	Compensation of officers (see instructions—attach Form 1125-E) ►			12	
13	Salaries and wages (less employment credits)			13	
14	Repairs and maintenance			14	
15	Bad debts			15	
16	Rents			16	
17	Taxes and licenses			17	
18	Interest			18	
19	Charitable contributions			19	
20	Depreciation from Form 4562 not claimed on Form 1125-A or elsewhere on return (attach Form 4562)			20	
21	Depletion			21	
22	Advertising			22	
23	Pension, profit-sharing, etc., plans			23	
24	Employee benefit programs			24	
25	Domestic production activities deduction (attach Form 8903)			25	
26	Other deductions (attach statement)			26	
27	**Total deductions.** Add lines 12 through 26 ►			27	
28	Taxable income before net operating loss deduction and special deductions. Subtract line 27 from line 11.			28	
29a	Net operating loss deduction (see instructions)	29a			
b	Special deductions (Schedule C, line 20)	29b			
c	Add lines 29a and 29b			29c	

Tax, Refundable Credits, and Payments

30	**Taxable income.** Subtract line 29c from line 28 (see instructions)	30	
31	Total tax (Schedule J, Part I, line 11)	31	
32	Total payments and refundable credits (Schedule J, Part II, line 21)	32	
33	Estimated tax penalty (see instructions). Check if Form 2220 is attached ► ☐	33	
34	**Amount owed.** If line 32 is smaller than the total of lines 31 and 33, enter amount owed	34	
35	**Overpayment.** If line 32 is larger than the total of lines 31 and 33, enter amount overpaid	35	
36	Enter amount from line 35 you want: **Credited to 2013 estimated tax ►** **Refunded ►**	36	

Sign Here

Under penalties of perjury, I declare that I have examined this return, including accompanying schedules and statements, and to the best of my knowledge and belief, it is true, correct, and complete. Declaration of preparer (other than taxpayer) is based on all information of which preparer has any knowledge.

► Signature of officer | Date | ► Title

May the IRS discuss this return with the preparer shown below (see instructions)? ☐ **Yes** ☐ **No**

Paid Preparer Use Only

Print/Type preparer's name	Preparer's signature	Date	Check ☐ if self-employed	PTIN
Firm's name ►			Firm's EIN ►	
Firm's address ►			Phone no.	

Schedule C **Dividends and Special Deductions** (see instructions)	**(a)** Dividends received	**(b)** %	**(c)** Special deductions **(a)** × **(b)**
1 Dividends from less-than-20%-owned domestic corporations (other than debt-financed stock)		70	
2 Dividends from 20%-or-more-owned domestic corporations (other than debt-financed stock)		80	
3 Dividends on debt-financed stock of domestic and foreign corporations		see instructions	
4 Dividends on certain preferred stock of less-than-20%-owned public utilities		42	
5 Dividends on certain preferred stock of 20%-or-more-owned public utilities		48	
6 Dividends from less-than-20%-owned foreign corporations and certain FSCs		70	
7 Dividends from 20%-or-more-owned foreign corporations and certain FSCs		80	
8 Dividends from wholly owned foreign subsidiaries		100	
9 **Total.** Add lines 1 through 8. See instructions for limitation			
10 Dividends from domestic corporations received by a small business investment company operating under the Small Business Investment Act of 1958		100	
11 Dividends from affiliated group members		100	
12 Dividends from certain FSCs		100	
13 Dividends from foreign corporations not included on lines 3, 6, 7, 8, 11, or 12			
14 Income from controlled foreign corporations under subpart F (attach Form(s) 5471)			
15 Foreign dividend gross-up			
16 IC-DISC and former DISC dividends not included on lines 1, 2, or 3			
17 Other dividends			
18 Deduction for dividends paid on certain preferred stock of public utilities			
19 **Total dividends.** Add lines 1 through 17. Enter here and on page 1, line 4 ▶			
20 **Total special deductions.** Add lines 9, 10, 11, 12, and 18. Enter here and on page 1, line 29b ▶			

Schedule J Tax Computation and Payment (see instructions)

Part I–Tax Computation

1	Check if the corporation is a member of a controlled group (attach Schedule O (Form 1120)) . . . . ▶ ☐				
2	Income tax. Check if a qualified personal service corporation (see instructions) . . . . ▶ ☐			2	
3	Alternative minimum tax (attach Form 4626)			3	
4	Add lines 2 and 3			4	
5a	Foreign tax credit (attach Form 1118)	5a			
b	Credit from Form 8834, line 30 (attach Form 8834)	5b			
c	General business credit (attach Form 3800)	5c			
d	Credit for prior year minimum tax (attach Form 8827)	5d			
e	Bond credits from Form 8912	5e			
6	**Total credits.** Add lines 5a through 5e			6	
7	Subtract line 6 from line 4			7	
8	Personal holding company tax (attach Schedule PH (Form 1120))			8	
9a	Recapture of investment credit (attach Form 4255)	9a			
b	Recapture of low-income housing credit (attach Form 8611)	9b			
c	Interest due under the look-back method—completed long-term contracts (attach Form 8697)	9c			
d	Interest due under the look-back method—income forecast method (attach Form 8866)	9d			
e	Alternative tax on qualifying shipping activities (attach Form 8902)	9e			
f	Other (see instructions—attach statement)	9f			
10	**Total.** Add lines 9a through 9f			10	
11	**Total tax.** Add lines 7, 8, and 10. Enter here and on page 1, line 31			11	

Part II–Payments and Refundable Credits

12	2011 overpayment credited to 2012			12	
13	2012 estimated tax payments			13	
14	2012 refund applied for on Form 4466			14	( )
15	Combine lines 12, 13, and 14			15	
16	Tax deposited with Form 7004			16	
17	Withholding (see instructions)			17	
18	**Total payments.** Add lines 15, 16, and 17			18	
19	Refundable credits from:				
a	Form 2439	19a			
b	Form 4136	19b			
c	Form 8827, line 8c	19c			
d	Other (attach statement—see instructions)	19d			
20	**Total credits.** Add lines 19a through 19d			20	
21	**Total payments and credits.** Add lines 18 and 20. Enter here and on page 1, line 32			21	

Schedule K Other Information (see instructions)

		Yes	No
1	Check accounting method: **a** ☐ Cash **b** ☐ Accrual **c** ☐ Other (specify) ▶ ______		
2	See the instructions and enter the:		
a	Business activity code no. ▶ ______		
b	Business activity ▶ ______		
c	Product or service ▶ ______		
3	Is the corporation a subsidiary in an affiliated group or a parent-subsidiary controlled group? If "Yes," enter name and EIN of the parent corporation ▶ ______		
4	At the end of the tax year:		
a	Did any foreign or domestic corporation, partnership (including any entity treated as a partnership), trust, or tax-exempt organization own directly 20% or more, or own, directly or indirectly, 50% or more of the total voting power of all classes of the corporation's stock entitled to vote? If "Yes," complete Part I of Schedule G (Form 1120) (attach Schedule G)		
b	Did any individual or estate own directly 20% or more, or own, directly or indirectly, 50% or more of the total voting power of all classes of the corporation's stock entitled to vote? If "Yes," complete Part II of Schedule G (Form 1120) (attach Schedule G)		

Schedule K Other Information *continued* (see instructions)

		Yes	No
5	At the end of the tax year, did the corporation:		
a	Own directly 20% or more, or own, directly or indirectly, 50% or more of the total voting power of all classes of stock entitled to vote of any foreign or domestic corporation not included on **Form 851,** Affiliations Schedule? For rules of constructive ownership, see instructions. If "Yes," complete (i) through (iv) below.		

(i) Name of Corporation	**(ii)** Employer Identification Number (if any)	**(iii)** Country of Incorporation	**(iv)** Percentage Owned in Voting Stock

		Yes	No
b	Own directly an interest of 20% or more, or own, directly or indirectly, an interest of 50% or more in any foreign or domestic partnership (including an entity treated as a partnership) or in the beneficial interest of a trust? For rules of constructive ownership, see instructions. If "Yes," complete (i) through (iv) below.		

(i) Name of Entity	**(ii)** Employer Identification Number (if any)	**(iii)** Country of Organization	**(iv)** Maximum Percentage Owned in Profit, Loss, or Capital

		Yes	No
6	During this tax year, did the corporation pay dividends (other than stock dividends and distributions in exchange for stock) in excess of the corporation's current and accumulated earnings and profits? (See sections 301 and 316.)		
	If "Yes," file **Form 5452,** Corporate Report of Nondividend Distributions. If this is a consolidated return, answer here for the parent corporation and on Form 851 for each subsidiary.		
7	At any time during the tax year, did one foreign person own, directly or indirectly, at least 25% of **(a)** the total voting power of all classes of the corporation's stock entitled to vote or **(b)** the total value of all classes of the corporation's stock?		
	For rules of attribution, see section 318. If "Yes," enter: **(i)** Percentage owned ▶ ________ and **(ii)** Owner's country ▶ ________		
	(c) The corporation may have to file **Form 5472,** Information Return of a 25% Foreign-Owned U.S. Corporation or a Foreign Corporation Engaged in a U.S. Trade or Business. Enter the number of Forms 5472 attached ▶ ________		
8	Check this box if the corporation issued publicly offered debt instruments with original issue discount . . . . ▶ ☐		
	If checked, the corporation may have to file **Form 8281,** Information Return for Publicly Offered Original Issue Discount Instruments.		
9	Enter the amount of tax-exempt interest received or accrued during the tax year ▶ $ ________		
10	Enter the number of shareholders at the end of the tax year (if 100 or fewer) ▶ ________		
11	If the corporation has an NOL for the tax year and is electing to forego the carryback period, check here . . . . . ▶ ☐		
	If the corporation is filing a consolidated return, the statement required by Regulations section 1.1502-21(b)(3) must be attached or the election will not be valid.		
12	Enter the available NOL carryover from prior tax years (do not reduce it by any deduction on line 29a.) ▶ $ ________		
13	Are the corporation's total receipts (line 1c plus lines 4 through 10 on page 1) for the tax year **and** its total assets at the end of the tax year less than $250,000?		
	If "Yes," the corporation is not required to complete Schedules L, M-1, and M-2 on page 5. Instead, enter the total amount of cash distributions and the book value of property distributions (other than cash) made during the tax year ▶ $ ________		
14	Is the corporation required to file Schedule UTP (Form 1120), Uncertain Tax Position Statement (see instructions)?		
	If "Yes," complete and attach Schedule UTP.		
15a	Did the corporation make any payments in 2012 that would require it to file Form(s) 1099?		
b	If "Yes," did or will the corporation file required Forms 1099?		
16	During this tax year, did the corporation have an 80% or more change in ownership, including a change due to redemption of its own stock?		
17	During or subsequent to this tax year, but before the filing of this return, did the corporation dispose of more than 65% (by value) of its assets in a taxable, non-taxable, or tax deferred transaction?		
18	Did the corporation receive assets in a section 351 transfer in which any of the transferred assets had a fair market basis or fair market value of more than $1 million?		

Schedule L Balance Sheets per Books

	Assets	Beginning of tax year (a)	(b)	End of tax year (c)	(d)
1	Cash				
2a	Trade notes and accounts receivable				
b	Less allowance for bad debts	( )		( )	
3	Inventories				
4	U.S. government obligations				
5	Tax-exempt securities (see instructions)				
6	Other current assets (attach statement)				
7	Loans to shareholders				
8	Mortgage and real estate loans				
9	Other investments (attach statement)				
10a	Buildings and other depreciable assets				
b	Less accumulated depreciation	( )		( )	
11a	Depletable assets				
b	Less accumulated depletion	( )		( )	
12	Land (net of any amortization)				
13a	Intangible assets (amortizable only)				
b	Less accumulated amortization	( )		( )	
14	Other assets (attach statement)				
15	Total assets				
	Liabilities and Shareholders' Equity				
16	Accounts payable				
17	Mortgages, notes, bonds payable in less than 1 year				
18	Other current liabilities (attach statement)				
19	Loans from shareholders				
20	Mortgages, notes, bonds payable in 1 year or more				
21	Other liabilities (attach statement)				
22	Capital stock: a Preferred stock				
	b Common stock				
23	Additional paid-in capital				
24	Retained earnings—Appropriated (attach statement)				
25	Retained earnings—Unappropriated				
26	Adjustments to shareholders' equity (attach statement)				
27	Less cost of treasury stock		( )		( )
28	Total liabilities and shareholders' equity				

Schedule M-1 Reconciliation of Income (Loss) per Books With Income per Return

Note: Schedule M-3 required instead of Schedule M-1 if total assets are $10 million or more—see instructions

1	Net income (loss) per books		7	Income recorded on books this year not included on this return (itemize): Tax-exempt interest $	
2	Federal income tax per books				
3	Excess of capital losses over capital gains				
4	Income subject to tax not recorded on books this year (itemize):		8	Deductions on this return not charged against book income this year (itemize):	
5	Expenses recorded on books this year not deducted on this return (itemize):		a	Depreciation $	
a	Depreciation $		b	Charitable contributions $	
b	Charitable contributions $				
c	Travel and entertainment $				
			9	Add lines 7 and 8	
6	Add lines 1 through 5		10	Income (page 1, line 28)—line 6 less line 9	

Schedule M-2 Analysis of Unappropriated Retained Earnings per Books (Line 25, Schedule L)

1	Balance at beginning of year		5	Distributions: a Cash	
2	Net income (loss) per books			b Stock	
3	Other increases (itemize):			c Property	
			6	Other decreases (itemize):	
			7	Add lines 5 and 6	
4	Add lines 1, 2, and 3		8	Balance at end of year (line 4 less line 7)	

Form **1120S**

Department of the Treasury
Internal Revenue Service

U.S. Income Tax Return for an S Corporation

▶ **Do not file this form unless the corporation has filed or is attaching Form 2553 to elect to be an S corporation.**

▶ **Information about Form 1120S and its separate instructions is at *www.irs.gov/form1120s*.**

OMB No. 1545-0130

2012

For calendar year 2012 or tax year beginning , 2012, ending , 20

	TYPE OR PRINT	
A S election effective date	Name	**D Employer identification number**
B Business activity code number (see instructions)	Number, street, and room or suite no. If a P.O. box, see instructions.	**E** Date incorporated
C Check if Sch. M-3 attached ☐	City or town, state, and ZIP code	**F** Total assets (see instructions) $

G Is the corporation electing to be an S corporation beginning with this tax year? ☐ Yes ☐ No If "Yes," attach Form 2553 if not already filed

H Check if: **(1)** ☐ Final return **(2)** ☐ Name change **(3)** ☐ Address change **(4)** ☐ Amended return **(5)** ☐ S election termination or revocation

I Enter the number of shareholders who were shareholders during any part of the tax year ▶

Caution. Include **only** trade or business income and expenses on lines 1a through 21. See the instructions for more information.

Income	1a	Gross receipts or sales	1a			
	b	Returns and allowances	1b			
	c	Balance. Subtract line 1b from line 1a			1c	
	2	Cost of goods sold (attach Form 1125-A)			2	
	3	Gross profit. Subtract line 2 from line 1c			3	
	4	Net gain (loss) from Form 4797, line 17 (attach Form 4797)			4	
	5	Other income (loss) (see instructions—attach statement)			5	
	6	**Total income (loss).** Add lines 3 through 5 ▶			6	
Deductions (see instructions for limitations)	7	Compensation of officers			7	
	8	Salaries and wages (less employment credits)			8	
	9	Repairs and maintenance			9	
	10	Bad debts			10	
	11	Rents			11	
	12	Taxes and licenses			12	
	13	Interest			13	
	14	Depreciation not claimed on Form 1125-A or elsewhere on return (attach Form 4562)			14	
	15	Depletion **(Do not deduct oil and gas depletion.)**			15	
	16	Advertising			16	
	17	Pension, profit-sharing, etc., plans			17	
	18	Employee benefit programs			18	
	19	Other deductions (attach statement)			19	
	20	**Total deductions.** Add lines 7 through 19 ▶			20	
	21	**Ordinary business income (loss).** Subtract line 20 from line 6			21	
Tax and Payments	22a	Excess net passive income or LIFO recapture tax (see instructions)	22a			
	b	Tax from Schedule D (Form 1120S)	22b			
	c	Add lines 22a and 22b (see instructions for additional taxes)			22c	
	23a	2012 estimated tax payments and 2011 overpayment credited to 2012	23a			
	b	Tax deposited with Form 7004	23b			
	c	Credit for federal tax paid on fuels (attach Form 4136)	23c			
	d	Add lines 23a through 23c			23d	
	24	Estimated tax penalty (see instructions). Check if Form 2220 is attached ▶ ☐			24	
	25	**Amount owed.** If line 23d is smaller than the total of lines 22c and 24, enter amount owed			25	
	26	**Overpayment.** If line 23d is larger than the total of lines 22c and 24, enter amount overpaid			26	
	27	Enter amount from line 26 **Credited to 2013 estimated tax** ▶		**Refunded** ▶	27	

Sign Here

Under penalties of perjury, I declare that I have examined this return, including accompanying schedules and statements, and to the best of my knowledge and belief, it is true, correct, and complete. Declaration of preparer (other than taxpayer) is based on all information of which preparer has any knowledge.

▶ Signature of officer | Date | ▶ Title

May the IRS discuss this return with the preparer shown below (see instructions)? ☐ Yes ☐ No

Paid Preparer Use Only

Print/Type preparer's name	Preparer's signature	Date	Check ☐ if self-employed	PTIN
Firm's name ▶			Firm's EIN ▶	
Firm's address ▶			Phone no.	

Schedule B Other Information (see instructions)

		Yes	No
1	Check accounting method: a ☐ Cash b ☐ Accrual c ☐ Other (specify) ▶		
2	See the instructions and enter the: a Business activity ▶ b Product or service ▶		
3	At any time during the tax year, was any shareholder of the corporation a disregarded entity, a trust, an estate, or a nominee or similar person?		
4	At the end of the tax year, did the corporation:		
a	Own directly 20% or more, or own, directly or indirectly, 50% or more of the total stock issued and outstanding of any foreign or domestic corporation? For rules of constructive ownership, see instructions. If "Yes," complete (i) through (v) below		

(i) Name of Corporation	(ii) Employer Identification Number (if any)	(iii) Country of Incorporation	(iv) Percentage of Stock Owned	(v) If Percentage in (iv) is 100%, Enter the Date (if any) a Qualified Subchapter S Subsidiary Election Was Made

		Yes	No
b	Own directly an interest of 20% or more, or own, directly or indirectly, an interest of 50% or more in the profit, loss, or capital in any foreign or domestic partnership (including an entity treated as a partnership) or in the beneficial interest of a trust? For rules of constructive ownership, see instructions. If "Yes," complete (i) through (v) below		

(i) Name of Entity	(ii) Employer Identification Number (if any)	(iii) Type of Entity	(iv) Country of Organization	(v) Maximum Percentage Owned in Profit, Loss, or Capital

		Yes	No
5 a	At the end of the tax year, did the corporation have any outstanding shares of restricted stock?		
	If "Yes," complete lines (i) and (ii) below.		
	(i) Total shares of restricted stock ▶		
	(ii) Total shares of non-restricted stock ▶		
b	At the end of the tax year, did the corporation have any outstanding stock options, warrants, or similar instruments?		
	If "Yes," complete lines (i) and (ii) below.		
	(i) Total shares of stock outstanding at the end of the tax year ▶		
	(ii) Total shares of stock outstanding if all instruments were executed ▶		
6	Has this corporation filed, or is it required to file, **Form 8918,** Material Advisor Disclosure Statement, to provide information on any reportable transaction?		
7	Check this box if the corporation issued publicly offered debt instruments with original issue discount ▶ ☐		
	If checked, the corporation may have to file **Form 8281,** Information Return for Publicly Offered Original Issue Discount Instruments.		
8	If the corporation: **(a)** was a C corporation before it elected to be an S corporation **or** the corporation acquired an asset with a basis determined by reference to the basis of the asset (or the basis of any other property) in the hands of a C corporation **and (b)** has net unrealized built-in gain in excess of the net recognized built-in gain from prior years, enter the net unrealized built-in gain reduced by net recognized built-in gain from prior years (see instructions) ▶ $		
9	Enter the accumulated earnings and profits of the corporation at the end of the tax year. $		
10	Does the corporation satisfy **both** of the following conditions?		
a	The corporation's total receipts (see instructions) for the tax year were less than $250,000		
b	The corporation's total assets at the end of the tax year were less than $250,000		
	If "Yes," the corporation is not required to complete Schedules L and M-1.		
11	During the tax year, did the corporation have any non-shareholder debt that was canceled, was forgiven, or had the terms modified so as to reduce the principal amount of the debt?		
	If "Yes," enter the amount of principal reduction $		
12	During the tax year, was a qualified subchapter S subsidiary election terminated or revoked? If "Yes," see instructions		
13a	Did the corporation make any payments in 2012 that would require it to file Form(s) 1099?		
b	If "Yes," did the corporation file or will it file required Forms 1099?		

Schedule K		Shareholders' Pro Rata Share Items			Total amount
Income (Loss)	1	Ordinary business income (loss) (page 1, line 21)		1	
	2	Net rental real estate income (loss) (attach Form 8825)		2	
	3a	Other gross rental income (loss)	3a		
	b	Expenses from other rental activities (attach statement)	3b		
	c	Other net rental income (loss). Subtract line 3b from line 3a		3c	
	4	Interest income		4	
	5	Dividends: **a** Ordinary dividends		5a	
		b Qualified dividends	5b		
	6	Royalties		6	
	7	Net short-term capital gain (loss) (attach Schedule D (Form 1120S))		7	
	8a	Net long-term capital gain (loss) (attach Schedule D (Form 1120S))		8a	
	b	Collectibles (28%) gain (loss)	8b		
	c	Unrecaptured section 1250 gain (attach statement)	8c		
	9	Net section 1231 gain (loss) (attach Form 4797)		9	
	10	Other income (loss) (see instructions) Type ▶		10	
Deductions	11	Section 179 deduction (attach Form 4562)		11	
	12a	Charitable contributions		12a	
	b	Investment interest expense		12b	
	c	Section 59(e)(2) expenditures **(1)** Type ▶ **(2)** Amount ▶		12c(2)	
	d	Other deductions (see instructions) Type ▶		12d	
Credits	13a	Low-income housing credit (section 42(j)(5))		13a	
	b	Low-income housing credit (other)		13b	
	c	Qualified rehabilitation expenditures (rental real estate) (attach Form 3468)		13c	
	d	Other rental real estate credits (see instructions) Type ▶		13d	
	e	Other rental credits (see instructions) Type ▶		13e	
	f	Alcohol and cellulosic biofuel fuels credit (attach Form 6478)		13f	
	g	Other credits (see instructions) Type ▶		13g	
Foreign Transactions	14a	Name of country or U.S. possession ▶			
	b	Gross income from all sources		14b	
	c	Gross income sourced at shareholder level		14c	
		Foreign gross income sourced at corporate level			
	d	Passive category		14d	
	e	General category		14e	
	f	Other (attach statement)		14f	
		Deductions allocated and apportioned at shareholder level			
	g	Interest expense		14g	
	h	Other		14h	
		Deductions allocated and apportioned at corporate level to foreign source income			
	i	Passive category		14i	
	j	General category		14j	
	k	Other (attach statement)		14k	
		Other information			
	l	Total foreign taxes (check one): ▶ ☐ Paid ☐ Accrued		14l	
	m	Reduction in taxes available for credit (attach statement)		14m	
	n	Other foreign tax information (attach statement)			
Alternative Minimum Tax (AMT) Items	15a	Post-1986 depreciation adjustment		15a	
	b	Adjusted gain or loss		15b	
	c	Depletion (other than oil and gas)		15c	
	d	Oil, gas, and geothermal properties—gross income		15d	
	e	Oil, gas, and geothermal properties—deductions		15e	
	f	Other AMT items (attach statement)		15f	
Items Affecting Shareholder Basis	16a	Tax-exempt interest income		16a	
	b	Other tax-exempt income		16b	
	c	Nondeductible expenses		16c	
	d	Distributions (attach statement if required) (see instructions)		16d	
	e	Repayment of loans from shareholders		16e	

Schedule K **Shareholders' Pro Rata Share Items** (continued)

				Total amount
Other Information	17a	Investment income	17a	
	b	Investment expenses	17b	
	c	Dividend distributions paid from accumulated earnings and profits	17c	
	d	Other items and amounts (attach statement)		
Recon-ciliation	18	**Income/loss reconciliation.** Combine the amounts on lines 1 through 10 in the far right column. From the result, subtract the sum of the amounts on lines 11 through 12d and 14l	18	

Schedule L **Balance Sheets per Books**

	Assets	Beginning of tax year (a)	(b)	End of tax year (c)	(d)
1	Cash				
2a	Trade notes and accounts receivable				
b	Less allowance for bad debts	( )		( )	
3	Inventories				
4	U.S. government obligations				
5	Tax-exempt securities (see instructions)				
6	Other current assets (attach statement)				
7	Loans to shareholders				
8	Mortgage and real estate loans				
9	Other investments (attach statement)				
10a	Buildings and other depreciable assets				
b	Less accumulated depreciation	( )		( )	
11a	Depletable assets				
b	Less accumulated depletion	( )		( )	
12	Land (net of any amortization)				
13a	Intangible assets (amortizable only)				
b	Less accumulated amortization	( )		( )	
14	Other assets (attach statement)				
15	Total assets				
	Liabilities and Shareholders' Equity				
16	Accounts payable				
17	Mortgages, notes, bonds payable in less than 1 year				
18	Other current liabilities (attach statement)				
19	Loans from shareholders				
20	Mortgages, notes, bonds payable in 1 year or more				
21	Other liabilities (attach statement)				
22	Capital stock				
23	Additional paid-in capital				
24	Retained earnings				
25	Adjustments to shareholders' equity (attach statement)				
26	Less cost of treasury stock		( )		( )
27	Total liabilities and shareholders' equity				

Schedule M-1 Reconciliation of Income (Loss) per Books With Income (Loss) per Return

Note. Schedule M-3 required instead of Schedule M-1 if total assets are $10 million or more—see instructions

1	Net income (loss) per books		5 Income recorded on books this year not included on Schedule K, lines 1 through 10 (itemize):	
2	Income included on Schedule K, lines 1, 2, 3c, 4, 5a, 6, 7, 8a, 9, and 10, not recorded on books this year (itemize)		a Tax-exempt interest $	
3	Expenses recorded on books this year not included on Schedule K, lines 1 through 12 and 14l (itemize):		6 Deductions included on Schedule K, lines 1 through 12 and 14l, not charged against book income this year (itemize):	
a	Depreciation $		a Depreciation $	
b	Travel and entertainment $			
			7 Add lines 5 and 6	
4	Add lines 1 through 3		8 Income (loss) (Schedule K, line 18). Line 4 less line 7	

Schedule M-2 Analysis of Accumulated Adjustments Account, Other Adjustments Account, and Shareholders' Undistributed Taxable Income Previously Taxed (see instructions)

		(a) Accumulated adjustments account	(b) Other adjustments account	(c) Shareholders' undistributed taxable income previously taxed
1	Balance at beginning of tax year			
2	Ordinary income from page 1, line 21 . . .			
3	Other additions			
4	Loss from page 1, line 21	( )		
5	Other reductions	( )	( )	
6	Combine lines 1 through 5			
7	Distributions other than dividend distributions			
8	Balance at end of tax year. Subtract line 7 from line 6			

Form **4562** Department of the Treasury Internal Revenue Service (99)

Depreciation and Amortization (Including Information on Listed Property)

▶ See separate instructions. ▶ Attach to your tax return.

OMB No. 1545-0172 **2012** Attachment Sequence No. **179**

Name(s) shown on return	Business or activity to which this form relates	**Identifying number**

Part I Election To Expense Certain Property Under Section 179

Note: *If you have any listed property, complete Part V before you complete Part I.*

1	Maximum amount (see instructions)	1	
2	Total cost of section 179 property placed in service (see instructions)	2	
3	Threshold cost of section 179 property before reduction in limitation (see instructions)	3	
4	Reduction in limitation. Subtract line 3 from line 2. If zero or less, enter -0-	4	
5	Dollar limitation for tax year. Subtract line 4 from line 1. If zero or less, enter -0-. If married filing separately, see instructions	5	

6	(a) Description of property	(b) Cost (business use only)	(c) Elected cost

7	Listed property. Enter the amount from line 29	7	
8	Total elected cost of section 179 property. Add amounts in column (c), lines 6 and 7	8	
9	Tentative deduction. Enter the **smaller** of line 5 or line 8	9	
10	Carryover of disallowed deduction from line 13 of your 2011 Form 4562	10	
11	Business income limitation. Enter the smaller of business income (not less than zero) or line 5 (see instructions)	11	
12	Section 179 expense deduction. Add lines 9 and 10, but do not enter more than line 11	12	
13	Carryover of disallowed deduction to 2013. Add lines 9 and 10, less line 12 ▶	13	

Note: *Do not use Part II or Part III below for listed property. Instead, use Part V.*

Part II Special Depreciation Allowance and Other Depreciation (Do not include listed property.) (See instructions.)

14	Special depreciation allowance for qualified property (other than listed property) placed in service during the tax year (see instructions)	14	
15	Property subject to section 168(f)(1) election	15	
16	Other depreciation (including ACRS)	16	

Part III MACRS Depreciation (Do not include listed property.) (See instructions.)

Section A

17	MACRS deductions for assets placed in service in tax years beginning before 2012	17	
18	If you are electing to group any assets placed in service during the tax year into one or more general asset accounts, check here ▶ ☐		

Section B—Assets Placed in Service During 2012 Tax Year Using the General Depreciation System

(a) Classification of property	(b) Month and year placed in service	(c) Basis for depreciation (business/investment use only—see instructions)	(d) Recovery period	(e) Convention	(f) Method	(g) Depreciation deduction
19a 3-year property						
b 5-year property						
c 7-year property						
d 10-year property						
e 15-year property						
f 20-year property						
g 25-year property			25 yrs.		S/L	
h Residential rental property			27.5 yrs.	MM	S/L	
			27.5 yrs.	MM	S/L	
i Nonresidential real property			39 yrs.	MM	S/L	
				MM	S/L	

Section C—Assets Placed in Service During 2012 Tax Year Using the Alternative Depreciation System

20a Class life					S/L	
b 12-year			12 yrs.		S/L	
c 40-year			40 yrs.	MM	S/L	

Part IV Summary (See instructions.)

21	Listed property. Enter amount from line 28	21	
22	**Total.** Add amounts from line 12, lines 14 through 17, lines 19 and 20 in column (g), and line 21. Enter here and on the appropriate lines of your return. Partnerships and S corporations—see instructions	22	
23	For assets shown above and placed in service during the current year, enter the portion of the basis attributable to section 263A costs	23	

Part V **Listed Property** (Include automobiles, certain other vehicles, certain computers, and property used for entertainment, recreation, or amusement.)

Note: *For any vehicle for which you are using the standard mileage rate or deducting lease expense, complete **only** 24a, 24b, columns (a) through (c) of Section A, all of Section B, and Section C if applicable.*

Section A—Depreciation and Other Information (Caution: *See the instructions for limits for passenger automobiles.***)**

24a Do you have evidence to support the business/investment use claimed? ☐ **Yes** ☐ **No** **24b** If "Yes," is the evidence written? ☐ **Yes** ☐ **No**

(a) Type of property (list vehicles first)	(b) Date placed in service	(c) Business/ investment use percentage	(d) Cost or other basis	(e) Basis for depreciation (business/investment use only)	(f) Recovery period	(g) Method/ Convention	(h) Depreciation deduction	(i) Elected section 179 cost
25 Special depreciation allowance for qualified listed property placed in service during the tax year and used more than 50% in a qualified business use (see instructions) .						**25**		
26 Property used more than 50% in a qualified business use:								
		%						
		%						
		%						
27 Property used 50% or less in a qualified business use:								
		%				S/L –		
		%				S/L –		
		%				S/L –		
28 Add amounts in column (h), lines 25 through 27. Enter here and on line 21, page 1 .						**28**		
29 Add amounts in column (i), line 26. Enter here and on line 7, page 1							**29**	

Section B—Information on Use of Vehicles

Complete this section for vehicles used by a sole proprietor, partner, or other "more than 5% owner," or related person. If you provided vehicles to your employees, first answer the questions in Section C to see if you meet an exception to completing this section for those vehicles.

	(a) Vehicle 1		(b) Vehicle 2		(c) Vehicle 3		(d) Vehicle 4		(e) Vehicle 5		(f) Vehicle 6	
30 Total business/investment miles driven during the year (**do not** include commuting miles) .												
31 Total commuting miles driven during the year												
32 Total other personal (noncommuting) miles driven												
33 Total miles driven during the year. Add lines 30 through 32												
	Yes	**No**	**Yes**	**No**	**Yes**	**No**	**Yes**	**No**	**Yes**	**No**	**Yes**	**No**
34 Was the vehicle available for personal use during off-duty hours?												
35 Was the vehicle used primarily by a more than 5% owner or related person? . .												
36 Is another vehicle available for personal use?												

Section C—Questions for Employers Who Provide Vehicles for Use by Their Employees

Answer these questions to determine if you meet an exception to completing Section B for vehicles used by employees who **are not** more than 5% owners or related persons (see instructions).

	Yes	**No**
37 Do you maintain a written policy statement that prohibits all personal use of vehicles, including commuting, by your employees?		
38 Do you maintain a written policy statement that prohibits personal use of vehicles, except commuting, by your employees? See the instructions for vehicles used by corporate officers, directors, or 1% or more owners . .		
39 Do you treat all use of vehicles by employees as personal use?		
40 Do you provide more than five vehicles to your employees, obtain information from your employees about the use of the vehicles, and retain the information received?		
41 Do you meet the requirements concerning qualified automobile demonstration use? (See instructions.) . . .		

Note: *If your answer to 37, 38, 39, 40, or 41 is "Yes," do not complete Section B for the covered vehicles.*

Part VI **Amortization**

(a) Description of costs	(b) Date amortization begins	(c) Amortizable amount	(d) Code section	(e) Amortization period or percentage	(f) Amortization for this year
42 Amortization of costs that begins during your 2012 tax year (see instructions):					
43 Amortization of costs that began before your 2012 tax year				**43**	
44 **Total.** Add amounts in column (f). See the instructions for where to report				**44**	

www.ingramcontent.com/pod-product-compliance
Lightning Source LLC
LaVergne TN
LVHW080037210926
848481LV00011B/3217